THE SOCIAL ORDER OF
THE SLUM

STUDIES OF URBAN SOCIETY

GENERAL EDITOR, *David P. Street*

Gerald D. Suttles

THE SOCIAL ORDER OF THE SLUM

Ethnicity and Territory in the Inner City

Preface by Morris Janowitz

THE UNIVERSITY OF CHICAGO PRESS

Chicago & London

ISBN: 0–226–78191–7 (clothbound); 0–226–78192–5 (paperbound)

Library of Congress Catalog Card Number: 68–26762

THE UNIVERSITY OF CHICAGO PRESS
CHICAGO 60637

The University of Chicago Press, Ltd., London

For Mr. and Mrs. I.,
my landlords and friends
from the Addams area

Preface

By the end of the 1950's, it would have appeared to the intellectual historian that the Chicago school of urban sociology had exhausted itself. Even at the University of Chicago, the intensive and humanistically oriented study of the social worlds of the metropolis had come to an end. The older figures had disappeared one by one, and a new generation of sociologists were interested in quantitative methodology and systematic theory. A few disciples of the traditional approach carried on in the shadows of the university or were scattered through the country.

But intellectual traditions are transmitted and transformed as much by the intrinsic vitality of their content as by the institutions of academic life. A mere decade later the themes of a reconstructed urban sociology are once again at the center of social science thinking. The complexity of social behavior in the urban setting and the rise of concern with policy issues has meant that urban sociologists have come to focus on a particular social grouping or on a specific social institution, such as the family, the juvenile gang, the slum school, or newly emerging community organizations. Nevertheless, in the reconstruction of urban sociology, the community study remains a basic vehicle for holistic and comprehensive understanding of the metropolitan condition.

Gerald Suttles' study of the Addams area on the Near West Side of Chicago is a powerful expression of the contemporary effort to maintain a continuity in the tradition of the urban community study and to contribute to an urban sociology based on a more precise methodological base and a sounder theoretical frame of reference. His work is grounded on the notion that intensive observation of microunits—that is, of the family and of age-graded groups—is the initial step in the analysis of community structure. He proceeds with an empirical orientation reflective of earlier periods of the Chicago school when social anthropology had not yet separated from sociology. At the same time, he is fully committed to the view that the intensive study of a few families or a single street corner gang is not an adequate strategy for an empirical community study in depth. He goes beyond the segmental findings of the sample survey and avoids reliance on excerpts from tape-recorded interactions.

As a sociologist, Suttles strives to develop quantitative indices to give depth to his observations on the ethnic and social worlds he explores. There is every reason to hope that the level of quantification that he develops will be surpassed, but this volume represents a benchmark in the perfection of the techniques of participant observation in a field setting. This massive collection of systematic data is essential to convey the subtle intricacies of the slum community.

Suttles spent three years in the Near West Side. The residents came to accept him as another intrusion of the outer world. Given the disruption of changed land usage and urban renewal, they had become accustomed to intrusions. By contrast his arrival was almost unnoticeable. No doubt, his reserved personal manner, his sympathetic detachment, and his skill as a field worker all contributed to the massing of essential details.

But the final intellectual result rests on the conceptual apparatus with which he proceeded. It is important that he does not present an elaborate framework which has an existence independent of his empirical findings. It is even more important that he does not feel it necessary to obscure his theoretical standpoint to demonstrate attachment to the humanistic traditions of community research. Concern with detail and elegance of presentation does not mean that the sociologist must renounce his search for analytical rigor and more precise language.

Suttles rejects by implication any over-simplistic theory of social change that might be derived from the well-known formulations of *gemeinschaft* and *gesellschaft*, or the folk-urban continuum. The idea of "ordered segmentation" supplies an impetus for handling the complexities of this multiethnic local area. There are common elements in the social order of any slum community. But there are variations which derive from ecological patterns, different internal institutions and from cultural elements which reflect ethnicity, religion, and racial composition. Ordered segmentation does not simply refer to the differentiation of ethnic groups such as the Italians, the Spanish-speaking people, and the Negroes. It becomes a device for explaining the discontinuities between family and community, and between various age groups. These discontinuities become greater as one moves from the Italian to the Spanish-speaking groups to the Negroes. Social solidarity and success in the larger society as well as the forms and types of deviant behavior found in these different groups are functions not only of cultural themes but of the extent to which younger and older age groups articulate with one another.

Suttles is fully aware of the difficulties of personal and social preferences in the study of the slum community. He has no romantic adoration of the slum, nor is his struggle for objectivity impaired by a sense of personal fear or distaste which leads to exaggeration. The social reality is grim enough. In the end, the image of the slum community that Suttles presents is different from that presented by much of the recent literature. The difference is due not to the fact that this slum is older and more settled and that it does not represent the very poorest and most repressive conditions of life in Chicago. The difference results from the more complete analysis Suttles presents of its internal relations and its links with the outside metropolis. The difference centers on his ability to observe, record, and analyze the realities of the search for a moral order in the slum community.

Of course, there is a value orientation in his attachment to the propelling formulations of Emile Durkheim, but it is a value orientation which permits the closest scrutiny of the social behavior of the Near West Side. First, Suttles emphasizes that the moral order existing in the Addams area is rooted in a set of very personalistic relations that the residents have with members of their own groups. The understandings and the misunderstandings that develop as the residents seek to impose order on a dangerous and uncontrollable outer world are fashioned out of direct, though often unreciprocated, confrontations of one human being and another. The stereotypes which make for individuality and personal identity and personal autonomy are undeveloped, fragmented, and unstable. Second, the moral order of the slum community reflects its ordered segmentation from the larger society. Provincialism is a dominant theme. Provincialism serves to organize daily life and restrain disruptive outbursts. When provincialism becomes too powerful, it hinders the pursuit of opportunities, but when provincialism becomes attenuated, it destroys social defenses and common assumptions.

Suttles joins a tradition that emphasizes the contributions of the sociologist to policy and professional practice. This tradition is not based on contrived research or vulgar popularization. Reasoned and responsible scholarship leads to empirical findings and to the formulation of delimited generalizations. It is hoped that such results are relevant both for sociologists and for all interested in policy issues. This book is no plea for utopia based on research to be completed in the distant future, but rather a contribution to immediate understanding.

MORRIS JANOWITZ
University of Chicago

Acknowledgments

The early field work for this study was carried out while I was a field associate with the Institute for Social Research at The University of Michigan. Subsequent support was generously provided by the Center for Social Organization Studies at the University of Chicago.

As a member of a larger research team, I am much indebted to my co-workers for the freedom and encouragement they provided. I would like especially to acknowledge the efforts of Hans W. Mattick, director of the Chicago Youth Development Project, Dr. Nathan S. Caplan, study director of this project, and Dennis J. Deshaies, my fellow field associate. At one time or another so many people were helpful to this study that it is difficult to mention more than a few. Among the most generous were Francis J. Carney, Ezra Smith, Fred Christie, Obern Simons, and Martin Dann, all with the Chicago Youth Development Project.

While in preparation, this study profited greatly from the direction and encouragement of Professor Daniel Glaser. For comments and advice on the study, I would like to thank professors Julian H. Steward, John P. Clark, and Morris Janowitz.

Naturally, any attempt at field work requires an immense amount of cooperation and tolerance from one's informants. While they cannot be mentioned here, it is to them that I owe my greatest debt.

Contents

xiii

Figures

Maps

xix

Tables

Part 1

---

*Territoriality and
Ordered Segmentation*

1

Slum Neighborhoods

The Addams area is one of the oldest slums in Chicago and researchers have invaded it almost as often as new minority groups. Like most slums, however, it remains something of a mystery hovering between two divergent interpretations. In some ways it is easiest to describe the neighborhood by how its residents deviate from the public standards of the wider community. There are, for example, a high delinquency rate, numerous unwed mothers, and several adolescent "gangs." Measured by the usual yardstick of success it is tempting to think that the local residents are simply inadequate and disadvantaged people suffering from cultural deprivation, unemployment, and a number of other "urban ills."[1] If the residents insist upon the irrelevance of public standards and the primacy of their own, this can be dismissed as sour grapes or only an attempt to make necessity a virtue.

Seen from the inside, however, the Addams area is intricately organized according to its own standards and the residents are fairly insistent on their demands. These demands require discipline and self-restraint in the same way as do the moral dictates of the wider community. Conventional norms are not rejected but differentially emphasized or suspended for established reasons. The vast majority of the residents are quite conventional people. At the same time those who continue in good standing by public measures are often exceptionally tolerant and even encouraging to those who are "deviant."

Neither disorganization nor value rejection are apt terms to describe the Addams area. Certainly the social practices of the residents are not just an inversion of those of the wider society, and the inhabitants would be outraged to hear as much. Also the neighborhood is not a cultural island with its own distinct and imported traditions. The major lineaments of the area's

[1] See for example, Robert K. Merton, "Social Structure and Anomie," *Social Theory and Social Structure*, rev. ed. (Glencoe, Ill.: Free Press, 1957), pp. 131–60; Richard A. Cloward and Lloyd E. Ohlin, *Delinquency and Opportunity* (Glencoe, Ill.: Free Press, 1960); Albert K. Cohen, *Delinquent Boys* (Glencoe, Ill.: Free Press, 1955); and Martin Gold, *Status Forces in Delinquent Boys* (Ann Arbor.: University of Michigan Press, 1963).

3

internal structure are such commonplace distinctions as age, sex, territoriality, ethnicity, and personal identity. Some ethnic customs have been preserved, and numerous localisms have been developed. Many of the residents are so thoroughly acquainted with one another that only personalistic standards are relevant. Frequently the residents emphasize these structural components to the exclusion of educational, legal, and occupational considerations. Taken out of context, many of the social arrangements of the Addams area may seem an illusory denial of the beliefs and values of the wider society. Seen in more holistic terms, the residents are bent on ordering local relations where the beliefs and evaluations of the wider society do not provide adequate guidelines for conduct.

The Provincial Morality of Slum Neighborhoods

In examining slum neighborhoods it is customary to accept compliance with public morality as a kind of high-water mark of organization from which departures must be "explained." It is possible, however, to look upon communities as a confederation of groups and organizations which support public morality primarily as a means of protecting themselves against one another. In this sense public morality is not so much the heart-felt sentiments of people as a set of defensive guarantees demanded by various minority members. Within the privacy of their own local groups, people may fall back on quite a different set of standards and practices. The morality practiced in a family need not be that which they would like their neighbors to observe. Those who share a neighborhood, in turn, may feel free to relax from the stringent code they support for the remainder of the community.

In the light of some empirical findings, this last point of view has a certain appeal. There is, first, the perplexing way that people may endorse a morality they do not expect to observe, as when we "vote dry but drink wet."[2] Second, there is the historical process of urban growth which tends to congregate various groups with different moralities of their own. Each may subscribe to "popular morality" but take a more relaxed posture when among "their own kind." Finally, as Julian Steward has shown, evolutionary changes toward urbanization need not altogether replace older forms of organization but often develop alongside them.[3] Thus, at one and the same time, different populations are enmeshed in several levels of sociocultural integration.

In some populations it is reasonable to assume that people can and do re-

[2] Charles K. Warringer, "The Nature and Functions of Official Morality," *American Journal of Sociology*, 64 (September, 1958): 165–68.

[3] Julian H. Steward, *Theory of Culture Change* (Urbana.: University of Illinois Press, 1955), pp. 43–63.

main heavily engrossed in their local neighborhood as a separate and rather distinct moral world. Variations here may run from the cosmopolitanism of the "jet set" to the parochialism of an Amish settlement. In southern mill towns, the townspeople, the white mill hands, and the Negroes advance in this order toward a national culture; each, however, keeps one foot in his local neighborhood.[4] Within some recently constructed "developments" the residents may be unable to appeal to anything other than the distinctions current at the most public level. The residents of Beverly Hills, however, seem to have perfected their own class system to augment the one used by sociologists.[5]

Obviously the balance between a person's involvement in his local neighborhood and alternative associations is unevenly distributed. To decipher these variations two central observations must be kept in mind. First, distinctions or earmarks that can be applied to an entire society—social class, education, and so forth—are often complemented by another set of distinctions that are specific to a single locality. Localisms of this type simply increase the degree of social differentiation and provide an additional basis for association. Sometimes local and national levels of sociocultural integration go along independent but parallel courses. In other cases national and local patterns may supplement one another, as in some elitist neighborhoods where family lineage and personal reputation become important in the absence of further distinctions on the basis of education and social class.

A second consideration is the *differential moral isolation* of a neighborhood from the wider society. In all societies there are probably people who fall short of existing standards that attest to their trustworthiness and self-restraint. The standards of American society are severe, and a very large proportion of our population is regarded with suspicion and caution. Typically, these are poor people from a low-status minority group and unable to manage very well their "public relations." The presence of such a group of people is disruptive because it undermines the trust residents must share to go about their daily rounds. In American society, a common solution to this difficulty has been to relegate all suspicious people to "slums" and "skid rows." As a result, respectable and essential citizens can carry on their corporate life undisturbed by their own apprehensions.

Slum residents, however, are subject to all the suspicions and bear those

[4] Hylan Lewis, *Blackways of Kent* (New Haven, Conn.: College and University Press, 1964), and John Kenneth Morland, *Millways of Kent* (New Haven, Conn.: College and University Press, 1965).

[5] Hortense Powdermaker, *Hollywood, the Dream Factory* (Boston: Little, Brown, 1950).

disreputable characteristics that turn people away from one another and interfere with joint activities. Seen from the standpoint of the wider community, slum residents do not inspire levels of trust necessary to the usual round of neighborhood activities. Out of necessity, then, they may fall back on local patterns which guarantee their safety and promote association.

In the Addams area, local forms of social differentiation complement some of the structual elements of the wider society but evade others. In terms of income, occupation, and education the residents are very similar and lack obvious leaders, patrons, and helpful associates. Distinctions known mainly to the residents help them to fill at least some of these roles. Moreover, the disreputable characteristics that so many of the residents share can be nullified by emphasizing other characteristics which are apparent to co-residents. The result is a progressive retreat into provincialism and a practical rather than an ideal set of guidelines for conduct.

Slum Neighborhoods as Culture-Building Worlds

On the basis of stochastic processes alone, one might expect that a distinct locality would become a common arena within which people arrive at a fairly standard code for deciphering and evaluating one another's behavior. All models of social behavior which emphasize frequency, convenience, and continuity of interaction generally imply that relatively separate local groupings provide the occasion for cultural patterns to become standardized and differentiated from those of other local groupings.[6] The early work of Park and Burgess on "natural areas" was an important beginning but was so couched in physicalistic terminology that it drew undue criticism.[7] Accordingly, later sociologists have neglected territorial groups in favor of structural ones. There is, of course, no scarcity of studies dealing with people who happen to live near one another. Spatial distributions have not been ignored but have been seen as a product of structural elements general to an entire society.

In anthropology, however, territorial grouping has been a subject of continued interest. Most anthropological studies begin by focusing upon social groupings that can be defined by areal distribution. In turn, many of the social units singled out for particular attention—the domestic unit, the homestead, the tribe, and so forth—frequently have locality as one of their

[6] Edwin Sutherland and Donald Cressey, *Principles of Criminology* (New York: J. B. Lippincott, 1955); George Homans, *The Human Group* (New York: Harcourt, Brace, 1950); and Dorwin Cartwright and Alvin Zander, eds., "Group Pressure and Group Standards," in *Group Dynamics* (White Plains, N. Y.: Row, Peterson, 1953), pp. 137–301.

[7] Robert E. Park, Ernest W. Burgess, and Roderick D. McKenzie, *The City* (Chicago: University of Chicago Press, 1967).

principles of organization. Alternatively, where locality and structural forms do not coincide, anthropologists have regarded this discrepancy as a distinct problem which raises a number of theoretical and methodological issues. In this respect, anthropologists have self-consciously addressed themselves to the question of how territorial and structural configurations are related.

The importance of territorial groupings has probably been most apparent in linguistic studies. As a rule, linguistics have approached separate language groupings as spatial units irrespective of the structural differences that obtain within them. In fact, one of the common methods of determining the time at which two groups separated themselves in physical space is a measure of changes in their language usage.[8] To the extent that standard linguistic forms parallel the routinization of other cultural patterns or become the media for perpetuating nonlinguistic structures, uniformity of linguistic practices within a given territory, then, should imply still other commonalities.

The analysis of territorial groups has been pursued most fully by British social anthropologists and their American counterparts. The relevance of their work lies not so much in their focus on localized groups as in their recognition of locality as a proper element of social structure. While this observation is very simple, it is a far cry from an abstract social system where general categories of people are related to one another irrespective of where they happen to be located. In fact, of course, managers do not manage all employees and doctors do not treat all patients: managers manage *their* employees and doctors treat *their* patients. Without some recognition of locality, the concept "social system" leads to an absurd juxtaposition of personnel.

The most obvious reason for centering in on locality groups is that their members cannot simply ignore one another. People who routinely occupy the same place must either develop a moral order that includes all those present or fall into conflict. Since almost all societies create a public morality that exceeds the capabilities of some of its members, territorial groups are always faced with the prospect of people whose public character does not warrant trust. In the United States a very large proportion of our population fails to meet the public standards we set for measuring someone's merit, trustworthiness, and respectability. Many locality groups have avoided compromising these ideals of public morality by territorial segregation: more exactly, they have simply retreated and left valuable portions of the inner city to those they distrust. Obviously this practice has its limits since it tends to aggregate those who are poor, unsuccessful, and

[8] D. H. Hymes, "Lexicostatistics So Far," *Current Anthropology*, 1 (January, 1960); 3–44.

disreputable in the same slum neighborhoods. These people must compromise the ideals of public morality or remain permanently estranged from one another.

In slum neighborhoods territorial aggregation usually precedes any common social framework for assuring orderly relations. Ethnic invasion, the encroachment of industry, and economic conditions constantly reshuffle slum residents and relocate them around new neighbors. Since they lack obvious grounds for assuming mutual trust, a combination of two alternatives seems to offer the most promising course.

First, social relations can be restricted to permit only the safest ones. Families can withdraw to their households where they see only close relatives. Age grading along with sex and ethnic segregation are maneuvers that will avoid at least the most unfair and likely forms of conflict and exploitation. Remaining in close proximity to the household cuts down on the range of anonymity and reduces the number of social relations. The general pattern, then, should be a "fan-shaped" spatial arrangement with women and children remaining close by the house while males move progressively outwards depending on their age.

Second, slum residents can assuage at least some of their apprehensions by a close inquiry into each other's personal character and past history. Communication, then, should be of an intimate character and aimed toward producing "personal" rather than formal relations. In turn, social relations will represent a sort of private "compact" where particularistic loyalties replace impersonal standards of worth.

Neither of these patterns will immediately produce a comprehensive framework within which a large number of slum residents can safely negotiate among one another. The segregation of age, sex, and territorial groups, however, provides a structural starting point from which face-to-face relations can grow and reach beyond each small territorial aggregation. The development of personal relations furnishes both a moral formula and a structural bridge between groups. Within each small, localized peer group, continuing face-to-face relations can eventually provide a personalistic order. Once these groups are established, a single personal relation between them can extend the range of such an order. With the acceptance of age grading and territorial usufruct, it becomes possible for slum neighborhoods to work out a moral order that includes most of their residents.

The withdrawal to small territorial groupings and the extension of personal acquaintances are strategies which slum residents can use to embark on a search for order. As with all strategies, a developmental sequence lies between their conception and completion. The Addams area itself lies between a starting point where people are fragmented into many independent and suspicious groupings and the other extreme where all residents are encompassed in a single moral order. Between these two extremes there is always the danger of ethnic invasion, transiency, and destruction. It is only under very idealized conditions that one can imagine all slum neighborhoods converging to a single type of social order. What seems to remain uniform among them is the way they pursue a local and provincial moral order.

The Addams Area

The Addams area consists of four different ethnic sections occupied predominantly by Negroes, Italians, Puerto Ricans, and Mexicans. Each of these ethnic sections falls into a somewhat different stage in its development of a provincial order. At one extreme is an old Italian population slowly being displaced by Mexicans, Negroes, and Puerto Ricans. Among the Italians, people from all walks of life are drawn together in a well-knit series of peer groups that range from childhood to the upper realms of adulthood. Both the "church people" and the racketeers are bound together in a common collusion at "impression management"[9] and are equally safe in each other's presence. Local business establishments, street corners, and other public facilities are categorized according to their proper "hangers-on," the license they may enjoy, and the behavior appropriate to "outsiders."

At the other extreme are the Negroes who, like the three ethnic groups, form a small but compact residential group. They are the most recent to invade the neighborhood and remain the most estranged from one another. Anonymity and distrust are pervasive, and well-established peer groups are present only among the adolescents. Sometimes those residents who are most "respectable" carry on a futile and divisive attack on those who are not so respectable. Occasionally they are incited and encouraged in this endeavor by the social welfare agents who find their neglect of public morality incomprehensible. Local businesses, street locations, and other spatial settings, with the exception of adolescent hangouts, are not well-differentiated according to who can be there and what behavior is required of them. In large part this seems due to the placement of the Negroes in public housing and the lack of private facilities within which the other groups can retire to practice their provincial morality. As will be reiterated in this study, the local integration of the Negro population seems to have been stymied by their inclusion in public housing.

[9] Erving Goffman, *The Presentation of Self in Everyday Life* (Garden City, N.Y.: Doubleday, 1959).

The Mexicans and Puerto Ricans seem to occupy a middle ground. The Puerto Ricans make up such a small and compact group that the problems of anonymity are less pressing; practically everyone can be known "as an individual." The Mexicans are most numerous and have well-developed peer groups among the adolescents. Beyond this age group, adult affiliations are tenuous although several Mexican adults have been absorbed into the older Italian groups and a few of the adult males have made incipient gestures toward forming groups of their own. All the same, the Mexicans who support public morality and those who violate it have not been entirely reconciled to one another. Unlike the Negroes, however, both the Puerto Ricans and the Mexicans have developed many local establishments and spatial boundaries where a limited range of persons may congregate and find a reliable code for deciding what can or cannot be done.

Despite these differences, all four ethnic sections share many characteristics and seem headed along the same social progression. The overall pattern is one where age, sex, ethnic, and territorial units are fitted together like building blocks to create a larger structure. I have termed this pattern "ordered segmentation" to indicate two related features: (1) the orderly relationship between groups and (2) the sequential order in which groups combine in instances of conflict and opposition. This ordered segmentation is not equally developed in all ethnic sections but, in skeletal outline, it is the common framework within which groups are being formed and social relations are being cultivated.

My own experiences within the Addams area and the presentation of this volume are heavily influenced by the ordered segmentation of the neighborhood. I took up residence in the area in the summer of 1963 and left a little less than three years later. At the outset the most evident finding was the distinctiveness of the Addams area and its opposition to adjacent neighborhoods. Since I had unwittingly settled near the boundary between the Italian, Mexican, and Puerto Rican sections, I soon became acquainted with some of the territorial, institutional, and communication arrangements that prevail between ethnic sections. Each of these topics is reviewed in the same order in the first two parts of this volume.

As I acquired friends and close informants, my own ethnicity became a serious problem. A few people worked over my genealogy trying to find some trace that would allot me to a known ethnic group. After close inquiry, one old Italian lady announced with peals of laughter, "Geraldo, you're just an American." She did not mean it as a compliment and afterwards I remember being depressed. In the Addams area, being without ethnicity means there is no one to whom you can appeal or claim as your own. The importance of ethnic solidarity is recounted in Part 3 of this volume.

Only after a year or more in the Addams area was I able to penetrate the private world of its families, street corner groups, and insular establishments. These are the groupings within which Addams area residents are least cautious and most likely to expose themselves. In large part my experience with these groups is limited to many adolescent male street corner groups and my own adult friends who formed a group of this type. In Part 4 I have concentrated on adolescent male street corner groups because they are so general an example of the primary groups that exist in the Addams area.

The ordered segmentation of the Addams area is a rather simple form of social organization and there is no attempt here to spell it out chapter by chapter. The general outlines of the neighborhood's social organization are presented in the next chapter while the remaining chapters show how the same principles of organization occur again and again in a variety of different situations. The findings, then, are seldom entirely novel but demonstrate how a rather limited set of organizational principles can be used to order social life in a number of contexts.

My own entry into the Addams area came about as a result of the Chicago Youth Development Project (hereafter called the CYDP), an action program aimed at reducing delinquency in the area.[10] While it was financed by the Ford Foundation, the project operated out of the local Boys Club. Throughout my stay, I was attached to this project as a research assistant, but the local people knew me principally as "someone who works down at the Boys Club." The residents took my position at the Boys Club as a "patronage job" and assumed that I had to live in the local ward as do many other people who receive "patronage." After a few months in the area I mentioned to some people that I wanted to write a history of the neighborhood before the city "tore it down." Since the residents were at the time very irritated at the city's plan to demolish a good portion of the area, they usually accepted my aim of recording the life of the neighborhood so as to correct certain stereotypes used to justify its forthcoming destruction.

The general method was that of participant observation, augmented by the long term use of informants and data available through public sources. The shortcomings of such methods have been often stated and do not need to be reiterated here. My own position is that these disadvantages are

[10] For further details see H. Mattick and N. Caplan, *The Chicago Youth Development Project* (Ann Arbor: University of Michigan, 1964).

counterbalanced by an intimate view of slum life which gains in validity what it lacks in representativeness. When observing from a great distance, one is apt to invent all sorts of irrational mental mechanisms to account for the behavior of slum residents. When observing close at hand, we are made all the more aware of how our own ideals have blinded us to the practicality of slum residents.

2

The Ecological Basis
of Ordered Segmentation

Geographic Setting

In its heyday the Near West Side of Chicago was the stronghold of such men as Al "Scarface" Capone, and Frank "The Enforcer" Nitti and was the kindergarten for several figures still active in the underworld. For convenience, I will call this part of Chicago the Addams area after Jane Addams, who founded Hull House there. The name is artificial since it is never used by the local residents.

To the north the area is bounded by a huge expressway that is the main east-west artery of the city. On the east is a large block of industry and then the "Loop" or the downtown part of the city. To the west is one of the world's largest complexes of hospitals and associated institutions. The southern boundary is a little less distinct, starting with a shopping district along Roosevelt Road that fades into the open air markets of Maxwell Street and then stops abruptly with a series of railroad tracks that cover two full city blocks.

None of these are natural boundaries in the sense that they can or do effectively block the establishment of human relations and social contacts. Yet according to local views, they are important landmarks used in making judgments about how one will behave as well as in assessing and describing the behavior of others. Across the expressway is one of Chicago's "skid rows," an area set aside for drunkenness, ill-dress, debauchery, minor prostitution, begging, and other vices.[1] Below Roosevelt Road is Maxwell Street or "Jew Town," where gypsy fortune tellers and Jewish merchants share the daytime hours with the Negro residents.[2] At night, however, this area is off limits to any whites. In the Medical Center there is a large number of doctors, medical students, and student nurses, most of whom commute to the area. For the most part, these people and the residents of the Addams area find each other's behavior incomprehensible and have neither grounds

[1] See Nels Anderson, *The Hobo* (Chicago: University of Chicago Press, 1923), pp. 3–39.

[2] Louis Wirth, *The Ghetto* (Chicago: University of Chicago Press, 1956).

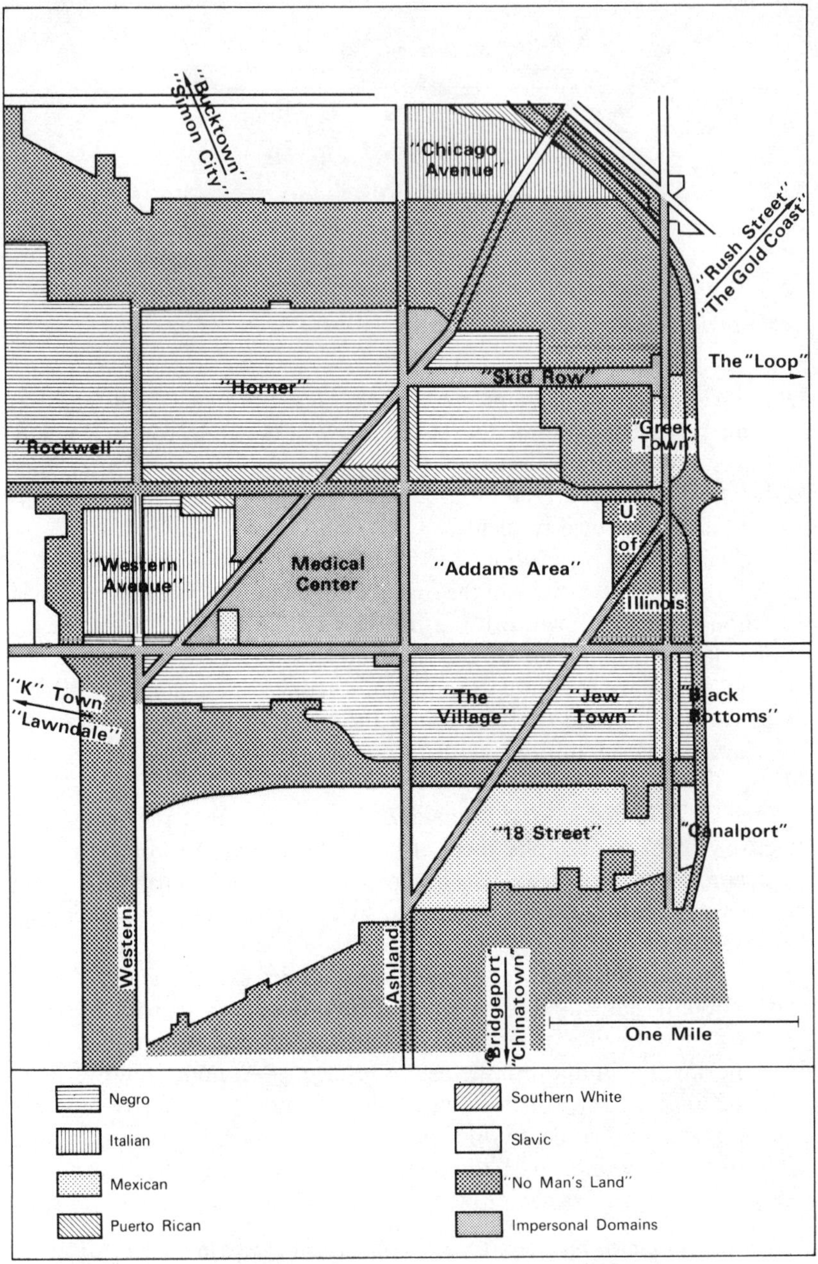

MAP 1. Neighborhoods Adjacent to the Addams Area ("Taylor Street")

for conflict nor peaceful exchange. In any case their lives are carried out in such different fashions that they seldom come in contact and can easily "keep their distance."

For persons in the Addams area only the adjacent neighborhoods are well defined (see map 1). Beyond this, their notion of established boundaries become vague and uncertain. Even when they are in unfamiliar territory, however, there is the general assumption that boundaries exist and that the area included must "belong" to someone.[3] Thus, the city is seen as something like an irregular lattice work from which a person's behavior and appearance can be gauged, interpreted, and reacted to depending upon the section to which he belongs. This does not mean, however, that Addams area residents believe that persons from other areas are secretly at war with them or have a way of life that is totally alien to their own. On the contrary, the general assumption seems to be that others are driven by much the same urges and needs as themselves. Each little section is taken to be a self-sufficient world where residents carry out almost all of their legitimate pursuits. A person who leaves his own area, then, is suspect so long as he has no visible and justifiable reason for straying from his home grounds. The first and most immediate evidence for making inferences about where a person "belongs" are his clothing, apparent ethnicity, demeanor, sex, age, companions, location, and plausible destination. In combination, these become the signs on which residents rely to define a person and to determine their own course of action. The demographic and ecological circumstances that give credence to this outlook will be examined in the remainder of this study.

History and Background

The Addams area was first settled around 1837 as a relatively well-to-do neighborhood, but by 1880 encroaching industry had already so jeopardized property values and the continuity of the area as a place of residence that the more affluent population left. From that time on the Addams area became a zone of transition where buildings were generally held as speculative property and rented without improvements lest they be replaced by other structures. Gradually some industry made its way into the area, and by 1964, 18% of the land was devoted to this purpose. For the most part, however, it has remained the first place of settlement for old-world immigrants and new-world migrants. First there were the Germans and Irish, who gradually gave way to the Greeks, Poles, French Canadians, Bohemians, and Russian Jews. Even before these groups fully occupied the area,

[3] See Harvey M. Zorbaugh, *The Gold Coast and the Slum* (Chicago: University of Chicago Press, 1929), pp. 159–81.

however, they were hard-pressed by the Italians. Only the Italians seem ever to have achieved any sort of hegemony over the entire area. The other nationality groups either occupied only portions of the area or were inter-mixed.[4] The dominance of the Italians, however, was short-lived. By 1930 the Mexicans began to enter the area and currently make up almost a third of its population. The Mexicans in turn are now being displaced at the periphery of the area by a small group of Puerto Ricans who are growing in number but who have never made up more than eight per cent of the population (see map 2).

Shortly after World War II, the Negroes almost totally occupied the Jane Addams Public Housing Projects. These housing projects, which are shown in map 3, contain about 975 apartments. To date, however, the Negroes have been almost entirely restricted to the projects, and before 1960 they made up only about 14% of the population.[5]

Except for the short period of Italian hegemony, the Addams area has never been ethnically homogeneous. As a rule most groups carved out only a small portion of the area and laid claim to it until some other group displaced them. In the course of time this has meant much cultural conflict, the constant readaptation of old facilities to new uses, and the acculturation of successive populations to an alien culture. As might be expected, the

---

[4] The Jews lived almost entirely below Taylor Street and, in later years, to the south of Roosevelt Road. The Greeks settled around Harrison, Blue Island, and Halsted on the northeast fringe of the area and remained there until the 1940's when the construction of the Congress Expressway more or less destroyed their community except for a few night clubs and coffee shops. The French Canadians were located mostly around Flour-noy and Loomis where their church (Our Lady of Provins) still stands. The Poles, Bohemians, and Germans seem to have been more dispersed. Italians filled up the open spots and gradually moved in until they almost entirely occupied the area between Roosevelt and Harrison, Ashland and Halsted. Then, between 1930 and 1960, the situation changed to what it is today (see map 2). This account of ethnic movements has been garnered from Jane Addams, *Twenty Years at Hull House* (New York: New American Library, 1961); E. W. Burgess, *Urban Areas of Chicago*, ed. T. V. Smith and L. D. White (Chicago: University of Chicago Press, 1929); Frank Carney "Experimental Area III–X (Addams)," Unpublished Report (Chicago Youth Development Project, 1961); Louis Wirth, *The Ghetto* (Chicago: University of Chicago Press, 1956); Welfare Council of Metropolitan Chicago, *Community Area 28—The Near West Side* (1953).

[5] Informants tell me that there was originally an "understanding" that the Negroes would have the projects south of Taylor while the Italians were to retain those to the north. However, this never really worked, and the Negroes soon took over the entire Jane Addams Projects. Available information seems to indicate that two different factors worked toward this end: (1) Local politicians were unable to contravene pressure brought by more militant Negro political action and (2) once the project had been defined as a "place for Negroes" the Italians moved of their own accord. Today, incidentally, over 92% of Chicago Public Housing is occupied by Negroes. Anyone who lives in the projects is automatically assumed to be a Negro or "like the Negroes." Just as there is guilt by association, so there is stigma by location.

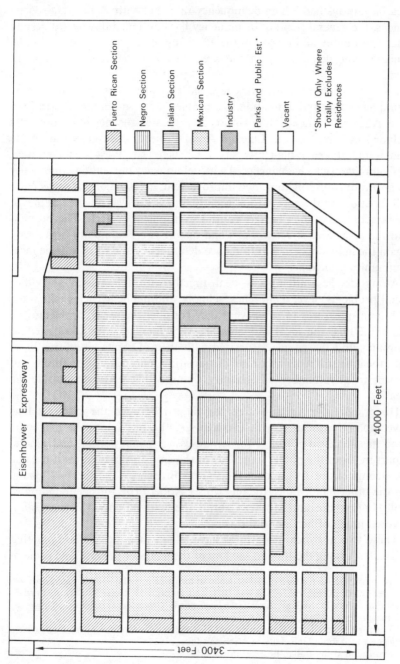

MAP. 2. Ethnic Sections as Defined by Local Residents

area has always had a high delinquency rate. Yet with all the area's vicissitudes, the general trend of delinquency has continued downward despite what is probably an increase in the efficiency of law enforcement.[6] Public concern over delinquency in the area, however, has taken a different turn.

For a long time the area has received special attention because of its delinquency rate and reputation as a problem area within the city. In 1889 Jane Addams founded Hull House there. Later the neighborhood was included as a part of the Chicago Areas Project which grew out of the studies undertaken at the University of Chicago. The West Side Community Committee, which is concerned with delinquency prevention, community organization, and neighborhood improvement, grew out of this project and still functions in the area. More recently, in 1961, it was selected as one of the target areas of the Chicago Youth Development Project.[7] This brought into the area three street workers and one or two community organizers. Again the main concern was to reduce delinquency and to encourage local community groups.

Alongside these attempts to deal directly with delinquency and other social problems, several churches, schools, and public agencies take some additional measures to solve what they consider the area's problems (see map 3). Thus, the local residents are very familiar with social welfare programs and the people associated with them. Despite all efforts, however, the area still remains a zone of transition, uncertain of its future and subject to any number of arbitrary changes that originate outside the area.

Historically the Addams area has ranged between the extremes that have become associated with Chicago. On the one hand, the neighborhood has achieved notoriety for its lawlessness, gangsterism, and general departure from the public standards of the city. In the twenties it became the stronghold of Al Capone, the "Gena Brothers" and the "40" gang. On the other hand, Jane Addams won a Nobel Prize for her founding of Hull House there, and Mother Cabrini, the first and only American saint, devoted much of her life to the area.[8]

These two historical departures have left in their wake traditions that still exist. Among the Italians the lore of the gangster persists, and some of

---

[6] During 1900–06 the rate of delinquency in terms of juvenile court appearances was 16.3 per 1,000; during 1917–23 it was 10.3; and in 1927–33 it was 9.8. See Clifford R. Shaw and Henry D. McKay, *Juvenile Delinquency in Urban Areas* (Chicago: University of Chicago Press, 1942), pp. 60–68.

[7] For further details see H. Mattick and N. Caplan, *The Chicago Youth Development Project* (Ann Arbor: University of Michigan Press, 1964).

[8] She founded the Italian hospital in the area.

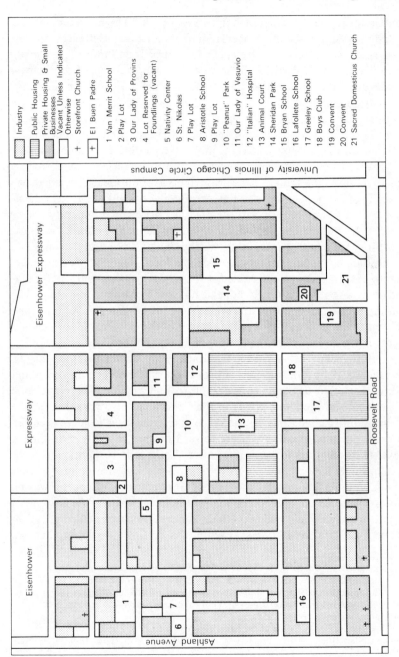

Legend:

- Industry
- Public Housing
- Private Housing & Small Businesses
- Vacant Unless Indicated Otherwise
- + Storefront Church
- + El Buen Padre

1. Van Merrit School
2. Play Lot
3. Our Lady of Provins
4. Lot Reserved for Foundlings (vacant)
5. Nativity Center
6. St. Nikolas
7. Play Lot
8. Aristotle School
9. Play Lot
10. "Peanut" Park
11. Our Lady of Vesuvio
12. "Italian" Hospital
13. Animal Court
14. Sheridan Park
15. Bryan School
16. Lafollete School
17. Greeley School
18. Boys Club
19. Convent
20. Convent
21. Sacred Domesticus Church

University of Illinois Chicago Circle Campus

Eisenhower Expressway

Expressway

Eisenhower

Roosevelt Road

Ashland Avenue

MAP 3. Significant Features within the Addams Area

the young boys can refer to such figures as Frank "The Enforcer" Nitti as casually as others might to a current baseball hero. Yet there are also unusually large numbers of Italians who can be found in both public and private agencies devoted to public welfare. Thus in a sense both conventional and illegitimate paths have provided the Italians with an escape hatch from the limitations of their ethnic beginnings. The Negroes and Mexicans, in turn, not finding their own heroes or patrons in these traditions, know far less about them and pay even less attention to them.

Currently the Addams area is the home of four different ethnic or minority groups: Negroes, Italians, Mexicans, and Puerto Ricans. According to general opinion the Italians have prior rights over the area. They make up a majority of the population, and the surrounding city also tends to authenticate their claim by referring to the area as an Italian community and by holding the Italians responsible for whatever happens within it.[9]

Most of the retail business as well as the available political patronage are in the Italians' hands. Moreover, even the local Negroes, Mexicans, and Puerto Ricans seem to acknowledge that their invasion will "naturally" end what was a "good thing" for the Italians. In combination these three conditions give credence to the widespread belief that the Addams area belongs to the Italians just as other sections of the city are said to "belong" to other ethnic groups for somewhat the same reasons.

More than any other group, the Italians are drawn together through mutual economic aid, common efforts at upward mobility, and an underworld that often demands considerable confidentiality. The coincidence of political and economic power in their hands has also provided some of the substantive conditions for the kinds of internal social control necessary to carry out this common venture toward upward mobility.[10] In fact, so well has this worked for them that after World War II the Italians in the Addams area saw themselves as enjoying a marked rise as an American ethnic group.[11] The general progress of their advance, of course, was not uniform or unidirectional. Often it meant ignoring some of the finer points of public morality and business ethics. It may also have entailed grovelling for petty political favors or legal exemptions. At times, no doubt, there was

[9] The members of the "West Side Bloc" in the Illinois legislature are largely from the Addams area. This group may be a myth, but the newspapers have turned it into a reality.

[10] The coincidence of power and responsibility as a basis for effective social control has been discussed by Marion J. Levy, *The Structure of Society* (Princeton, New Jersey: Princeton University Press, 1952), pp. 468–503.

[11] See Daniel Bell, "Crime as an American Way of Life," *The End of Ideology* (New York: Collier Books, 1961), pp. 127–50. During World War II the Italians suffered a setback, and it was at this time that many of the older residents learned English to avoid the suspicion and disapproval of non-Italians.

even an appeal to outright violence and coercion.[12] And finally, in the background there was certainly a good deal of conniving to keep all this as secret as possible. Still, in the course of time, a kind of myth of respectability, power, and wealth had been created and, in fact, by the time of this study it had probably become less a myth than a blueprint for general conduct.

In retrospect, the Italians seemed no sooner to have achieved their ascendancy over the area when the other ethnic groups became a significant part of its population. This was just as the Italians were beginning to "lift the face" of the area to suit their new found status. Houses were repaired and painted, new furniture purchased, tiny flower gardens fenced and planted, old furnaces, wiring, and plumbing replaced. But all of these efforts rested on the assumption that the area would remain in the Italians' hands. With the arrival of low status Negroes, Mexicans, and Puerto Ricans, everything became as indeterminate as it ever had been in the past. Whether or not they happened to like the members of these minority groups, there was no escaping the uncertainty and instability of such things as property values, physical upkeep, business opportunities, political favors, and the set routine of familiar day-to-day encounters and exchanges.

A far more comprehensive movement eventually took the shape of an "urban renewal program" that started in 1959. Although partially initiated and supported by the Italians, their reactions to the renewal program were mixed. On the one hand, it was hoped that rental and property values would be raised out of the reach of the low income members of the other ethnic groups.[13] At the same time, it also meant that building inspectors would be "snooping around" and enforcing rulings that had been overlooked for years. There was also the suspicion, and in some cases the conviction, that these rulings would be enforced arbitrarily or changed unpredicably.

Within a short time, however, all these hopes or misgivings were overshadowed by a still more important move on the part of the city government. Shortly after the renewal project got under way, it was decided that the University of Illinois should have a branch in the city. Initially there was much indecision about its location, but ultimately the area between

[12] A month or so before I arrived in the area (June, 1962), there was one "gangland" style killing at Taylor and Halsted. There have been none since. As Zorbaugh points out, most of these disciplinary measures are carried out against members within an ethnic group (*The Gold Coast and the Slum*, pp. 170–77).

[13] Well-to-do Mexicans are received into the Italian community without many reservations. It is doubtful if Negroes or Puerto Ricans would receive similar treatment. Since I know of no well-to-do Negroes or Puerto Ricans in the area, the question remains academic.

Morgan and Halsted, Congress and Roosevelt was chosen (see map 1). By 1960 there was a considerable reaction to this choice, and a number of court appeals, accompanied by several more or less obvious political moves, sought to forestall this location of the university. For present purposes it would be pointless to chronicle even the highlights of this movement except to point out that it never succeeded and that by late 1963 the bare skeletons of the university buildings were rising above the rubble. The immediate result was the clearing of the eastern third of the area and the removal of about the same fraction of its population.

The remaining two-thirds of the area, excluding the Jane Addams Housing Projects, is still subject to the original urban renewal plan that was anticipated for the entire area. According to the official plan, the residents that are left will benefit from the general improvements and be assured of a stable community. The actual outcome, however, is less sure. Lying between the medical center and a growing university, the residents question just how tolerant either of these institutions will be of a rather unruly and unappreciative conglomeration of minority groups.[14]

The Italians in the area are especially apprehensive and often blame the other groups for "ruining" the area's prospects. Still, this has not kept members of all these groups from joining forces and commiserating with one another over a common dilemma. At least one inter-ethnic committee was formed; housewives complained understandingly to each other; and when Florence Scala, the leader of the opposition to the university, ran for alderman she drew votes from all minority groups. Divided as they might be, many of the residents of the Addams area could still recognize a common enemy.

Conditions During the Present Study: 1962–65

Of the 30,000 people who lived in the Addams area during the 1950's, only about 20,000 are left in the western two-thirds of the neighborhood. The racial and ethnic composition of this remnant has not changed dramatically: approximately one-third are Italian, a quarter are Mexican, 17% are Negro, and 8% or less are Puerto Rican. A few isolated Greek families and persons from various ethnic groups, many of whom have married Italians, round out these figures.

The extent to which all of these changes affect the present study must be examined from several different vantage points. Certainly, many of the residents initially suspected that any outsider who asked questions was

---

[14] The University's first official recognition of the surrounding population was to assure the city that sufficient walls and fences would be built to keep out the local "undesirables."

somehow associated with the changes in the area. By living there for three years between 1962 and 1965 and by meeting people regularly, however, it was generally possible to overcome most of these fears.

In some ways the changes in the area only brought into relief persisting themes always present in the neighborhood. With the choice of the university site, people were only quicker to voice the general view that "you can't beat city hall." The Italians became even more convinced that their neighborhood was considered a "slum" and themselves expendable. Misgivings about how the invasions of lower status minority groups had undermined the previous gains of the area may have been exaggerated. But all of these views were present beforehand and the urban renewal program and the university site only tended to focus them.

Again, most of these consequences tend to highlight the existing arrangements in the area and make them more accessible to the researcher. In this respect the changes in the neighborhood are rather like a natural experiment which elicits the basic lineaments of its structure. Taken in this light, the most remarkable observation is that in many aspects the neighborhood has hardly changed at all.

Life in the Addams area is extremely provincial and what goes on a few blocks away may hardly affect the daily routine of commercial transactions, social engagements, and family life. After the eastern portion of the area had been demolished, those who remained carried on their lives much as they always had. The lack of marked disruption of the entire neighborhood is due largely to its general structure. The Addams area consists of several ethnic segments which are relatively independent, although they sometimes combine in an orderly way. With the clearance of the eastern portion, one Italian and one Mexican section were excised. While these ethnic sections could no longer combine with those remaining in the area, the remaining sections were left almost wholly intact. In turn, these sections continued to observe the same principles both in their opposition and in their alliances.

Probably the hardest hit were several home owners and businessmen at the western periphery of the university site. Typically, Addams area residents do not buy or improve a building for speculative purposes, but as a home which they can outfit to please themselves and a few long-term friends, relatives, and neighbors. It is useless to assure them that they will be adequately compensated for the loss of their home or that the remaining buildings and rentals will rise in value. If their friends, relatives, and neighbors are removed, they are like an actor with a huge but empty auditorium.

In the Addams area, most business establishments are not just a way of making a living but also of enjoying an enduring set of social relations where money is only one of the tokens that change hands. Besides, businesses in the Addams area cater to the very restricted needs, preferences, and background of a specific group of persons. In this case, customers are simply not interchangeable. Reimbursement for a lost business thus can never quite be translated into its equivalent elsewhere.

Similarly, the local owners of a small number of dwelling units can survive only if they do most of their own repair work and depend upon a measure of tolerance and cooperation that goes well beyond that of an ordinary economic contract.[15] Those whose property is demolished find both their economic interests and their social relations permanently impaired. In the Addams area the two are inextricably combined.

Nevertheless, it should be emphasized that the present study pertains only to that remnant of the Addams area which is still intact. Certainly this is a rather unusual area with many peculiarities of its own and situated in a unique historical context. Currently it is subject to a variety of social welfare programs, and its future as a residential area is in jeopardy. In addition, it is undergoing a progressive cycle of invasions, with the Mexicans pressing upon the Italians, and the Puerto Ricans and Negroes not far behind. But ethnic invasions, residential uncertainty, and social welfare programs are long standing forces in the area. It is, after all, a zone of transition, and change is its most permanent aspect. Indeed, there is every reason to believe that the segmentary structure of the area is itself an adaptation to such abrupt and uncontrollable changes. Broken up into a number of ethnic sections, each of them can manage to survive despite the disappearance of neighboring sections. The flexibility with which they can combine makes it possible for each to become allied with an exceptionally wide range of adjacent territorial units. So long as the territorial unities around them remain equally uncertain, there seems little reason to think that residents in the Addams area have any grounds for giving up their present system of ordered segmentation.

The Public View

For many Chicagoans the Addams area is only an indistinct part of the "West Side." At that distance, it is generally labeled an impoverished Negro slum, not only dangerous but also a center of criminal activity. Among

---

[15] Present realistic values make it "uneconomical" for absentee landlords to build anything less than an eight-story building. Since most of the buildings are two- and three-story affairs, local owners must exploit every personal aspect of their relationship with their renters. This, of course, does not mean that their sentiments are not thoroughly captured by the diffuse relationships they so often establish.

Negroes alone, it is often contrasted with the "South Side," which is adjudged more sophisticated and affluent.[16]

The newspapers and, among those persons who know of the West Side, a smaller number of individuals make a finer distinction by referring to the "Near West Side." Here the emphasis shifts from Negroes to Italians. Generally this appelation connotes the "West Side Bloc," "The Capone Mob," "gangs," the need for urban renewal, and Mrs. Scala's abortive attempt to save the Italian neighborhood by honoring the memory of Jane Addams. More recently the area has added to its doubtful honors that of being the birthplace of Jack Ruby, the killer of President Kennedy's assassin.

Among a more select group of people who live adjacent to the Addams area, it is known simply as "Taylor Street." Above all, this name implies a connection with the Outfit and Italians. It is also known that there are "gangs" and that "a lot happens on Taylor Street." At night it is supposed to be dangerous and inhospitable to outsiders. Occasionally, people say that it is "mixed" and "anything can happen."

Doubtless, all these preconceptions are a sort of myth; and any statistician could point out that most of the residents are not criminals, that pedestrians are usually left unmolested, that local children are seldom arrested, and that the majority of the residents are neither Italian nor Negro. These observations, however, provide most Chicagoans with very little comfort; and they would probably only smile and add that these are only the "official figures." Most Chicagoans, of course, do not rely much on official statistics to regulate their entry into various neighborhoods. Statistics always turn every act into a gamble; public stereotypes convey a sense of certainty.

Insofar as people from outside the Addams area accept these stereotypes as a reasonable guideline for their own actions, certain consequences follow. At the very least, it means that outsiders avoid the area unless they have to go there during work hours or pass through to get somewhere else. A second consequence is the humiliation brought upon the local population. However, for reasons that may be apparent, this is not too important; Addams area residents have many ways of circuiting or "neutralizing" these public definitions of themselves. Privately each of them knows that he is neither so despicable nor omnipotent as the general public thinks.

---

[16] Also, the South Side is more likely to be acknowledged as the natal home of the Chicago Negroes. In some areas of the South Side, the Negroes are in more dire economic straits than in the West Side. However, the South Side also includes well-to-do Negro communities and, besides, the Negroes on the West Side are simply regarded as more "country."

What they find far more difficult, however, is to be equally assured that the *other residents* are not so bad as they are said to be. Here they must resort to public signs of consistency, trust, and predictability. Four alternatives seem possible.

1. Since public definitions and social signs do not provide a gradation of trustworthy types within the Addams area, the residents may take refuge in those ethnic orbits of trust they brought with them from another region. In this case, the range of trust or suspicion will vary from one ethnic group to another depending upon the public signs they acknowledge. At most, however, they can never exceed the boundaries of a particular ethnic group.

2. Residents may also retreat from all social contacts beyond those of the nuclear family, which, in any case, cannot be avoided. Children are kept off the street, watched every minute, sent to a safe parochial school, and warned against strangers. Adults view their neighbors with suspicion and remain circumspect in their admissions. Local events are derided or avoided and, at most, nonrelatives are faced in the confines of a church or other "safe place." In the meantime, children may revolt to be with their peers, parents may be regarded as unsociable by their neighbors, and the remainder of the residents may abandon such isolationist families to meet their individual difficulties "on their own."

3. Where ethnic and kin unities are insufficient to fill the normative void between them, residents may take things in their own hands and establish a "personal relation." In this way people create a safe little moral world that is based on private understandings rather than public rulings. Necessarily, this means a relationship where assumed individual proclivities map out the range of permitted behavior. A most serious limitation, however, is that a personal relation requires a massive exchange of information and cannot be extended beyond the immediate participants. In fact, individuals must be felt out one-by-one without assuming very much about those connected with them. The business of society can hardly wait for such a meticulous examination of its members' individual credentials. Even in the Addams area, where personal relations are probably extended to a maximum, they can include only a minority of those encounters which are unavoidable.

4. Even though the public stereotypes applied to Addams area residents do not identify an acceptable morality, they do offer, for some residents, a certain honor and, for others, a determinate way of defining other people. Thus, some persons may thoroughly embrace one of the images that the wider community provides: "hood," "gangster," "tough guy," or "big shot." Others may personally reject those labels, but assume their truth regarding other people. Subsequently, they may either gloat over the wider community's inability to curtail such heroic escapades or simply condemn

them outright and avoid them at all times. Either way a certain definition of self and other has been established, and some measure of order has replaced a situation of ambiguity.

These alternatives are only a series of analytical exigencies that can be worked out on paper. In the language of game theory, they are "pure strategies"; in actual practice most of the residents seem to follow a "mixed strategy." There are the "hoods" who have many friends, show great concern for their families, and never miss Mass; the isolates who become sociable when they meet someone with whom they are personally acquainted; the ethnic purists who make an exception of some of the people in other ethnic groups; the sociables who make many people their friends but remain on guard against those who are especially notorious. Still, these patterns are not so compatible that all combinations and permutations are possible. At least on any one encounter, they map out the alternatives that the residents confront moment-to-moment.

The major value of this outline is that it shows how nearly the Addams area resembles a prison community or any other population that is not initially credited with a capacity to behave in an approved social manner. Insofar as the residents depend upon the public definition of each other, there is very little basis for trust except through the exercise of brute force or economic sanctions. By relying on these definitions alone they would truly descend to Hobbes' "war of all against all." To escape this disorder, they must discover some further set of social signs that indicate those they can or cannot trust.

The Local View

Although the reactions of the wider community have been fundamental to the development and current definition of the Addams area, most of the immediate consequences are realized within more limited bounds. The Addams area is surrounded by several other ethnic neighborhoods (see map 1) which have their own history and public standing in the wider community. To the northeast is "Greek Town," where the remnant of a Greek neighborhood survives in a few restaurants, nightclubs, and coffee shops.[17] The residents are mostly Mexican, and Addams area residents usually acknowledge that it is the stronghold of a Mexican "gang" called the "Potentates."[18] Directly to the north, across the Eisenhower Expressway,

[17] For a sentimental remembrance of Greek Town when it was intact, see Constantine D. Orphan, "Good Bye Greek Town," *Inland: The Magazine of the Midwest* (Chicago), Spring, 1963.

[18] Addams area residents never seem to use the term "gang" when referring to persons in the same ethnic group from the area itself. They are "clubs" or "SAC's."

along Van Buren, there is a small Puerto Rican area, which acts like a Balkan "buffer state" to fend off the Negroes further north (see map 4). This is the stronghold of the Van Buren Royals, too insignificant to threaten the Addams area, but sufficient to ward off the Negroes between Van Buren and Madison Street. Thus the Negroes to the north are not considered a problem by the people in the Addams area. Madison Street itself is sufficiently far away that Addams area residents can regard it half humorously and half sympathetically; it is the rialto of derelicts and drunks who are a nuisance but not dangerous. To the northwest is a tiny colony of southern whites, so busy fighting among themselves that they are harmless to anyone else. Most Addams area residents do not know they are there.

Directly to the west is a more difficult situation. Beyond Ashland, the Medical Center stretches for almost a half mile. Within this area there are so many policemen and impersonal bodies of social control that safe passage is almost impossible for anything resembling a gang of "troublemakers." On the other side of the Medical Center is another Italian neighborhood that probably resembled the Addams area before it was invaded by the Mexicans, Negroes, and Puerto Ricans. At one time, however, there was no Medical Center and the Italian community extended from Halsted Street to the railroads (see map 1). Even so, my older Italian informants told me they never "had much to do with each other." Possibly one of the major thoroughfares (Ashland or Damen) intersected their common interests and created an "impersonal domain" that divided them.[19] Whatever the reason, the Italians "over on Western" stand in opposition to those on Taylor Street. In the meantime the sanctity of the Medical Center keeps them at arm's length. Mostly this is a "private matter" between the Italians in the two areas; but once, when hostilities seemed sure to advance beyond mere rhetoric, it was suspected that Mexicans, Puerto Ricans, and even the Negroes in the Addams area might all join forces with their Italian co-residents. Unfortunately this test between ethnic and territorial loyalties never came to issue; the Italians in the two areas kept hesitating until the issue was "forgotten" or settled by some other means.[20] Still, many of the Italian boys on Taylor Street are able to recognize the names of their counterparts "over on Western." There are, for example, the "West O's" and "Roman Spectres." Collectively, they stand in a vague opposition to the Italian groups in the Addams area.

[19] Also, there is some evidence that a remnant of the old Irish residents remained to separate the Italians in the two areas. Later in this chapter I will point out how major thoroughfares may create a similar occlusion.

[20] Originally a boy from the Addams area was "beat up" at a beefstand "over on Western." There were threats of retaliation and counterretaliation. Eventually, however, the issue disappeared from public consideration.

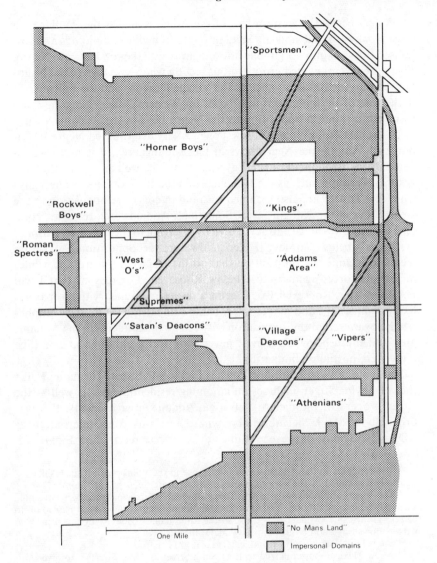

MAP 4. Dominant Groups in Areas Adjacent to the Addams Area

Directly below the western half of the Addams area is the "Village," a large block of public housing including several high rise buildings and row houses.[21] As in almost all public housing, nearly all the residents are Negro. There are several named groups in this section who are known to the Negro boys in the Addams area; such as the Village Deacons and the Falcons. As in the case of the Italian groups "over on Western," the Village boys are assumed to stand in opposition to the Negro boys in the Addams area.

To the east of the Village is Jew Town, a very deteriorated Negro neighborhood. Among the Negro boys in the Addams area, it is best remembered as the stronghold of the Egyptian Vipers as well as a few other less notorious groups, such as the Honchos, and the Red Ambers.[22] The "guys from Jew Town" are also assumed to stand in collective opposition to the Negro boys in the Addams area. Sometimes Addams area residents combine against the Village and Jew Town by referring to them as the "people" or "guys" below Roosevelt. Here, however, the oppositional structure seems to include the supposition that all the residents (Negro and white) might join forces against those below Roosevelt. For reasons that I will point out later, Roosevelt Road seems a powerful boundary that separates likely companions and makes improbable compatriots. It must be emphasized, however, that this opposition between all the residents in the Addams area and those below Roosevelt never took form, although at one time there were hostile preliminaries.[23]

South of the Village and Jew Town is Eighteenth Street. The name,[24] like that of Taylor Street, includes an adjoining residential area as well as the street proper. In the memory of some Addams area residents, this was originally a Slavic neighborhood whose residents some referred to as "DP's."[25] Today, however, ethnic invasion has reclassified Eighteenth

[21] The residents in the Addams area (and those in the Village) call it the "Village." Officially it is called by the various names of its separate "courts" or "homes."

[22] The Vipers still hold sway in Jew Town although the original members have long since passed into adulthood. The fame and reputation seem to have been passed on to certain groups in Lawndale who took up the same name. Today, they are somewhat overshadowed by another group in Lawndale: the Vice Kings.

[23] See below "Rumors and Rumbles: Trageatore," chap. 12.

[24] A few Mexican boys referred to Eighteenth Street as "Shit Street"; however, this appellation was not in wide usage.

[25] "Displaced persons." The older Italians do not use this label and refer to the people on Eighteenth Street as "Polacks." However, the more recent immigrant Mexican adults speak of them as "DP's," either in the firm conviction that they are actually "Displaced persons" or without the vaguest notion of what "DP" means. Aside from the Italians, many Addams area residents regard the Slavs as a single, homogeneous grouping. Another report, however, makes it clear that the Croats, Serbs, Bohemians, and Poles who live there are much less likely to share this view. Chicago Board of Education, "Montefiore Special School," unpublished report (1942), pp. 12–21.

Street as a Mexican neighborhood. To the Mexican boys in the Addams area there are several known gangs that hang out on Eighteenth Street, such as the Athenians and Roughshods. In the minds of the Mexicans these groups may not form a confederation, but certainly they are more likely to favor one another than their fellow nationals in the Addams area. In turn, it is also suspected that the Mexicans in the Addams area are more sympathetic with one another than with anyone else and that they might even be able to enlist the help of some of the Italians, Negroes, and Puerto Ricans. This suspicion is more than myth; on two or three occasions between 1961 and 1964 it became a reality.

There are many other areas that some of the residents recognize: Bridgeport, Horner, Rockwell, "K" Town, Lawndale, Bucktown, Simon City, Thirty-fifth Street, the Casbah, Six Tray, Tray Nine, Chinatown, and so forth. Like most Chicagoans, however, the majority of them have only heard of these areas, and in actual fact they are of little more concern to Addams area residents than to people in the suburbs. What especially distinguishes Addams area residents is that they must somehow manage to live there despite Eighteenth Street, Jew Town, the Village, and the "guys over on Western." According to Addams area residents, this is very difficult because all the people in these surrounding sections are "against them." Within each of these sections, of course, one can hear somewhat the same complaint: Individually they know themselves to be badly divided; it is only the united stand of the Addams area residents that puts them on the defensive. Perhaps in this way each of them husbands the other's reputation.

The Order of Segmentation

From a distance all of these antagonisms seem to take on the formal characteristics of a "segmentary system."[26] First, each group is a sociospatial unit. Second, inclusion in these groupings is mutually exclusive. Third, opposition is between "equivalent" units. Fourth, the order by which groups combine preserves the equivalence of oppositional units. While segmentary systems are usually restricted to corporate groups, however, the ones here include groups that are no more than corporate units of responsibility. Addams area residents are a group only in the sense that they are jointly held liable for each other's behavior. The following diagrams show how this system works.

[26] See M. Fortes and E. E. Evans-Pritchard, *African Political Systems* (London: Oxford University Press, 1940), pp. 1–23; E. E. Evans-Pritchard, *The Nuer* (Oxford: Clarendon Press, 1940), pp. 94–266.

First Level of Opposition: groups of the one age grade vis-à-vis groups of the same age grade from a different area but of the same ethnicity.

Separate Italian groups in the Addams area. ⟶ Separate Italian groups "over on Western" who are in approximately the same age range.

Separate Negro groups in the Addams area. ⟶ Separate Negro groups in Jew Town who are in approximately the same age range.

Separate Negro groups in the Village who are in approximately the same age range.

Separate Mexican groups in the Addams area. ⟶ Separate Mexican groups from Eighteenth Street who are in approximately the same age range.

Separate Puerto Rican groups in the Addams area. ⟶ Separate Puerto Rican groups from "Van Buren" who are in approximately the same age range.

At this level the opposition (↔) is group-to-group within a single age range. However, it is not group-specific; i.e., any two groups of the same ethnicity and about the same age but from different areas are in opposition.

Disputes at this level are fairly common but minor. Ordinarily they involve only teenage males and occur "on the spur of the moment" when two groups "accidentally" meet and a few "words are exchanged," ending in a very brief altercation (verbal or physical). There is little planning or warning in the form of a rumor or other communication. Often, but not always, these are clashes between named gangs. However, where the groups involved are unnamed, it is likely that both antagonists will "mistakenly" assume that its opponent is part or whole of some named gang and label them as responsible. Frequently this has the consequences of drawing additional people into the issue and, along with other events, introduces a secondary level of opposition.

Italians in the Addams area ⟷ Italians "over on Western"
Negroes in Addams area ⟷ Negroes from the Village
Mexicans in Addams area ⟷ Mexicans from Eighteenth Street
Puerto Ricans in Addams area ⟷ Puerto Ricans from "Van Buren"

At this secondary level, the opposition is definitely between territorial units of the same ethnic groups. Usually when disputes reach this level they involve persons in all age ranges, especially the males. Street groups coalesce; some of the adult men go get their guns and sit on the front steps, waiting; older women retire inside the house or at the doorway;

young unmarried girls stand in wait for the spectacle. Most generally, this situation is the aftermath of some dispute at the first level of opposition or the outcome of a series of rumors or other signs of conflict. Necessarily this degree of mobilization presupposes some sort of forewarning that is sufficiently public to alert those concerned. Frequently this takes a matter of days, and never does it happen "on the spur of the moment." Once delayed this long, however, this oppositional structure seldom matures to become anything more than a "preparation." Either it dies altogether or advances to the third level of opposition.

Addams area residents ⟷ "Western Avenue" residents
Addams area residents ⟷ The "people who live below Roosevelt"
Addams area residents ⟷ The "people from Eighteenth Street"
Addams area residents ⟷ Those "people over on Van Buren"

Here both age and ethnic differences are muted by the single fact of territorial unity. At best this is a suspected level of opposition. It almost never matures into actual combat, although it does occasionally reach the level of a "rumor." Once this stage is reached, however, several other factors come into play. First, there are grave misgivings about the unity of all the ethnic groups in each of these areas. Aggressors suspect territorial unity on the part of their enemies, but the defenders feel insecure about this unity. Second, by this time the potential conflict has reached the ears of several impersonal bodies of social control—the police, street workers, YMCA officials, and so forth[27]—who at this point usually intervene and take matters outside the residents' hands.

It may seem odd that all the ethnic groups in the Addams area would join forces no matter what the enemy. However, in order to understand how this system works, two points must be made. First, these three levels of opposition follow a time sequence in which the first level almost always has temporal priority. Almost invariably, antagonisms start *within* the same ethnic group and extend to other ethnic groups. Thus, no single ethnic group in the Addams area *is enlisted* to oppose its own members in another territorial unit. If, for example, the Mexicans "start something" with the Negroes below Roosevelt, it is very doubtful that the Negroes in the Jane Addams Project would come to their aid. However, this situation is very unlikely to occur. The Mexican boys have very little reason to go below

---

[27] It must be remembered that there are several such people located in the area. At least six policemen, one congressman, one state legislator, one Democratic committeeman, and several precinct captains live in the area. In addition, there are several street workers, youth agency people, priests, nuns, ministers, and civic personnel who either work or live in the area. Over a period of time, it is almost inevitable that some of them should hear of any large-scale antagonism.

Roosevelt Road and are well warned to shy away from the area. What usually happens is that the Negro boys in either area "get something started" and the other ethnic groups are "pulled in." The same sort of progression holds for all the other coalitions.

Second, any doubts about the undying unity of the ethnic groups in the Addams area are also shared by the residents themselves. Once disputes draw in more than one ethnic group, there are grave misgivings on everyone's part. Their hope is that if the other ethnic groups join either side, it will be that of their own area. In the eyes of their opponents this may appear a more likely outcome than in the eyes of the people in the Addams area. The residents themselves, however, make the same mistake when they assess the chances of other "guest" groups joining their "hosts" in the Village, Jew Town, Eighteenth Street, Western Avenue, or Van Buren.

Each of these points demonstrates the sense in which Addams area residents and others on the "Near West Side" assume that spatial unity automatically leads to social unity and concerted action. On the one hand, there is the bifurcation of ethnic groups once they have been separated in physical space. All that divides the Mexicans, Negroes, Italians, and Puerto Ricans in the Addams area from their fellow nationals in other areas are roads, vacant lots, and buildings. Yet, once they stand in opposition, they never seem to doubt that each street corner group within a single ethnic group will ally itself with other groups from the same territory. Moreover, there is the suspicion, if not the certainty, that all street corner groups within a territory might join forces irrespective of ethnicity.

By their assumption that residential unity implies social collaboration, inner city residents may help create the situation they imagine. Given their conviction that persons from another area will act in concert, they have little alternative except to go into collusion with their own territorial compatriots. To some extent, of course, this emphasis on territorial unities has its background in a cultural history wherein spatial groupings are one of the most frequent forms of social combination. This general pattern, however, is given credence by still another condition. Addams area residents are forced together in rather intimate and congested confines. Somehow the Mexicans, Puerto Ricans, Negroes, and Italians must manage to live together. If one day they joined a group from outside the area against others in their own territory, the following day they might meet their co-residents in the same store, church, playground, youth center, or school. They are even more likely to cross each other's pathway at the same street corner, bus stop, or beefstand. Much as they may dislike each other, Addams area residents always face the prospect of having to see one another on "the next day." By comparison, it is far more comforting to have an enemy from outside the area.

In contrast, people who live in the suburbs or more impersonal residential areas seem relatively indifferent to the location of their enemies. In fact, old and bitter enemies may pass each other without even knowing it. Persons in these areas often carry out their antagonisms by proxy through a series of voluntary and formal organizations and seldom meet their opponents face-to-face. In the Addams area, encounters usually take just the opposite course. Most often the residents carry out their antagonisms face-to-face and are only too well aware of whom their enemies are. Also it is very difficult for them to pretend that their relationship has no history, and an impersonal and "polite" form of exchange is not only unfamiliar, but a marked deviation from precedent. In any case, one of the antagonists is likely to be accompanied by "intimates" who know of their mutual grievances and may wonder at such an obvious failure to broach the issue.

In the Addams area this segmentary system of spatial and ethnic units is so well understood that the residents seldom bother to tell you of it. If you ask why it exists, they will usually answer that it is "only natural" or say "that's just the way it is." It would be easy to label this as a myth and dismiss the segmentary system outlined above as a reification. All the same, it is a myth that is shared by all the people of the Addams area. In this sense, it is one of those myths that is taken as information and becomes the basis on which people predicate their action.

The Ecological Basis for the Corporate Unity of the Addams Area

The Addams area gains its unity from the common accusations, insults, and fears of those immediately around it. This process of unification, however, is paralleled by certain ecological conditions. The Addams area, like its adjacent neighborhoods, is outlined by a series of geographic features that separate it from the wider community. Broadly speaking, these features fall into two different classes.

1. *No-man's lands*—Usually these are areas being razed, places of industrial concentration, or expressways. All of them are sections where people do not live permanently and over which no one exercises a personal surveillance. Given local ideas about who an area can "belong to," this creates a kind of social vacuum where the usual guarantees of social order and control are lacking. Ordinarily they are viewed as dangerous, and people cross them "at their own risk." On either side, residents take some comfort in knowing they are safely separated by a border of moral chaos.

In actual fact, this does not mean that these no-man's lands are never crossed, even in the late hours of the night. What is far more important is the way crossing one of these areas casts suspicion over the purposes of someone who does so at certain hours of the day. Unless their good intentions are obvious, they expose themselves to every suspicion. Momentarily they are "adventurers," and their status as well-intended citizens is suspended. Some people avoid them; some don't care what happens to them; a few take them as "fair game."

Adjacent to the Addams area, the Eisenhower Expressway and the upheaval of the University of Illinois constitute such no-man's lands. Beyond them there are several others which subdivide their enemies: the railroads along Sixteenth Street, the industry that lies between Twenty-first Street and Bridgeport, the mass of industry that separates Lake and Grand streets, the railyards and industry that lie just across from Western (see map 1).

2. *Impersonal Domains*—These are areas subject to periodic anomie. They are nonresidential areas where the safety of a passerby is mostly in the hands of impersonal authorities who are either acting on behalf of someone else's interests or whose responsibilities do not include the entire day. For the most part, these are major thoroughfares flanked by impersonal business establishments or public institutions. During the daytime these areas are patrolled fairly well by businessmen, bureaucrats, policemen, and customers. At night, however, when people are free of their duties and therefore most likely to be dangerous, these areas are abandoned by almost everyone but the police. There is no street life, there are no lights in the windows, and there is almost no reason for anyone to be there.

In the first place, Addams area residents have serious doubts about the efficiency of anyone appointed to look out for the interests of someone else. As individuals, policemen are "no worse than anyone else." But that is exactly the problem—they can't be expected to extend themselves beyond the minimum. Second, there are also grave doubts about the effectiveness of social control where people are relatively anonymous and have limited liabilities.

Alongside the Addams area, Roosevelt Road and the Medical Center are subject to such periods of anomie. Roosevelt Road is a major thoroughfare bordered by impersonal business places that serve people from all over the city. By nightfall, however, it is nearly vacant except for a few Negro "night spots" that are uncertain in their clientele.[28] There are a few

---

[28] Most of the customers come from Jew Town and the Village, but they do not seem to make up a daily clientele where everyone knows everyone else. Besides, there are strangers who come to these places from all over the West Side.

policemen in patrol cars, but their presence is undependable and does not penetrate all the nooks and crannies of Roosevelt Road.

The Medical Center is somewhat different because some of its business continues throughout the night. Also, it is especially well patrolled, and the least sign of danger elicits an even more intense surveillance.[29] All the same, this area draws a strong cleavage between the residents on either side. The very effectiveness of impersonal surveillance seems to remove the threat of people from either side as well as the necessity of establishing some working relationship between them.

The responses to both kinds of areas show the importance that people in the inner city place on residential unity to define the extent and limits of adequate social control. First, only the people who live in a given area are expected to take a heartfelt interest in its safety. Second, this amnesty is considered to cover only the residents themselves and not outsiders. Third, if an area is unprotected by the interests of people who must live there, it is judged unsafe.

To some extent, this reliance on territorial unities probably reflects the cultural background of inner city residents. Originally all of them depended heavily upon small territorial unities whose safety from one another was assured by distance and the lack of any reason for contact. Rare outsiders might be treated as "guests." In part, however, this reliance on residential unities may be shared by most Chicagoans. What seems to be especially disturbing for inner city residents is the relative abundance of non-residential areas. West of the river, Chicago stretches out like a hand, the fingers of industry and business getting thinner, while the enclosed residential spaces include more and more people. For those at the fringes, residential unity may include almost all those occasions where people must face each other without the benefit of daylight or prior acquaintance. By contrast, the inner city is a set of little residential islands surrounded by dangerous expanses of industry, business, and government.

It would be a serious mistake to dismiss each of these regions as only an artifact of temporary ethnic advances. The Medical Center divides two Italian neighborhoods; Roosevelt Road separates two groups of Negroes. In fact, disputes between Addams area residents and those around them usually start within a single ethnic group. Only later are the others drawn in. Despite all that has been said about ethnic antagonisms, this is not an illogical progression. The incipient steps that lead to opportunism and predation are easiest to begin within one's own ethnic group. Each ethnic

---

[29] The Medical Center is probably one of the safest places in the inner city. Yet, once when a few boys attacked two nurses in the center, it became a *cause célèbre* for increased police protection. Similar cases in the inner city never got the same kind of attention.

group knows that old grudges, new girls, and novel "kicks" are most accessible and approachable among their "own kind." The Negroes, for example, assume that the others are too distant to have personal grudges, be familiar with their girls, or know when there is to be a little "action." The situation is analogous for the other three ethnic groups.

Part 2

---

*Institutions and Patterns
of Communication*

3

Institutional Arrangements

The ordered segmentation that characterizes the Addams area's relationship with adjacent neighborhoods is repeated by its internal structure. The basic segments are those defined by race, ethnicity, territory, sex, and age. There is strong opposition between equivalent segments, but they can be combined according to a definite order.

The major division in the neighborhood occurs among its four ethnic groups. Not only are the Negroes, Italians, Mexicans, and Puerto Ricans separated by location, but they are divided still further by a host of ecological and institutional arrangements. Generally, the religious, commercial, recreational, and educational institutions help sustain these ethnic boundaries. These institutions, however, are not fully controlled by local residents and are subject to other ecological fluctuations. The overall structure, then, is one in which local institutions either mirror the ethnic sections in the neighborhood or bring out the opposition between them.

Religion

Religion is one of the most significant ways in which Addams area residents assure one another of their willingness to sacrifice personal designs in favor of joint concerns. This does not mean that they are particularly religious or moral. Instead, religious affiliation must be taken for what it is —a public guarantee of one's amenability to group concerns, whether one happens to be "moral" or not. Thus, even the most "immoral" of Addams area residents tend to distrust someone who openly flaunts his irreligiosity.

The most apparent cleavage between Addams area residents is in terms of dogma. Almost all of the Italians are Catholic. Many of them have only a nominal affiliation to the church, but still they regard an open break with their faith as an act of ultimate arrogance. (Such a person would probably not be trusted even to help in some immoral exploit.) Only a slight majority of the Mexicans are Catholic. As in the case of the Italians, many of them are only nominal Catholics. Those who have become Protestants are converts and seem somewhat more rigorous about religious practices and formal morality. Rarely, Protestant Mexicans will discredit their Catholic counterparts as "people who only say they are religious." In turn, some of the Italian and Mexican Catholics are still doubtful that anyone who openly eats meat on Friday could really care what God or *other people* think. Still, most Italians and Mexicans assume that they are coreligionists without bringing up the question. The Puerto Ricans are divided into Protestant and Catholic wings, and by now they cannot assume that they will have the same faith. Most Negroes are Protestants and usually assume as much of each other, even when it is untrue.

Differences of faith alone seem relatively unimportant because they are seldom raised in conversation. Churches are another matter, since they provide a common establishment where a continuing group of people waive their individuality in favor of their common welfare. Formal beliefs, then, are most significant in the way they conspire with other conditions to separate people into different religious establishments.

Because of their differences in faith, most of the ethnic groups in the Addams area make up separate congregations. By their location, their service, and past usage, the churches go still further toward preserving the divisions between ethnic sections. In all there are ten separate places of worship in the area. None of them brings together different ethnic groups.

1. *Our Lady of Vesuvio* (*Catholic*)—Almost all the Italians in the area either go to this church or consider it "their church." Architecturally it is modeled after a church of the same name in Naples, and the interior is decorated with pink carrara marble. The church was originally built by Italians, and Italian priests still manage it. Most masses are in English, but one is in Italian. Almost all the Italians use this church for their weddings, christenings, funerals, and so forth. This church is considered the most powerful single institution in the area, and it is often the scene of informal arrangements between the Italians and the other ethnic groups. The local priests are probably the most trusted of all intermediaries, and they faithfully honor the "private settlements" that are so common in the area.

2. *St. Assisi* (*Catholic*)—This church lies on the southern boundary of the Addams area. At one time this was a Mexican neighborhood; and since then the church has remained in their hands, although it is nearly surrounded by a Negro population. The local pastor is Italian but speaks excellent Spanish. Practically all services are carried out in Spanish. Aside from precedent and language, the Mexicans do not have much claim on the church. The congregation is almost entirely Mexican, however, and the continuity of their control may be due to the fact that the local Negroes have not challenged it. Because of the location of this church and the scarcity of

Spanish-speaking churches in Chicago, many of the congregation come from outside the Addams area. Also, there are some Mexicans in the Addams area who go to still other churches. Its congregation, then, is not a residential unity. Correspondingly, the church is not in a good position to arbitrate differences or settlements within the Addams area.

3. *Sacred Domesticus (Catholic)*—The congregation is almost entirely Negro. The priests, however, are all white, and the Negroes' claim to the church lies solely in their residential proximity. A few of the Negroes in the Addams area go to this church, but most of the congregation comes from south of Roosevelt or to the southwest. As in the case of St. Assisi, then, its congregation does not form a territorial unity. Occasionally, however, a local priest does try to act as intermediary with the whites in the Addams area. Still, the Negroes' hold on the church is tenuous; and their past difficulty in getting into the church was so great that they are now ambivalent about appealing to its pastor. Another difficulty is that anyone who attempts to sponsor the Negroes' interests must also take an explicit stand on integration and the civil rights movement. Necessarily, this makes it hard to enter into all of the *sub rosa* compromises that are so much the practice among the whites. Whites in the Addams area will accede to almost any working arrangement between ethnic groups. However, they are most unwilling to commit themselves to an explicit set of principles that are relatively inflexible and general to all people or situations. The civil rights movement is aimed at just such an arrangement.

4. *Our Lady of Provins (Catholic)*—Originally this church was built by a group of French Canadians who had settled around it. Today it is not a parish church but is owned and operated by a French-Canadian order. The congregation, however, is largely Mexican with a smattering of Puerto Ricans and Italians. Most of these people are from the local area, but they have not been able to assert much claim over the church. The services are in English and, in general, the priests do not speak Spanish. Recently, however, the church has become a center for Mexican social affairs. At the same time, it remains a meeting place for a Catholic men's organization that has members (many of whom are of French-Canadian descent) from all over the city. Accordingly, the Mexicans still seem to view the church with uncertainty and to regard themselves as "guests." Consequently they seldom rely upon it as a clearing house for their secular problems.

5. *West Side Christian Mission (Presbyterian)*—The congregation is entirely Negro, but only a portion comes from the Addams area. The staff are entirely white, live outside the West Side, and are very much involved in the civil rights movement. As a rule, they cannot engage in the sort of *ad hoc* and temporary expedients that are common elsewhere in the area.

Instead, they usually press for an open confrontation of issues and a formal settlement that is both permanent and binding. Under these circumstances they are often unable to bargain effectively with the local whites or to act as intermediaries among their members when the members seek a "private" rather than a public solution.

6. *St. Nikolas (Greek Orthodox)*—Originally this was a Jewish synagogue; but when the Jews moved out, the Greeks bought the building. Now the Greeks in turn, are gone, and almost all the congregation comes from outside the area. On one day of the week they suddenly appear and as suddenly leave. To the Addams area residents they are of little concern and are not significant in local affairs. The Greeks' control of the church is thoroughly uncontested, and no one else would think of going there. Since the church's congregation is not located in the area, there is also no reason to seize upon the church as a body which could speak for local residents. The Greeks are viewed as utter foreigners who owe nothing to anyone and to whom nothing is owed. On two occasions local boys have broken into the church. During the three years of my study no other church was so treated.

7. *Church of the Valley and the Voluntary Pentecostal Church*—These are two storefront churches that are almost entirely Puerto Rican in their membership. Each of them is dominated by an extended family and is extremely intimate. Practically no one enters these churches unless brought in by someone else. Within their own congregation they are probably very effective at providing a common setting for settling differences, but they are so unapproachable that no one else appeals to them as intermediaries.

8. *Lighthouse Missionary Baptist Church and Vineyard Spiritual Temple*—These are Negro storefront churches along Roosevelt. Like the Puerto Rican churches, they are extremely intimate and unapproachable except by becoming a member. Necessarily they cannot act as intermediaries with outsiders.

9. *El Buen Padre (Methodist)*—This is a Mexican church that carries out its services in Spanish and has a Mexican pastor. Practically all of its congregation comes from the Addams area, and they concern themselves mostly with local issues. The church, however, can speak for only a minority of the Protestant Mexicans.

10. *First Testament Church*—This is a Mexican storefront church. Like the others in the area, it is unapproachable except by becoming a member of its congregation. Consequently it has little significance beyond its own congregation.

The overwhelming majority of Addams area residents go to these ten churches. A few local Puerto Ricans and Negroes go to several storefront churches along Van Buren and Halsted. These churches are not significant either as clearing houses for local difficulties or as a basis for establishing trust among the residents.

It is obvious that each local congregation draws exclusively from a single ethnic group. Only the Italians, however, have a church that unites them as a residential and ethnic congregation. As a result, Our Lady of Vesuvio can usually act as spokesman for the Italian section and a clearing house for settlements either among the Italians themselves or with the other ethnic groups. None of the other churches can represent an entire ethnic section since each of the other sections is divided among more than one congregation.

The lack of single churches able to represent the Mexican, Negro, and Puerto Rican sections makes it difficult for each ethnic section to carry on private negotiations with the other. In the winter of 1964, for example, some Italian boys robbed two Mexican boys. Some Mexican men went to the priest at Our Lady of Vesuvio and made vague threats about what would happen unless the stolen wallets were returned. The priest, with the aid of a precinct captain, found out where the wallets had been discarded and returned them along with certain papers. The priest was happy to do this for the Mexicans, but he deplored their inability to reciprocate "because you never know which church they belong to."

Since most other bodies of social control refuse to acknowledge the ethnic sections in the Addams area, the lack of a church to represent each section is a serious deficiency. Of all the institutions in the area, the church is virtually the only one that local residents can potentially make their own and whose services they can feel are simply what is due them. All the other bodies of social control operate somewhat like charities, dispensing their services as if they were gratuitous acts of benevolence. Thus the residents either shy away from them or receive their services without any sense of debt.[1] The church is different. Ultimately, it can belong to a local group. The receipt of benefits is not humiliating, and the residents can meet its ritual acts of obeisance without feeling themselves the victims of outsiders.

As has been observed, however, the churches in the Addams area cannot, except in isolated instances, effectively represent its four ethnic sections. Aside from the Italian section, the churches are too divided to arbitrate for

[1] Most of the local welfare agencies complain that the residents are ungrateful or exploitative. Yet, these same agencies go to great lengths to emphasize their liberality and the fact that local residents "really" have no right to demand them. In turn, the local residents can obtain these services only by undergoing some humiliation while submitting to the qualifications of the particular institution. So far as the residents are concerned, they owe nothing to such institutions, and their own humiliation more than compensates for whatever they receive.

the remaining ethnic sections, even though they provide their separate congregations with a basis for trust and association. The result, then, is that the other ethnic sections remain distinct but still lack the sort of effective representation provided by the Italian church.

Commercial Exchanges

Economic life in the Addams area consists primarily of commercial exchanges rather than occupational membership. Outside the nuclear family it is rare for people to know each others' occupational titles. School teachers, lawyers, doctors, social workers, and policemen are recognized as distinct categories of people. Persons in these occupations are scarce in the Addams area, and most of the residents' occupations are identified by where they work rather than what they do. If you ask what a person does for a living, an informant will usually mention the place where he works. The "stockyards," "the Loop," "medical center," and "Angelo's Restaurant" are typical replies.

Actually, occupational identities are pushed aside by more important considerations. In introducing one another, local residents will usually mention where they live, their personal name, their ethnicity, or some local group to which they belong. If pressed, a person will tell where he works, but it is somewhat impolite to ask what he does. No doubt income and occupation are important conditions that help determine the consumer practices of Addams area residents. Within the neighborhood, however, these practices are often ignored while the pattern of commercial relations is closely observed.

In the Addams area the ideal form of commercial exchange is one that follows intra-ethnic boundaries. Preferably a person should confine his transactions to places where he "belongs." As with the churches, almost all the local business places are categorized according to their proper clients. These classifications are regulated by a series of criteria well-acknowledged by the residents:

1. *Merchandise*—A business place that specializes in ethnic products is invariably said to belong to that group.
2. *Operators*—Where the operator is a member of one minority group, this is taken into consideration to the extent that members of another ethnic group cannot call it "their own."
3. *Hangouts*—Businesses that are hangouts for a group from a particular minority group are generally said to belong to that group.
4. *Decor, language usage, and "line" of operation*—Business places that adopt a decor, language, or "line" (conversational style, radio

programs, music, etc.) that is appropriate to a local minority group are assigned to that group.

5. *Location*—Where a business is located in an area of residence that has been conceded to a particular minority group, the latter is generally defined as the "owner."

In the summer of 1964 there were 267 business establishments in the Addams area. One hundred and seven of them were regarded as the sole property of a single ethnic group. While most of the remaining business places are assigned to a local ethnic group, many of them are on the boundaries between ethnic sections and are subject to inter-ethnic encounters. Aside from one unique business place, all the others are owned and managed by outsiders.

Among the residents of the area, the ideal form of commercial relations is one in which each ethnic group conducts its business entirely among its own members. This ideal, however, can never be fully realized. Gradations away from this ideal are accompanied by a similar departure from the residents' ideal of social behavior, as demonstrated by the various relationships and adaptations described below and summarized in table 1.

Seclusiveness and Suspicion

Many business establishments are so thoroughly acknowledged the property of a single minority group that customers outside the group seem like intruders. When I first went into the Addams area, I entered several places where I was asked, "Whatta you want?," as if I were lost. At the time I thought them inhospitable or "prejudiced." What I did not know was that these places are almost never confronted by someone they have not known for years and that they are thoroughly tailored to the needs and personal peculiarities of a small network of friends within a single minority group. To them my presence was totally inexplicable. At worst, I could be a policeman, some sort of city inspector, or a troublemaker. At best, I might have got there by accident, not knowing any better. Whatever had led me there could not have been their products because they were too expensive, of questionable quality, badly displayed, and usable only to an ethnic group quite other than my own.

All the ethnic groups in the area have such establishments, and the general public seldom enters them. When someone from outside the area or from another ethnic group enters, the proprietor and regular customers view them with great suspicion and, in some cases, use *ad hoc* measures to insure their safety. Sometimes they will simply wait for the intruder to get his bearings and leave. If that fails, the proprietor may eventually get

TABLE 1

INTERETHNIC RELATIONS IN 267 COMMERCIAL ESTABLISHMENTS

RELATION	CHARACTERISTICS OF ESTABLISHMENT	NUMBER OF ESTABLISHMENTS IN EACH ETHNIC SECTION					TOTAL
		Italian	Mexican	Puerto Rican	Negro		
Seclusiveness/Suspicion	Not located on boundary; some ethnic products or decoration; proprietor's ethnicity same as that of clients.	56	14	19	3		92
Guests/Hosts	Specializes in ethnic products.	12	2	...	1		15
Taking Turns	Short order cafe on boundary between ethnic sections.	1	...	...	...		1
Mutual Tolerance	Few or no ethnic products; on boundary between ethnic sections or proprietor's ethnicity differs from that of clients.	91	26	18	3		138
Mutual Exploitation	Proprietor from outside Addams area or establishment located in ethnic section where proprietor does not live.	6	2	2	11		21
TOTALS		166	44	39	18		267

around to asking what he wants. In the meantime, everyone in the store stops and stares.

The treatment of regular customers, of course, is exactly the opposite. Commercial relations with these people are intimate, and all economic transactions are buried in the guise of friendship and sentiment. In large part this is the reason they cannot tolerate the presence of strangers from another ethnic group. Among themselves the customers set aside their public face and disclose much of their private life to one another. Their conversations, their exchanges, and their understandings are simply too intimate to be carried out before the general public.

There are ninety-two such places in the area. All of them are quite small and specialize in ethnic products or carry out their services in a manner attuned to a particular ethnic group.[2] At the same time, their products or services are not of such a quality that they could expect to attract "guest-clients." Invariably they are the gathering place for people who have long since forgotten their role as customers and have become habitués.

Occasionally, as ethnic invasions progress, an establishment of this sort is slowly engulfed by members of another ethnic group. As these new people begin to frequent the business, their presence causes great distress and antagonism. For the old habitués it is equivalent to having a stranger enter their own home and insist upon sitting at the dinner table. Yet the newcomers have a claim over the area which surrounds the business. At the very beginning, when the newcomers are still small in number and relatively humble, they may gain entry and be treated as "guests" or may even be included among the old habitués.[3] As their confidence increases, however, the newcomers seem to become more arrogant and insistent. Momentarily they may receive the "tolerant" treatment. In the long run, no comfortable resolution can be found; as the old habitués withdraw, the business place either loses all ethnic characteristics or takes on the ethnicity of the new-comers.

Guests and Hosts

Within the area there are a few business places that specialize in ethnic products that have become popular with members of other ethnic groups. Within these establishments outsiders are treated as "guests" and must

---

[2] For example, some of the Italian barber shops specialize in techniques and styles that are appreciated by the Italians. Similarly, some of them have radio programs, newspapers, posters, and a "line of chatter" that is directed to a specific ethnic group.

[3] In the Addams area, some of the Mexicans who came earlier into the area seem to be so thoroughly incorporated into Italian groups that they regard the more recent wave of Mexicans as "invaders" and side with the Italians in disagreements between the two groups.

take the part of someone who appreciates the product and has come there for that special purpose. Like guests everywhere, however, they must show respect for the establishment and concede to its practices rather than force their own.

A good example of this type of business place is an Italian restaurant on Taylor Street. Altogether, there are four different ways in which customers are handled. Along the bar there is a group of Italian men who come there regularly. As "ordinary," "everyday" customers they are treated with a familiarity that verges on contempt. On their own part, they banter with the proprietor and feel no need to "dress up." Their presence is appreciated, however, because they "fit" the ethnic identity of the restaurant. In the rear there are a number of tables where two other types of customers are served. The first is a grouping of local Italians, usually a family or a party of businessmen. These people are treated as old clients who are due a familiar greeting and are even allowed to make suggestions about how their food ought to be prepared. They are usually well enough dressed to clearly indicate that they are "out for dinner." The other group that eats here are non-Italians. They are also well dressed and clearly have come there to enjoy the ethnic color along with the food. The proprietor treats them as sight-seers and, so long as they let him manage the relationship, they can come to feel almost like insiders. To do this, however, they must defer to the proprietor's judgment and wait for him to initiate each progressive level of intimacy. The fourth group which frequents this restaurant are customers who come to the front of the bar for pizza to "carry out." This group is the "sore spot" of the restaurant. In the first place, the impatient and mute presence of these people is out of place in the restaurant and tends to detract from its atmosphere of gaiety, relaxation, and tribute to Italian cookery. Since many of these people have just stepped out of their house to get a pizza, their dress is also likely to indicate no particular concern for Italian culinary arts. This is all the more obvious if the customer happens to be non-Italian or someone who cannot be credited with a special appreciation for Italian food. In particular, the Negroes who live close by are regarded by the proprietor, and especially by his wife, as harmful to the restaurant. In the first place, the proprietor fears that they will somehow damage the ethnic color of the restaurant and bring into question the authenticity of his product. Second, he is also concerned that the presence of the Negroes will cast doubt on his restaurant's respectability and exclusiveness. This is an important consideration because one of the establishment's products is its ability to furnish non-Italians with a claim to being on the "inside" and having knowledge of those restaurants known only to a select few.

The Negroes fail to appreciate the burden they place on the establishment's impression management and tend to view most Italian dishes as a "short order"—a snack that is not the occasion for "dressing up." The Negroes detect the proprietor's dislike but generally assume he is eager for their money. The proprietor says he does not want their money but can find no practical or legal way to avoid their trade. Being on the boundary between the Negro and Italian section, the Negroes feel they have a right to receive the services of the restaurant even if their approach is ill conceived.

The Negroes possess a similar establishment on Roosevelt Road where a combo plays rock and roll on weekends. Rarely, whites will go there when escorted by a Negro. Usually these are whites from outside the Addams area because most of the whites in the area are very fearful of this place. Of all the establishments in the Addams area, this is probably the most exclusive in the guests it receives.

The host-guest pattern is probably the least problematic of all relations between members of different ethnic groups in the area. It is not a relationship where people ignore each other's ethnicity. The infrequency of this relationship shows not only the small number of occasions where ethnic groups can meet in a congenial context but also the necessity of clear guarantees when they do so. The host-guest pattern is essentially a non-equalitarian relationship where the host ethnic group is guarded by its own ability to dictate what cultural practices are appropriate.

Taking Turns

In the Italian section, no more than half a block from the Mexican and Negro sections, is a "short order" cafe selling hot dogs, pop, french fries, and the like. Its products, together with a juke box and pinball machine, especially encourage the patronage of young people. The operator himself is a young Italian male widely known among the teenagers. For many Negro and Mexican teenagers, it is the nearest place to procure a snack. Almost always, the boys come into the restaurant in groups, chiefly because they usually travel in groups, but also because such "snacks" are often a social occasion where there is a pooling of money and sharing of food.

Since the establishment is rather small, it is almost impossible for two separate groups to maintain any privacy while there. Thus the typical practice is for one group to enter only when they notice that the cafe is empty. Occasionally, then, one will see a group pass by, look in, and pass on because it is already occupied. However, the group may wait at some distance from the cafe and later, after the first group leaves, the second will enter.

As most groups are uniform in their ethnicity, the cafe is almost always occupied by boys from only one ethnic group. Apparently there is no specific timing to their occupancy, and the common practice is occasionally to "drop by" until one finds it empty. Naturally there are times when one or two individuals may stray into the cafe while another group is there. This occurrence, however, elicits so oppressive and colorless a reception that one can easily understand why it seldom recurs.

Mutual Tolerance

A relationship of mutual tolerance between ethnic groups seems likely to occur where a business (1) is operated by members of one ethnic group, (2) draws most of its customers from that ethnic group, (3) does not specialize in an ethnic product, and (4) is located in close proximity to members of other ethnic groups. A typical example is a local drive-in that serves short orders. The lady who operates the place is Italian, and most of the customers are young Italian boys and girls who live in the vicinity. The Italian boys and girls hang around the place and engage in a kind of banter with the proprietress. At the same time several Negro and Mexican families also live close enough so that they frequently go there. They approach the drive-in, however, with some trepidation and assume a mute, humble, and somewhat sullen appearance. In turn, they are served without comment or any particular show of interest. Once they eat, they are expected to leave. In the meantime their presence appears to be tolerated only as an economic exigency.

Establishments of this sort are protected somewhat by a clientele predominantly from one ethnic group. Eventually, however, as the ethnic boundaries change and as the old customers move away, the new clientele may become more prominent, and a pattern of mutual exploitation seems a likely sequel.

At present there are 138 businesses where this pattern is in effect. For the most part they are at those points where ethnic groups intersect or on certain thoroughfares where an ethnic group must cross another's pathway. Mutual tolerance, then, is a kind of halfway house that pleases no one but is lived with for the moment.

Mutual Exploitation

Generally a pattern of mutual exploitation by both proprietor and shopper seems to occur where: (1) the business is operated by the members of one minority group, (2) the business is located in an area conceded to another minority group, and (3) neither the operators nor the local residents have any further ethnic claims to the business establishment. A good example of this is a grocery store on Roosevelt. The store is run by whites.

The area is entirely Negro and almost all the customers are Negro. The merchandise is not tailored to the tastes of a particular local minority group, and there are no other signs that would establish its ownership. Accordingly, it is hard for the Negroes to explain the presence of the white operators except as rank opportunism that takes advantage of their own weakness. In turn, the Negroes see very little reason to not respond in kind. The store suffers greatly from shoplifting and unpaid bills, and has been broken into twice during the period 1963–65. Probably only a very small proportion of the Negroes actually engage in these forms of predation. Nonetheless, those who do are not much disapproved of, and their actions are regarded as only "fair." To steal from a thief is not exactly the same as theft.

From the white operator's viewpoint, this indifference to his losses is totally unjustified, and over the years he has taken several precautions to guard against the immorality of his customers. He has special locks on the doors and has hired a detective agency that regularly investigates it after business hours. He reminds his customers if their bills are past due and occasionally harangues a creditor for payment. Higher prices are charged to cover expected losses. These maneuvers are not exploitative from the operator's point of view. To the Negroes, however, they only confirm their initial suspicions.

Altogether there are twenty-one businesses where this pattern holds sway. Most of them are white-operated and cater to Negro trade. The store described here is fairly typical, but sometimes the relationship between customer and proprietor becomes much more vicious. One local liquor store, owned by Italians but often serving Negroes, Mexicans, and Puerto Ricans, is rumored to use strong-arm methods to collect debts. There is also a general understanding that the liquor store is an "Outfit" place.[4] Outside the Italian community, few people have any compunction against exploiting the store in any way they can. Actually, successful attempts at exploitation may be regarded as either humorous or as a kind of "poetic justice."

Mutual exploitation represents the furthest departure from the seclusiveness of the establishments which cater exclusively to one ethnic group. Each step away from a strictly ethnic establishment is marked by an increase in distrust and apprehension. Thus, the businesses that do not

---

[4] That is, it belongs to the Syndicate. All the local bars and liquor stores are presumed to have Outfit connections. The liquor store referred to here has a branch in Dixmoor which was the center of the riots there in 1964. The common complaint was that the liquor store used "strong-arm" methods. The owner is a fairly well-known figure, and the newspapers generally define him as a member of the underworld.

restrict relations to a single ethnic group also demonstrate the preexisting importance of ethnic and territorial segments within the Addams area.

A little over half the local business establishments are shared by more than one ethnic group. The difficulty of relations in these establishments does not diminish the residents' desire to retreat into their respective ethnic sections, but it is apparent that they are not fully able to do so. As the ethnic boundaries in the area have changed, members of each ethnic group have been thrust together and are unable to fully realize the residential and ethnic unity they prefer. The residents have only limited control over these residential changes, and the range of inter-ethnic relations within business places is an adaptation to this lack of control.

Recreation

In the Addams area there are eleven places explicitly set aside for play. As in the case of business establishments, the local residents try to assign each of these to one or another of the local ethnic groups. In going about this, they depend upon the following criteria:

1. *Location*—If a recreational establishment is located in an area of residence conceded to a particular ethnic group, the latter have a claim on it.
2. *Staff*—If the recreational establishment has a staff, their ethnicity is one of the grounds on which a claim may be asserted.
3. *Precedent*—If a recreational place has a history of usage by one ethnic group, that group has a claim on it.

Here again, not all these criteria always coincide to give a particular ethnic group an uncontested claim to a recreational establishment. Table 2 gives their distribution as of 1964.

Where a recreational establishment is the unquestioned property of a single minority group, the pattern of usage is fairly clear-cut. For the most part, participation is restricted to the incumbent minority group. Others come there either as guests or as intruders. As guests, they are treated with temporary courtesy. As intruders, they are regarded as persons who have taken the first step off the known path of orderly social relationships.

In the cases of two recreation areas, however, more than one ethnic group has a valid claim. Originally, the Van Merrit school lot was a hangout for young Italian boys. As the Puerto Ricans moved in on Harrison, they eventually took over the school lot. The Italian boys conceded it grudgingly but without overt opposition.[5] Today some Italians still refer to

---

[5] The Italian boys were not a named group, and it is doubtful that they could have acted in concert.

TABLE 2
RECREATIONAL ESTABLISHMENTS

NAME	RESIDENTIAL LOCATION (ETHNIC SECTION)	ETHNICITY OF STAFF	PRECEDENT	RIGHTS OF USAGE	GUESTS
Sheridan Park	Italian	Italian	Italian	Italian	Mexican
Nativity Center	Italian	Outsiders[b]	Italian	Italian	Mexican
Greek Social Center	Puerto Rican	Greek	Greek	Greek	...
"Peanut Park"	Boundary between Negro and Italian	...	Italian	Negro Italian	Mexican
Boys Club	Negro	Negro	Negro	Negro	Mexican
Greeley[a]	Negro	...	Negro	Negro	...
Bryan[a]	Italian	...	Italian	Italian	Mexican
Lafollette[a]	Mexican	...	Mexican	Mexican	...
Van Merrit[a]	Boundary between Puerto Rican and Italian	...	Italian	Puerto Rican	...
Sacred Domesticus[a]	Italian	...	Italian	Italian	Mexican
Our Lady of Provins[a]	Italian	...	Italian	Italian	Mexican
St. Alonzo[a]	Italian	...	Italian	Italian	Mexican
Play Grounds[c] (1) (1)	Italian Mexican	... ...	Italian Mexican	Italian Mexican	... ...

[a] School play grounds.
[b] Later the staff changed to Mexican and the rights of usage also shifted to them.
[c] Two small asphalt sections that belonged to the Park District.

it as "ours." Generally, however, the Puerto Ricans' hegemony is uncontested, and Italian mothers are beginning to warn their children to stay away from the play lot lest they get in trouble.

"Peanut Park" is far more problematic. It forms part of the boundary between the Negroes in the projects and the Italians to the north (see map 2). Until about 1961, the Negroes practically never used the park. Since then, the Negroes have progressively made inroads so that by now the question of who "owns" it is unsettled. Both the Negroes and whites make use of the southwest softball diamond, although they usually take turns. The northeast diamond is still used almost exclusively by the Italians. Map 5 gives a detailed picture of how the park is used. During the day, relations between ethnic groups are amicable enough, but at night each has some concern over its safety. The Negroes assume that the Italians will resist their invasion. The Italians assume that the Negroes want the park for themselves. In the meantime, each group hesitates in an uneasy silence waiting for someone to make the first move.

With each advance of the Negroes into the park the whites have automatically retreated. Thus, as ethnic groups meet, each measures its gains by the other's losses. Since the park is underused, both the Negroes and Italians would probably gain by opening all the facilities of the park to everyone. But for Addams area residents this is no more possible than for two separate families to join forces and share both their dwelling units and their income. It might be practical, but who would ever trust the other party to such an agreement?

Aside from "Peanut Park," inter-ethnic encounters in recreational establishments are rare. A few times each year ethnic groups play each other at ball games, but these occasions are closely watched by a number of street workers and policemen. Without these safeguards, both participants would fear violence.

Uninvited youngsters from one ethnic group seldom intrude into another's recreational establishments. They are well warned by the adults not to do so lest they "get in trouble." This does not deny that there is some contact between ethnic groups in these places of recreation. In recent years some of the workers in these recreational places have made a concerted attempt to hold inter-ethnic events. Where these events are well-supervised they pass with few incidents. On a few occasions, however, supervision was inadequate, and small scale riots or frays took place. In either case, the local residents point out that street workers and policemen are necessary to keep the peace when ethnic groups come together at the same recreational establishment.

Education

Although Addams area residents share the same school district, this does not provide a setting in which members of different ethnic groups can assume each other's good intentions. Approximately 60% of the white children attend parochial schools[6] compared to only about 10% of the Negro

---

[6] Based on a random sample of eighty-one boys in the area.

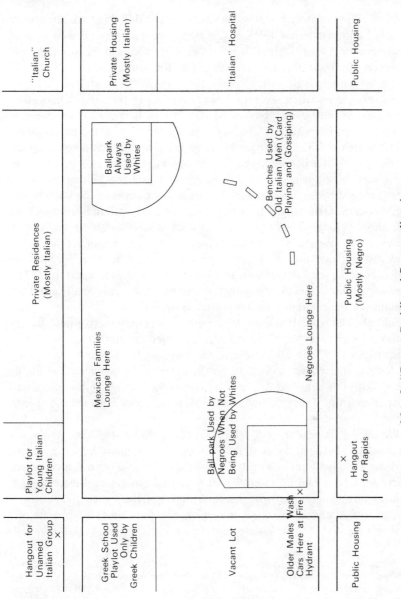

MAP 5. "Peanut Park" and Surrounding Area

children. For the most part, this disparity is probably due to differences of religion, although a few families mention parochial schools as a way of evading contact with Negroes. Among Catholic parents in the Addams area, however, the most frequent reason given for sending their children to parochial schools is that they "make them learn."

However, even when several ethnic groups go to the same school, they must contend with the established rights of usage assigned to the dominant ethnic group. Each school "belongs" to a particular ethnic group. Most Addams area children are divided among fourteen different schools. Of the public schools, five belong to the Negroes, two to the whites, and two are in the process of changing hands. All the parochial schools belong to whites; three are held by the Italians and two are at issue between the Italians and the Mexicans. Generally, a look at the student body will indicate to whom the school belongs. This, however, is not an infallible sign. Bryan School, for example, has recently been assigned such a large number of Negro students that they now make up a majority of its student body. Still, the Italians call the school their own and regard the Negroes as interlopers. The Negroes acknowledge that they are not welcome and occasionally taunt the Italians for their inability to bar the intruders.[7]

Schools, like recreational establishments, are consigned to ethnic groups on multiple criteria: location, precedent, ethnicity of staff, and ethnicity of student body. Where all these criteria coincide, the few minority group students that remain usually take on the ingratiating manner of a humble guest. With this behavior they can survive and sometimes even advance to close friendship. If they do not accept this status, they must fend for themselves.[8]

Where the ownership of a school is still in doubt, the alternatives for relationships between the contesting groups follow much the same pattern as those already discussed for other institutions whose control is disputed. There may be a mutual tolerance or a mutual arrogance. Members of a minority group may court with danger by ignoring the prerogatives of those in control. A mutual wariness may give rise to a series of precautions against potential danger. Where supervision is exceptionally well planned,

---

[7] Since the Negroes were transferred, neither they nor the local Italians have behaved very well. There have been a few fights, minor thefts, and vague threats. Far more common, however, is a sort of constant abrasive arrogance that keeps them at arm's length. This is especially noticeable when the students leave school to go home and the Negro boys and girls walk through the area.

[8] Some research seems to show that where one ethnic group dominates an area, instances of inter-ethnic conflict and delinquency diminish in number. See Bernard Lander, "An Ecological Analysis of Baltimore," *The Sociology of Crime and Delinquency*, ed. Wolfgang, Savitz, and Johnston (New York: John Wiley, 1962), pp. 184–90.

both groups may engage in an explicit but orderly jousting for honor and status through athletics. But there is no relationship where persons of different ethnicity simply assume each other's good intentions.

Of all the institutions mentioned, the schools are the least able to accommodate the cleavages between ethnic groups in the Addams area. Four of the nine public schools and two of the five parochial schools lie outside the Addams area and draw students from more than one neighborhood. Only the nine schools located within the Addams area correspond closely to its territorial and ethnic divisions. As a result, many of the remaining schools are seen as dangerous and a source of "trouble." Thus, while the schools do not always follow local ethnic divisions, neither do they engender orderly relations between ethnic groups. Indeed, the schools often provide the occasions for inter-ethnic conflicts and confirm the local view that children should not stray outside their ethnic section.

Although many of the schools depart sharply from the ethnic divisions in the Addams area, the consequences of such departures parallel those found in the other institutions. Most of the business places can be consigned to a single ethnic section and thus help sustain intra-ethnic relations. Where a business establishment cannot be clearly defined as the property of a single ethnic group, it becomes an occasion for opposition and conflict. The recreational and religious institutions subscribe more closely to ethnic sections, and here again conflict breaks out once these ethnic boundaries are crossed.

All these institutions illustrate again the continuing importance of ethnic solidarity within the Addams area. The residents behavior, however, is not merely a result of "prejudice" or a dislike of other ethnic groups. All the local ethnic groups assume that members within one minority group have exceptional claim on each other's trust, help, association, and understanding. Necessarily this carries with it the obverse implication that persons of a different ethnicity cannot be depended upon to extend themselves to each other in a similar manner. So long as Addams area residents maintain this conviction of the nature of ethnic loyalties they are unlikely to place themselves at the mercy of another ethnic group.

In this sense, the institutional arrangements in the Addams area demonstrate a constant effort to restrict relations to the safe confines of one's own ethnic section. The residents are not always successful, but the ensuing conflicts impress upon them the necessity of ethnic divisions. The schools, whose placement and composition cannot be controlled by the local residents, arouse particularly strong apprehensions. The residents are better able to control the religious and recreational institutions, and thus these provide safer ethnic enclosures.

By relying so heavily upon common minority group membership as a basis for trust, Addams area residents are not being unreasonable. The residents are well aware of the public status of each ethnic group in the area. Negroes know that they are publicly defined as inferior to Italians, Mexicans, and Puerto Ricans in that order. Moreover, they have good reason to suspect that members of these three groups who extend themselves to be friendly must have some design that would take advantage of the Negroes' vulnerability. Similarly, Italians find it equally hard to conceive of a Puerto Rican who would neglect to exploit an equalitarian relationship with them. In this sense, Addams area residents are sensitive to each other's relative position and to the ulterior motives they might have for overlooking these distinctions. Thus, it is often their very ability at "taking the role of the other" that eliminates the hope of any trusting relationship.

The institutions in the Addams area often help sustain its ethnic divisions but they do not seem fundamental to these divisions. The status of each ethnic group in the wider society is such that overtures to equalitarianism arouse suspicion. A more basic problem, however, is the residents' search for trustworthy associates in a population where the grounds for trustworthiness are so scarce. In the absence of any other grounds for trust, they rely upon ethnic and residential unities.

4

___

Communicative Devices

Ethnicity is the major basis of division within the Addams area, but practically every resident has at least one acquaintance in another ethnic group. These relationships are usually rather superficial and often consist of little more than a nod between adults living in adjoining buildings. Occasionally, the host-guest relationship advances to become an acquaintanceship that is acknowledged beyond the establishment where it started. Sometimes there is common membership in a street corner group. More rarely, there is an open covenant such as a marriage, business partnership, or landlord-renter relation.

Relations between ethnic groups, however, are like an off-color joke: they are not recommended for others, they are seldom publicly revealed, and they are taken as a kind of promissory note toward still other "irregularities." Parents who have friends in another ethnic group discourage their children from following the same practice for fear of trouble. Almost all the youngsters in the area have acquaintances outside their ethnic group and place a considerable value on "being in" with another ethnic group. Italian boys brag that they know the Poles up on "Milwaukee;" Mexican girls protest that they know the guys in the projects and "they won't hurt me;" sometimes the Puerto Ricans insist that they personally have safe passage on Laflin street. These are relations, however, which are hidden from adults and seldom expressed in a public form such as a common group membership. Inter-ethnic relations in the Addams area are a very private matter and a part of the neighborhood's "underlife."

Once under way, inter-ethnic relations are subject to a number of misunderstandings and may follow an abortive course. If a Mexican girl is friendly with Negro boys, she is apt to be seen as "on the make." A Negro boy who is friendly with Italians is typically received in one of four ways: (1) he is "conning you," (2) he is different from other Negroes, (3) he is gullible about ethnic group distinctions, or (4) he is the hope of his race.

Often the residents interpret the unconventional character of inter-ethnic relations as an invitation to further unconventionalities. Italians sometimes ask friendly Negroes to procure prostitutes and marijuana for them. Negroes may solicit an Italian's help in fixing a traffic ticket or bad check. Neither party may be able to furnish the expected service, but a person willing to engage in inter-ethnic relations is thought willing to try almost anything else.[1]

These barriers to inter-ethnic relations in the Addams area are common to all the groups in the area and arise chiefly from ethnic stereotypes that are widely shared throughout the United States. Even after an inter-ethnic relationship has surmounted these hurdles, however, it encounters an additional set of obstacles in the different communicative devices used by each local ethnic group.

Each ethnic group in the Addams area has a set of cultural practices unfamiliar to the others. Traditionally this sort of social misunderstanding between ethnic groups has been called "culture conflict." The cultural differences that divide Addams area residents, however, usually do not extend to an obvious and uncompromising contradiction of basic norms or values. Mexicans, Negroes, Italians, and Puerto Ricans all believe that killing, fighting, stealing, and insolence are "bad." Similarly, they almost invariably agree that cleanliness, motherhood, education, money, and kindness are "good."[2] The differences that become serious in local relationships, then, are not so much in norms, goals, or general standards, but in the *notational devices* that each group relies upon to express and encode their adherence to these basic social rules. In this regard, the participants are like schoolboys using different number systems while trying to explain to one another the same arithmetic problem. Behind their misunderstanding is the same mathematical system and possibly the same answer. However, unless they can make the necessary transformations, they cannot possibly agree. Quite possibly, there is also a correspondence between the meanings attached to the gesture of Italians and Negroes. Yet, so long as each group does not know how to translate this correspondence they go on misunderstanding one another and incorrectly interpreting each other's behavior.

---

[1] During my stay in the Addams area there were at least three instances of flagrant sexual misbehavior. All of them involved members of two or more ethnic groups. There were many more instances of sexual misbehavior, and some of them occurred among members of the same ethnic group. Generally, however, these were fairly discreet affairs carried out with considerable secrecy. What was outstanding about the first three instances was the overt manner in which they were carried out—almost as if they were being endorsed as the norm rather than the exception.

[2] These statements are little more than tautologies. Of course, all these groups value such things as kindness, because one of the bases on which we determine what is considered "kindness" in different cultures is whether or not its particular occurrences are regarded as "good." If they were not defined as good, then we would call them something else.

For purposes of this study, it might as well be assumed that each minority group subscribes to exactly the same general norms, even if this is not quite true. The approach here has been narrowed down to specific differences in the behavioral code that each group depends upon to serve notice of its good or bad intentions, its goals, and its beliefs. The question whether each of these notational systems can be translated into the same or completely different normative systems is relatively unimportant because in any case local residents usually cannot bridge the gaps between them.

Language

The most obvious restriction on communication between the ethnic groups in the Addams area is their differences of language and dialect. For many of the older residents, Spanish and Italian are still the working languages for everyday life. Even within each of these speech communities, however, the dialects are often so far apart that they lead to grave misunderstandings, invidious comparisons, and mutual avoidance. Where English is spoken, the range of common understanding is not much greater. With the older Italians, Mexicans, and Puerto Ricans, their English is often badly broken and is either a source of embarrassment or a tool by which only the bare rudiments of communication can take place. All the subtleties that are usually incorporated into speech are suddenly lost. Thus persons are left adrift without the ordinary innuendos, graces, overtones, and insinuations that play such a critical part in the constant reassurances they furnish one another.

Lacking these essentials, verbal behavior often loses the easy continuity that we call spontaneity and takes on a halting and rehearsed manner that is usually attributed to calculation. At the same time, the participants are reduced to presenting only the most mundane and blatant information about themselves and their intentions. It becomes almost impossible to hint at one's objectives before fully broaching them, to use circumlocutions or idioms that evade overt admission of vulgarity, and to employ metaphors that protect the participants from the full light of social exposure. A more subtle but no less important deficiency is that inflection and intonation cease to be dependable indices that persons can use to judge the appropriateness of their own reactions. For the older residents, this last shortcoming means that they cannot reliably distinguish between demands, questions, and polite requests. A common greeting by the older Italians and Mexicans, for example, is a bland, "Whadda you want?" Since members of the various groups in the area prefer to be requested rather than required to meet each other's expectations, such an inability to detect nuances in speech is a serious handicap to comfortable social relations.

When the residents are reduced to speech patterns that are coarse, abrupt, and lacking in polite forms, their own self-presentation becomes equally coarse, abrupt, and impolite. Since they can be no more than the shared symbols that represent them allow, most Addams area residents would be embarrassed and humiliated to appear as such crude and incomplete persons or to have to deal with someone who can only be overt, uncompromising, and impolite. Thus, it is not surprising that those among them who depend upon broken English either avoid those encounters requiring communication in English or at best submit to them with considerable uneasiness.

Linguistic embarrassment is most acute among the older residents, and they are most likely to apologize for their language. Italians explain that they speak a "dialect" rather than "real Italian." As for their English, the older people only laugh at their broken English if you are a good friend; otherwise they avoid you and say as little as possible. The Puerto Ricans tell you that their Spanish is not quite "right." Their English is a new and somewhat uncertain way of getting people to understand them. The older Mexicans have a good deal of confidence in their Spanish but regard their English as something of an experiment.

Among the younger people, English is almost invariably spoken, although a few of the Mexicans and even more of the Puerto Ricans maintain varying degrees of familiarity with Spanish.[3] Both the Mexican and Puerto Rican youngsters seem to have learned a dialect of English very similar to that of the Italians. The Negroes, on the other hand, still preserve a measure of several different southern dialects along with their accompanying vocabulary and syntactic forms.[4] Sometimes the Negroes and whites will "make fun" of each others' English, but this is not common.

More often there is an acceptance of the historical origins of their language differences. Both Negroes and whites, for example, will simply point to their regional origins to explain why their language is different. Unfortunately this does not much help them to assign any interpretation to these

[3] In all the Mexican street corner groups, English is used, and most of the boys cannot speak adequate Spanish. Quite a few of the Puerto Rican boys use Spanish among themselves and speak English with differing degrees of success. However, even in most of their groups, English is the common language, and they differ in their ability with Spanish. All the Italian groups use English, and it is rare to find a member who knows Italian. Incidentally, it is quite common for a child to grow up in a household where Spanish or Italian is used and never come to speak that language. Apparently the children learn most of their language from their peers.

[4] For example, the use of the present tense and the use of the first person verb form with all pronouns. See Raven McDavid and Virginia McDavid, "The Relationship of the Speech of American Negroes to the Speech of Whites," *American Speech*, 26 (February, 1951): 3-17.

differences. Like most people, Addams area residents are not likely to dismiss speech differences simply because they are "justifiable." Their life, safety, self-enhancement, and knowledge of the other person's intentions all depend upon being able to decipher these differences. At times, no doubt, these differences between Negro and white speech may not be significant even within their own speech communities. But Addams area residents do not know this. All they know is that differences do exist and, so long as they cannot understand their significance, they are hesitant to expose themselves to a relationship with no recognizable guidelines.

For the most part, syntactic and phonological differences divide the white and Negro residents in the area. An interesting departure is the use of "jive." This special vocabulary of argot or "slang" terms is restricted according to both age and ethnicity, but its usage overlaps the Negro-white distinction. Negro boys are most expert at this sort of discourse, but the English-speaking Mexican and Puerto Rican boys are also somewhat conversant with "jive." The Italians seldom use any of this vocabulary even to the point of not understanding it.[5] In the case of "jive," however, the Italians do not regard language differences so much as an unexplained phenomena as an attempt to talk behind someone's back, "show off" one's knowledge of urban ways, or display one's emancipation from the homely virtues of family, ethnic group, and neighbors. To the Italians, the use of "jive" often indicates a person who has scuttled the surest signs of human feeling and concern for the bonds that secure personal relations within the neighborhood. To the Negroes, and less so among the Mexicans and Puerto Ricans, a familiarity with this youthful jargon is only a sign of a willingness to expand the magic circle of trust beyond that of family, ethnic group, and territorial compatriots. As should become apparent later, there is good reason for the Italians' backwardness. More than any other ethnic group in the area, they are firmly ensconced in a network of kinfolk, family friends, and intergenerational relations. Among themselves, they are hardly ever anonymous and can ill afford to flaunt their emancipation from traditional relations.

[5] Once it was suggested to me that this showed that the Italians no longer need to rely upon secrecy to disguise their underlife. However, this is very unlikely because they are certainly the most involved in the rackets and the most difficult for an outsider to approach. Indeed, it seems that their withdrawal from the wider community and their provinciality are the major reasons for not bothering with the fads of language. The Negroes, Puerto Ricans, and Mexicans are very eager to show they are hipsters, familiar with the most advanced of urban speech, clothing styles, and learning. The Italians, lost in their own provincial world, just don't seem to care. More than any other group, they ignore the fads and fashions that attest to one's place in the forefront of urban life. Whether or not they were always equally indifferent to these new modes of expression is something I have not been able to determine.

Gestures

Language differences between each ethnic group are often exacerbated by nonverbal acts which accompany or supplant speech. First-generation Italians, for example, have an entire repertory of gestures that are not even fully understood by their own children. Negro boys, in turn, have a "cool" way of walking ("pimp's walk") in which the upper trunk and pelvis rock fore and aft while the head remains stable with the eyes looking straight ahead. The "pimp's walk" is quite slow, and the Negroes take it as a way of "strutting" or "showing off." The whites usually interpret it as a pointed lack of concern for those adjacent to the walker. Negro girls provide a parallel in a slow "sashay" that white males sometimes take as an unqualified invitation to their attentions.

These subtle differences in posture, stance, and gestures are the source of considerable interest among Addams area residents. The other ethnic groups think it odd that a group of Mexican men should strike a pose of obliviousness to other people and even to their nearby wives and children. Puerto Ricans, on the other hand, are disparaged because they stand painfully close during a conversation and talk in such a voluble manner as to "jabber." Whites say that Negroes will not look them in the eye. The Negroes counter by saying the whites are impolite and try to "cow" people by staring at them.

The residents do not report these gestural differences as a part of each other's cultural heritage or as a general attribute common to all members of a single ethnic group. Often it is useless for an investigator to ask informants to make a blanket statement about the gestural behavior of another ethnic group. They will simply say that "there's really no difference."[6] When asked about a specific historical event, however, they often provide an account in which ethnic social types are almost always joined to specific gestures. The most subtle accounts are those which describe almost entirely nonverbal encounters: "When I went over to the Negro nurse, she didn't even look up;" "I'd go again (to an Italian restaurant) but they really stare

---

[6] Negro informants seem to be especially unwilling to generalize about differences among the four minority groups in the area. The other groups, however, also insist upon qualifications that exempt at least some members of each minority group. In this respect, Addams area residents are truer to the facts than most investigators who have dealt with the problem of minority groups. They recognize that the members of any minority group are both exceptional and typical. This point was once brought home to me by an Italian lady who, pointing to another woman, said, "Do you see that woman? She is Mexican but she is a wonderful person." The Italian lady went on to tell me why the Mexican woman was so wonderful. Later I found out that the two were close friends. Nonetheless, the Italian lady continued to confide to me her sorrow at seeing the Mexicans move into the area. Incidentally, as a landlord, she steadfastly refused to put a "for rent" sign in her window for fear that she might have to rent to a Mexican or Puerto Rican family.

you down;" "Those Mexican men were just standing there while the kids ran in the street and, you know, one of them was their father!"; "I was walking by the Projects, and those Negro girls were just sitting there, their legs all sprawled all over, and I didn't feel right."

If asked to generalize from their own commentaries, the residents protest that no gestural forms are general or even common to another ethnic group; it is just that some members in a single ethnic group behave this way. Thus, while particular gestural forms are thought to be restricted to a single ethnic group, their use is not usually regarded as a custom or habit but as a calculated and voluntary individual act. Unlike language differences, then, gestural differences are taken as an intentional affront. As one Negro informant put it, "I can understand why those guys (older male Italian street group) can't half speak English, but, dammit, why they gotta eyeball everybody walk past?"

These fragmentary observations on gestural forms only serve to illustrate how nonverbal communications estrange ethnic groups in the Addams area. Often these differences are rare and hardly perceptible, but they do not escape the experienced scrutiny of the local residents. Nonetheless, the residents are no more able than contemporary sociologists at divining the import of these communicative signs. Unlike sociologists, however, Addams area residents cannot afford the academic curiosity that a distant observer might entertain. Many of these gestural forms precede inter-ethnic encounters and thus become the first warning received of the subsequent course of interaction. After the initiation of inter-ethnic relations, gestural behavior is constantly referred to as a source of corroborating or contrary evidence for judging a person's verbal claims. Such subtle and minor signs loom large when evaluated against the residents' suspicions of other ethnic groups.

Clothing, Grooming, and Personal Display

Clothing, grooming, and personal display add another area in which Addams area residents can look for and find ethnic differences. Local peculiarities of dress also contribute in varying degrees to the cleavages between each age and sex group within the neighborhood. On weekdays old Italian women in black shawls, print cotton dresses, and low-heel shoes trudge along the streets, occasionally crossing themselves before a church. Younger Italian girls wear bright "capris," blouses, and "flats." Except on ceremonial occasions, Mexican females follow much the same pattern as the Italians. Although less elaborate and less stylish, the dress of the Puerto Rican women is not easily distinguished from that of their Italian and Mexican counterparts.

The males show much greater differentiation in their apparel. They seem the primary bearers of those emblems of clothing that express ethnic differences and it is among them that examples of this differentiation are most apparent.[7] Examples of this differentiation are easily observed. Italians often gather on the sidewalks in sleeveless undershirts and standard (unpegged) pants. Young Italians wear the same "old-fashioned" undershirts but sometimes deviate by wearing none at all. Older Negro men are inconspicuous in their work clothes and standard suits. Younger Negroes, however, stand out with their dress shirts, blazers, pointed shoes ("points"), tight pants ("hiphuggers"), and expensive hats ("lids"). Mature Puerto Ricans unbutton their flowered shirts to display a decorative St. Christopher's medal. Felt collars, ruffled shirts, and cummerbunds are formal dress for some of the Mexican males. The Negroes crop their hair and shave their forelocks to achieve a higher brow. Italian barbers "shape" hair with a straight razor, and adult Mexican males let their sideburns grow and allow their forelocks to hang directly over a portion of their forehead.

The most pronounced and consistent differences between male adolescents in the Addams area are summarized in table 3.[8] The widest differentiation is between the Negro and the Italian boys; the Mexican and Puerto Rican boys falling somewhere in the middle.

The Negro boys are caught up in the avant-garde of current clothing fads. However, despite its "oddity" from an outsider's point of view, their clothing is sufficiently formal that it can be worn outside the Addams area. The style "ivy" is an extreme version of an "ivy league" suit; very thin lapels, tight sleeves and trousers, a small tie pin at the throat, and the entire ensemble immaculately creased. Ivy is widespread among the adolescents but also occurs among the adult males. "Gauster" is more casual, consisting of a "half coat" belted in the back and wide ("baggy") trousers of a different material, and may be worn with or without a tie. This style is worn only by adolescents, but like sports clothes it can be worn downtown or to a dance.

---

[7] Talcott Parsons ("Age and Sex in the Social Structure of the United States" in *Essays in Sociological Theory* [Glencoe, Ill.: Free Press, 1954], pp. 82–103) states that expressive variations in dress are mostly restricted to women, while men still wear something like a uniform. His observations, however, seem restricted to a segment of the American public where males are drawn into multiple loyalties while females are left with the task of expressing the consumer preferences of the nuclear family. In the Addams area, males are divided into quite discrete segments and thus become the main standard bearers of the ethnic sections to which they belong.

[8] This table was constructed on the basis of various "counts" made at several locations or events (street corners, youth centers, dances, schools, etc.) in the Addams area.

TABLE 3

DISTINCTIVE TYPES OF CLOTHING WORN BY BOYS IN EACH ETHNIC GROUP

TYPE	NEGRO	ITALIAN	MEXICAN	PUERTO RICAN
"SAC" Sweater	Does not occur	Very rare	Common	Only if boy in Mexican group
Gauster	Common	Does not occur	Very rare	Very rare
Ivy	Common	Does not occur	Does not occur	Does not occur
Heavy workshoes	Very rare	Common	Common	Rare
Black pants	Rare	Common	Common	Common
Black leather jacket	Rare	Common	Common	Common
Blazer	Common	Does not occur	Rare	Rare
Ruffled shirt	Does not occur	Does not occur	Common	Common
Vests	Rare	Does not occur	Common	Common
Hat	Common	Does not occur	Rare	Rare
Casual sweater	Common	Does not occur	Does not occur	Does not occur
Spanish shoes	Does not occur	Rare	Common	Common
Sleeveless undershirt	Rare	Common	Rare	Rare
The "Rag"	Common	Does not occur	Does not occur	Does not occur

On the other hand, the Italian boys' workshoes, sleeveless undershirts, and black denim pegged pants are worn only locally and on everyday occasions. Thus their distinctive costume is geared almost entirely to a local self-presentation. The Italian boys recognize this and when they "dress up" to go out of the area or to a dance, they wear standard suits or sports clothes.

The Mexicans and Puerto Ricans seem to form an intermediary group between the Negroes and Italians. Apparently they have borrowed most items of their own style from both groups. Still, their wardrobe lacks the formality of the general style "ivy" which is the uniform most suitable for wear in all places and among all age groups. By and large, then, their self-presentation is restricted to the local area of their own age group. There are two items (Spanish shoes and ruffled shirts) that they share to the exclusion of the Italians and Negroes. The ruffled shirts may be a carry-over from their traditional culture. The Spanish shoes have exceptionally high heels and may be worn because the Mexican and Puerto Rican boys are self-conscious about their small stature. However, this explanation is quite tentative; a few Mexican and Puerto Ricans mentioned their "smallness" to me, but seemed reluctant to discuss it further.

In general, these observations on clothing seem to warrant two separate conclusions. First, insofar as these differences are not understood by all ethnic groups, they constitute another occasion for wariness and avoidance between ethnic groups. Second, each style of clothing tends to reiterate local ethnic differences that have been observed elsewhere. The Negro boys do not have a distinctive costume for purely local situations but address themselves to a wider audience. The style of dress associated with the Italians can be worn only locally and governs a self-presentation that can be appreciated only within their own ethnic section. The Puerto Ricans and Mexicans lie between the other two ethnic groups. A few items in their wardrobe seem to be a part of their traditional culture and might appeal to other Mexicans and Puerto Ricans all over Chicago. Otherwise the Mexicans and Puerto Ricans selectively share various items that are provided by the Italians or Negroes. Differences in clothing, then, reflect the degree of provincialism prevalent in each ethnic group.

Dance styles show similar levels of provincialism in each ethnic group. Negro teenagers are almost invariably a step or two ahead of the Italians in the kinds of dances and music with which they are familiar. Between April 1962 and June 1964 at least ten different dance styles passed through the Addams area.[9] At all times the Negroes were at least one dance style ahead of the Italians. Generally, the Mexicans and Puerto Ricans were in between the Negroes and the Italians in their current dance styles.

In general, then, the Italian and Negro boys seem to be at opposite poles in their use of clothing and dances as communicative devices. Those elements shared by the Italian boys declare either a commitment to their own ethnic section or an indifference to wider social rulings. The Negro boys seem to lack any specific ways of expressing a similar prejudice for local acquaintances and to have a surplus of emblems that can be used beyond the local neighborhood. The Negro boys were, as one white woman put it, "always dressed up like they thought they were going somewhere."

This same pattern of self-presentation was present in the earlier observations on language, gestures, and grooming. The Negroes are very "hip" to linguistic novelty, "jive," and the avant-garde of personal appearance. The Italians are not so venturesome in their language, and many of the

[9] The twist, bird, hounddog, monkey, watusi, swim, uncle willi, frug, twine, and jerk.

adults draw back into a dialect that can be understood only by their local *paisani*. Their gestures are either drawn from a past tradition or are indicative of the informality and intimacy of their ethnic section. Grooming among the Negroes is often meticulous and stylish; in contrast the Italians seem ordinary and "square."[10] Drugs and other "far out" experiences are most prominent among the Negroes. The Italians lay equal emphasis on a domestic round of "basement parties," *paisani* picnics, and winemaking.

On their own part, the Mexicans and Puerto Ricans either represent an intermediate case or an accommodation to the adjacent Italians and Negroes. Both the Mexican and Puerto Rican boys pick up some of the dance styles and "jive" after they have been introduced by the Negroes. Mexican and Puerto Rican clothing is either like that of the Italians or carries its own distinctive stamp.

No doubt some of these differences between ethnic groups are drawn from their separate cultural traditions. In the South the Negroes were a country peasantry[11] with almost no level of organization beyond that of the nuclear family and the church. Even then, their churches were tiny operations with no standing relation among them. Subsequently, the urban Negro has been the most transient and least capable of all the ethnic groups of gathering around kinfolk, people from a common region, or persons of the same religious denomination. Sicilians and Southern Italians were townspeople who brought with them all the petty distinctions, collusions, and trivial skills that townsmen seem to cultivate. Their churches were large enough to serve a sizeable settlement, and a common faith brought them together into a single local establishment. Like the Negroes, the Sicilians and Southern Italians were an oppressed minority, but they reacted jointly as a community rather than as independent domestic units.

Within the Addams area, however, the continuity of traditional expressive orders seems less important than the way each communicative device is fitted into the area's ethnic segmentation. These differences in gestures, language, and style are not simply a barrier to convenient communication; they are emblems of each ethnic group's position in the Addams area and its stance toward the wider community. The daily life of the Italians is heavily restricted to their own local business places, church, and ethnic section. Historically and politically they are still closely identified with the area. The Negroes are regarded as recent invaders and have little political

[10] Negro hair styles are either very neat and unobtrusive or tailored to advanced styles by use of the "process" ("conk"). Italian haircuts are either ordinary or show signs of neglect. In the case of adult Negroes, a thin, well-trimmed mustache is the rule; among the Italians it is the exception.

[11] Even today, one of the worst insults is to say something like, "Man, you're real 'country.' Like forty acres and a mule."

control over the area. In their daily rounds Negroes must spend a good deal of time in establishments and institutions that are not identified with them. Less attached to the local area, the Negroes are thereby more able to borrow cultural forms from the wider society.

The Mexicans and Puerto Ricans are intermediate in ethnic status and share territorial boundaries with both the Negroes and Italians. Much of their daily life can be spent in their own establishments, but they fall far short of the Italians in their control over a full complement of ethnic institutions. Also the Puerto Ricans and Mexicans are caught in the cross fire when the Negroes and Italians are drawn into conflict. Usually the Puerto Ricans and Mexicans avoid taking sides and try not to offend either group. In their predicament it is useful to share some of the communicative devices of both the Italians and the Negroes.

Thus, when examined in the full context of the Addams area, cultural variations in communicative patterns seem to reflect different levels of sociocultural integration within each ethnic group.[12] The Italians are much involved in their local ethnic neighborhood and tend to ignore the fads and fashions of the wider society. The Negroes are far less dependent on their coresidents and are quick to orient themselves to at least some national patterns of dress and style. Each group may have derived some of its distinctive communicative devices from traditional sources and borrowed others from diverse sources. Whatever their source, however, these communicative devices form a composite that conveys an appropriate image of how each group balances its relations to the local neighborhood and the wider community.

---

[12] Julian H. Steward, *Theory of Culture Change* (Urbana: University of Illinois Press, 1955), pp. 43–63.

5

Communication Channels

The segmental structure of the Addams area places certain rough metes and bounds on communication among the residents. Items of information usually originate in a particular sex, age, territorial, and ethnic group and only gradually work their way across these boundaries. These are intimate groups whose most outstanding characteristic is the way their members can and do dwell on items of local interest and personal reputations. The "facts" the local residents learn of one another are drawn from verbal histories that include many personal disclosures. Thus, their knowledge of personal reputation often overrides the importance of categoric and normative rulings.

While these face-to-face groups are very intimate and tolerant of what a person exposes about himself, they are not isolated and much of what is said in confidence eventually becomes public knowledge. For reasons already discussed, the residents themselves consider such private knowledge the most dependable way of knowing another person's individual character and actively search for such information. Since face-to-face relations are sharply restricted, three occasions provide the sources from which they can learn about one another: the informality of street life, the license permitted in establishment groups, and the congestion of domestic life.

Street Life

For someone first entering the Addams area, the most striking aspect is its street life. This institution plays an interstitial role that bridges the privacy of the area's family life and the seclusiveness of its internal segments. On the streets, age, sex, ethnic, and territorial groups share boundaries that open them to mutual inspection, thus giving the occasion for transient interaction between groups, for gossip, and for interpretive observation. Street life, then, is a vital link in the communication network of the Addams area and, as a result, governs much of what the residents know of one another beyond the range of personal acquaintance. Because of the informality of street life, most of the information that circulates within its confines is of a very personal or private nature. The residents' expectations then tend to derive more from private disclosures than from public standards of morality.

During the summer months the streets in the Addams area are thronged with children, young adults, and old people. Street life is especially active in the afternoon after school or work. The front steps are crowded with old people chatting back and forth between households while some occasionally bring out chairs when sitting space gets scarce. Young girls stand in clusters a little distance from the "stoop-sitters," giggling, squealing, and glancing at the passersby. Young unmarried men seem to occupy every street corner or unused doorway. Small two- and three-year-olds stumble, crawl, and toddle along the sidewalks in front of their homes.

On warm nights there is hardly a stoop, corner, alley, or doorway that has not been staked out by some of its regular habitués. The adults get the door stoops. The young girls stay close by, just out of earshot. The small children are given the run of the sidewalks in front of their mothers. The unmarried males are relegated to whatever little nooks or crannies are left.

By and large, the most persistent spatial arrangement is one where peers of the same sex share the same location. Among age and sex groups there is a rough gradation corresponding to a progressive isolation from the household. Nearest their house stoops are the women and the old people followed by infants, young girls, young boys, and adult males in that order. This particular ecological arrangement, however, is not a result of any explicit set of social rules or prohibitions. Young males sometimes sit on the door stoops but generally wander off once the older people take up their positions. Like all the other peer groups of the same sex, the content and style of their conversation does not provide any common framework within which persons of different ages and sex can participate. The married women talk about household duties, family sickness, neighborhood scandals, and their infants. The older men talk about their youth, pronounce judgments on local politics, and tell stories and jokes about their peers. The young girls examine the latest word on clothing and pop tunes and tease each other about boys. The younger boys follow the pattern of their fathers and converse about the exploits of their peers.

In each group the conversation is heavily restricted to the known world of persons and events of the Addams area and its adjacent neighborhoods. Abstract issues, general trends, and objects which have some significance outside the Addams area are rare topics for routine conversation. There are a few exceptions: ball games and the races among the adult males, and pop music and clothing among the teenagers. The standard prefabricated joke is uncommon, and most humor is an extemporaneous commentary on local people. A stranger to the area finds it very hard to contribute to such conversations.

Since conversation is so heavily laden with personal experiences and confidential disclosures, there is simply no meeting ground for persons of different age and sex because their lives are usually carried out in different social establishments and touch on persons and things that are relatively foreign to one another.[1] In fact, social gatherings which bring together different age and sex groups are uneasy and awkward affairs. There is often no common focus of discussion, or the younger people and men listen in a painful silence while the older women run on about a variety of household chores and family tragedies.

Undoubtedly the prevalence of street life among Addams area residents is continuous with their separate cultural histories where the home is essentially a place for sleeping, eating, protection against the weather, and ritual occasions. All the ethnic groups in the Addams area have come from a warmer region where the dwelling unit is limited in space and function. In Chicago, the heat, unattractiveness, and congestion of living quarters may have continued this pattern. On closer inspection, however, the streets are probably less attractive and almost as crowded as their homes. On mild days, when one could comfortably stay home, the streets seem about as active as at any other time.[2] Seemingly there is a distinct preference for encountering people on more neutral grounds than one's own household. Among teenage boys this attachment to street life is especially great. After being arrested and released they do not speak of going home but of going "back to the streets."

The interior of most Addams area homes suggest a further reason for this preference for street life. Most homes are well-kept and cared for, but it is impossible to conceive of them as something other than a "woman's world." The curtains are of lace, the bedspreads are chenille, the furniture elaborate with design and doilies, the colors light and delicate. Here, there is simply no place for a male with his dirty hands, informality, and coarse manners. In fact, the well-kept household in the Addams area is less a place for carrying out day-to-day life than a "show place" to demonstrate the housewife's diligence and domestic skills. Among its furnishings, there are hardly any provisions for male activities or, for that matter, any form of joint family life except for meals. There are no games for males to play,

---

[1] Actually the problem goes deeper than this. Since the conversations implicate actual persons rather than abstract categories of people, they often contain admissions that are improper in "mixed company."

[2] On occasion I have seen older women come out on their door stoops and sit in the rain with their umbrellas.

no rooms set aside for their private use, or objects they can claim as their own. Ultimately, the home is a kind of ceremonial center used only at those rare moments when visitors are permitted to look into family life. Apart from these rather special occasions, the household is not even an appropriate setting for the casual exchanges of women.

With our imagery of lower class households, this characterization of the dwelling unit as a woman's world may seem strange, but for all their external decay and dirt, most Addams area homes are well-kept on the inside. There is, of course, a difference in esthetic taste. Most middle income people would be appalled at the "calendar art" pictures, the overstuffed furniture, the gargoyle-like bric-a-brac, the cheap finish of metal goods, and the mementos that seem far too numerous for the space. These, however, are the extremes that make households in the Addams area a woman's world. The neuter decor of middle income households reflects not so much a difference in housekeeping standards as a lack of sexual differentiation in household appointments.

Not all homes in the Addams area are well-kept, of course, and a few are downright messy. Even so, if there is a mess, it is usually a "woman's mess." Males almost never take an opportunity to introduce into its furnishings or upkeep any sign identifiable as their own.[3] The males have their own special province, but it is not in the household. Here, as elsewhere in the Addams area, the separation of male and female worlds is repeated in spatial arrangements.

Weather permitting, then, most Addams area residents must go to the streets to find a place befitting the ordinary nature of their "weekday" life. For their purposes the street is ideal. The setting itself is informal and open to many possibilities. Its activities can be entered or abandoned almost at will because they are relatively unscheduled or easily changed to meet the number of participants. Close at hand are most of the people they are interested in and the content that makes up their conversation. And, along with these attractions, there is the advantage that peers of the same sex can separate themselves as a group and take up their private concerns.

So thoroughly do Addams area residents appreciate their street life that by now it has been given some permanence through a series of understandings and arrangements. Almost every doorstoop, fence, alley, and sidewalk has its claimants, and their usufruct is usually respected. Over 270 households have constructed a makeshift wooden bench or set up an old couch

---

[3] However, it was my impression that unmarried males were more likely to "hang" in poorly kept households because they were less apt to be considered "underfoot" or "out of place." Certainly those households where teenagers spend some of their time during the winter months are of this type.

or discarded set of automobile seats between the sidewalks and street.[4] Excluding the projects, where such permanent seating arrangements are illegal, almost every (80%) block in the Addams area possesses one or more of these accommodations. In the afternoon and evening, people supplement these permanent seating arrangements by bringing out chairs and cushions. The fences and steps are worn smooth by years of use. Occasionally a television set is brought out where people can enjoy it. And everywhere boys and girls have written their names, like dogs leaving their scent.

Aside from its obvious color, convenience, excitement, and sociability, street life has a further attraction that is not nearly so apparent. Addams area residents are still very mindful of the rather diffuse obligations between people once they have been drawn into the interior of each other's home. To the residents it is a large step toward intimacy and implies a set of expectations that include the right to "drop in" without warning on subsequent occasions. As one woman explained, "I like to be able to talk to lots of people on the street but not in the house. I don't want to get that involved."

This preference for carrying out extra-familial relations outside the dwelling unit is supported by two other considerations. First, most of the interaction that takes place within their homes is of a very informal nature and exposes most of a family's "secrets" or "private life." In the Addams area, this can be especially threatening because the local informal communication network is so elaborate that the slightest admission can be spread throughout the neighborhood. The residents acknowledge this and frequently complain about how much other people "talk" or "gossip."[5]

Second, the household planning and preparation for visits which are so prominent in more affluent neighborhoods is almost entirely lacking in the Addams area. Telephone calls are seldom made before people "drop in." Advance invitations are even more uncommon and most prearranged domestic gatherings follow the annual cycle of customary holidays (Christmas, Thanksgiving, New Year's Eve, Lent) rather than individual convenience. Formal gatherings tend to be equally rare; cocktail parties, formal dinners, teas, and invitational parties are almost unheard of. Once started, then, domestic exchanges subject the residents either to unpredictable exposures or to additional confrontations from which they cannot easily

---

[4] This count was taken in the summer of 1964 and represents a decline from when the area was intact. This does not include any of the benches constructed by the city, although there are many of them in the projects.

[5] In fact, the residents' fears on this point may be exaggerated because they often assume that more of the local people know each other than is actually the case. Often, they will dismiss a whole section of the area by saying, "Oh, everybody over there knows each other."

retreat. Moreover, the gatherings within their households are not sufficiently guarded by the formalizations that keep a "safe distance" between
present. Thus, residents remain cautious and hesitant about bringing
"new" persons fully into their home and domestic circle.

One advantage to street life, then, is that it permits the residents to enjoy
friendly and informal social relations without exposing the very private
nature of their family life to subsequent unexpected visits. Perhaps this is
one reason why researchers have found that domestic gatherings among
working class people are so restricted to relatives.[6] The same is true of
domestic gatherings in the Addams area, but this does not mean the
residents lack extra-familial relations. Indeed, street life in the Addams
area seems to provide for exceptionally frequent associations outside the
family.

Street life in the Addams area carries with it a number of consequences.
The homogeneity of its groupings and its informal setting encourages an
exchange of intimacies that might otherwise be kept secret, or, at least,
withheld from explicit admission. Since the facts of one's private life
inevitably contain an element of shame, they invariably expose one's failure
to meet the ideal standards of public morality and taste. In most of the local
street groupings these intimacies have been regularly and persistently exchanged to the point that practically no one can claim an unblemished
social character. Since almost everyone has fallen so far from grace, there
is little attempt to keep up pretentions or to appeal to public standards as
an effective blueprint for action. In turn, having been party to so many little
personal disclosures, each individual has implicitly acceded to the primacy
of personal loyalties at the expense of public standards of behavior. Social
sanctions, then, are exercised primarily when someone deviates from personal precedent rather than from public standards.

The highly personal and private nature of these street groups is their
most apparent characteristic to an investigator or new member. Conversations assume so much knowledge of personal history that at first I could
neither understand nor contribute to their line of discourse. Nicknames
not used in other contexts are common, and kin terms are avoided as a form
of address even when they would be appropriate. Sentences are started and
not completed on the assumption that those present already know the

---

[6] M. Young and P. Willmont, *Family and Kinship in East London*, New York: Pelican
Books, 1962); A. J. Reiss, Jr., "Rural, Urban and Status Differences in Interpersonal
Contracts," *American Journal of Sociology*, 65 (September, 1959): 182–95; Bennett M.
Berger, *Working Class Suburb* (Berkeley: University of California Press, 1960); E. Litwak,
"Geographic Mobility and Extended Family Cohesion," *American Sociological Review*,
25 (February, 1960): 385–94; and Mirra Komarovsky, "The Voluntary Associations of
Urban Dwellers," *American Sociological Review*, 11 (December, 1946): 686–98.

remainder. Sometimes a person will simply mention a name or topic followed by a sage, "you know." The others barely bother to nod understanding.

Open criticism seldom is based on general mores but measures each individual according to the promises and commitments laid down in his known history. What might be praiseworthy behavior for one individual can be shameful to another. Actions that might be disconcerting if committed by one person, are only shrugged aside if someone else is responsible for them. The only general rule is the imperative that personal loyalties take precedence over moral principles. So long as an individual does not betray the trust that has been invested in him, the general attitude appears to be, "Let him who is without fault cast the first stone."

None of this, of course, means that the street group members in the Addams area do not resort to open criticism or that they give blanket approval to deviant conduct. In fact, they are very liberal with their criticisms and by no means do they ignore every deviant act. The point is that it is simply inappropriate to speak of *the norms* of a group irrespective of the accepted reputation of those in it. A man who has a reputation as a petty thief may be made fun of if he gets caught or admired if he gets away with his ventures. Another in the same group who is perfectly "straight" would be thought foolhardy or stupid if he took similar risks. At first sight each group seems to include a variety of utterly incompatible individuals. But the members of these street groups have been compromised together and assurances of personal trust exempt them from the fears and apprehensions that might otherwise develop. Even the best-known prude or thief is assumed to put his friends above his principles.

Since the conversations of these street groups tend to dwell so much on the local world of persons, events, and objects, their disclosures include the reputations and presumed activities of many other residents and street groups. Considering the extent to which persons know each other's private shortcomings, this kind of discourse tends to discredit anyone's claims or pretentions to an unrelenting moral uprightness. As a result, a much larger number of people are robbed of their capacity to appeal effectively to public standards in making demands upon each other.

In short, gossip and scandal are so rife in the Addams area that they destroy the illusion that public norms either provide a dependable picture of reality or a reliable view of each other. The residents do not seem to reject public norms and, when dealing with an utter stranger, they can be stern and unrelenting moralists. With each other, however, their own personal identities and past relations take precedence. Having shared the "true" facts of each others' lives, they simply descend from the pedestal of universal morality and enter a different normative world. The general rules and ideal images of society are not depreciated, then, but merely set aside as inappropriate.

Within the dialogue of street life, Addams area residents usually start by knowing one another's personal shortcomings and only later come to discover their mutual appreciation for the ideals of public morality. This sequence is the opposite of that where individuals start as "required persons" whose good behavior is guaranteed by the social amenities. In time, such individuals may come to know each other better and steal off into the sanctuary of informal relations. However, in their past there is always the precedent that binds them to a collusion of formal impression management. In the Addams area, people are more likely to be first committed to a highly personal relation and to find it equally hard to deviate from this precedent.

Since many of the residents draw their confirmed personal identity from the acknowledgment of their local street group, any attempt to discredit or cast doubt on their character brings into question not only a specific individual's pride but also the judgment and honor of his companions. On the streets, Addams area residents are seldom alone, and disputes or arguments between any two persons are usually felt to affect the self-evaluations of those around each protagonist. Thus, it is nearly impossible for an Addams area resident to carry on a dispute that is "nobody else's business." Almost invariably every juxtaposition of social personalities produces reverberations that disturb others and that pose the necessity of "taking sides." The order of segmentation within the area is an example of how these disputes can grow to include additional persons. The visibility of street life and the constant presence of one's street companions facilitate this type of accretion. Not only does street life make available those ready to take sides, but it also affords little opportunity for combatants to "back down" without everyone knowing of their lack of constancy.

The total communication network created by street life makes it especially difficult for the residents to separate their self-presentation and their interpersonal commitments. In their leisure hours Addams area residents, and especially the teenagers, tend to travel in the company of their street group. Moreover, even when they are outside each other's immediate presence, it is likely that word will get back about any "additional" associations. Ultimately, then, all one's friends must submit to judgment by one's street group. Thus, it is only by great secrecy and cunning that a street group member can meet new acquaintances on terms different from those to which he is already committed. Not only does this lack of privacy engender a rather inflexible approach to "outsiders," but it also makes it almost impossible to spread one's eggs about in several baskets.[7]

The difficulty of managing relations outside one's street group is especially pronounced among teenage males. Two boys I knew fairly well would wave or talk to me whenever they were alone. When they were with their street corner group, however, they would make a great pretense of not knowing me. Later, when I asked one of them about this, he explained, "Well, the rest of the guys don't know you. And with you, well, you know, I don't act exactly like I do with them." Boys also steal off to see their girls, take measures to avoid a common confrontation with their parents and "the guys," or engage in all sorts of surreptitious maneuvers to acknowledge outsiders without being discovered by their street group. The overshadowing presence of the street group is probably most evident in the contrast between the boys' behavior when alone and when they are with "the guys." Alone they are often sullen and tight-lipped, or so humble they nearly deafen you with "yes sirs." Together, they are a rowdy and independent crew, sometimes uncooperative, but always sure of themselves.

The problem of separating dyadic relations from the entire range of street life can be seen in these field notes taken one night when it was rumored that E and M were going to fight.

As I arrived at the club, E approached me and asked if I could arrange for him and M to fight at a place where others could not "jump into the fight." I took E to S, a street worker who was working with a group to which E belonged. E explained that a rumor had started that he and M were going to fight. Already a crowd had gathered in front of E's home, and his sister had had a fight with one girl in an effort to get rid of the crowd. There was no alternative, E said, but that he and M "do battle."

S agreed to the fight, and we took E in the car to pick up M. When we found M, a crowd of teenagers flocked around the car and asked where we were going "for the fight." S said, "Peanut Park." The kids ran off in that direction while we went to Addams Park.

Once there, S let the boys out of the car and told them, "OK, now." The boys began to spar around in a wide circle covering a quarter of the park. S and I did not bother to get out of the car. They talked constantly and occasionally we could hear the boys laugh. Each of the boys worked up a sweat without touching the other. They took a recess and one of them asked and got a cigarette from the other. After they finished their cigarettes they began to spar again. M scratched E with his fingernails. "Hey, you draw first blood," said E.

The boys continued to go through the motions of fighting. Finally, M came over out of breath and said, "We through. E, there, he say he defeated."

[7] See Alvin W. Gouldner, "Reciprocity and Autonomy in Functional Theory" in *Symposium on Sociological Theory*, ed. L. Gross (White Plains: Row, Peterson, 1959), pp. 241–70.

In the car M told E how he should conduct himself.

"E, you gotta tell how I whipped your ass."

"I'll take my sweater off so's they see my shirt torn," said E.

M told S and me that we should back up his story or no one would believe it. We said "OK." As we arrived near the boys' home a crowd of teenagers met us.

"Who won? Who won?" they yelled. M said he won.

"That's right, E?" somebody asked.

"Yeah, I got defeated," said E.

"Who won, S?" another asked.

"Oh, M," said S.

The kids began to laugh and jump around in the street. E walked sheepishly off to his home. M strutted off among the other kids.

This incident is fairly typical and illustrates the way street life constantly intrudes on dyadic relations. In the above instance the fight itself was started by a rumor fabricated by two street groups who had overheard E and M signifying. Both boys were somewhat surprised that they were supposed to fight but could not easily back down once several street groups had gathered at E's housefront. Only the intercession of a streetworker made it possible for the two boys to steal off and privately settle the issue by a mock fight.

Street workers try hard to bring such disputes to a private settlement. Often, of course, they are too late; and a dispute may grow by accretion until it includes several street groups. At these times the local residents usually avoid the arbitration of specialists such as the police, lawyers, welfare workers, and priests. In large part this seems due to the nature of street life and the sorts of conflicts that emerge out of it. Each street group permits an exchange of highly personal and often vulgar information. Disputes that arise out of these private disclosures generally start with the assumption that they will continue to be handled privately, and a shift to formal methods of settlement seems like a kind of betrayal. In addition, it is not only embarrassing to openly admit this sort of information to still other people, but formal authorities are likely to view it as "petty." The "fight" between E and M, for example, was supposed to have originated from an occasion where E called M "a name."[8] On these grounds, M could hardly run to the Illinois Youth Commission or Chicago Police Department and claim foul play against E.

The street workers in the Addams area were in a better position to know the disclosures of street life and the importance the residents attributed to them. The street workers' willingness to keep the residents' secrets and accept their evaluations was especially important in those altercations that

[8] No one was sure exactly what the "name" was. But some of them insinuated that it must have been the "worst" name, i.e., "motherfucker."

grew out of an accumulation of grievances reaching far back into the residents' personal history. The communication channels of street life keep alive a body of information that includes numerous personal faults and interpersonal grievances. Thus an insult, confrontation, or rivalry is judged against a background of "facts" that would be inadmissible in most courts of law or would seem trival to a non-resident. By accepting the way street life keeps these "facts" alive, the local street workers can intercede without belittling or violating the confidence of the local residents.

The above observations are meant to apply to all street groups whether it be a cluster of old Italian ladies with shawls thrown about their shoulders or a group of young boys drinking in an alley. In certain respects these groups are all alike: in their intimacy, their bawdiness, and their tendency to appraise persons in terms of what is known of them rather than in terms of their official social capacity. However, some of the personal identities these groups hold in store for their members are age-linked and others are sex-linked. The old ladies, for example, do not and cannot confide the same falls from social grace as do the males and the young girls. An elderly woman can be a bad housewife or a "bitch," but try as she might, she simply cannot get others to take her as a "mellow cat" (a successfully "cool" young male) or a "fox" (a self-consciously "sexy" young girl or woman). These and similar identities are generated by the departures that are possible from one's publicly proper social roles. Since each age and sex group starts with different publicly proper social roles, the personal identities open to members branch out in somewhat different directions. What remains constant is the process which removes a person from consideration as someone whose behavior can be anticipated simply by resorting to the official typology of roles. By definition, this does not fulfill the "ideal" of Addams area morality, but it does help somewhat to make life tolerable for people who "know too much about each other." The immunities they grant each other are mutually comforting.

Business Establishment Groups

Street life is not an isolated institution but overlaps all other institutions in the Addams area. Because street life occupies so central a position in the neighborhood's communication network, information broached in one setting usually works its way along the streets to another setting. Most of the information that is expelled into street life is as personal and revealing as that disclosed on the streets themselves. This is especially true of the informal exchanges that go on in business establishments where the social life of habitués merges with that of street life.

In some ways the inner city seems the last outpost of the country store.

In the Addams area itself, most businesses are locally owned or, at least, operated by local residents.[9] Generally, these places are quite small and able to serve a correspondingly small number of people. There is no full-scale supermarket,[10] and the two establishments that might be mistaken as chain stores are actually operated by local residents known to many people in their ethnic groups.

Usually the social relations that take place in these establishments parallel those occurring on the streets.[11] People laugh, argue, insult one another, extend their sympathies, and confide their troubles. Some people spend a good portion of the day bantering in these business places and then leave without buying anything. In fact, business transactions are often treated as a kind of afterthought and something of a nuisance. The smallness and longevity of each business' clientele, of course, favors this sort of informal arrangement. Many of the businesses in the Addams area date back to the 1920's when many people converted the lower story of their homes to some sort of small service trade. Zoning restrictions were lax; and business establishments and residences became thoroughly interwoven, appearing on the same streets, occupying the same buildings, and bringing together the same people. Their small scale and the ease of starting such a place of business undoubtedly brought about a strong competition for customers. Expensive measures like advertising, elaborate displays, price-cutting, and new furnishings, however, were not generally within their means. Under these conditions, survival depended upon exploiting those marginal competitive devices available to the operator at the expense of his own endeavors. Friends and relatives provided the labor supply. Personal connections were seized upon to furnish customers. Such favors as extending credit, catering to someone's particular tastes, or hanging up a church poster were ways of transforming new customers into a clientele. However, the easiest and most common competitive device was to grant customers such license as to exempt them from their narrow social role and thus allow them to extend their relationship in whatever direction their additional disclosures might lead. Older people were asked about their health. Housewives were flattered through the safe measures of kidding and teasing. Young boys and girls were allowed to hang around the doorways.

[9] Seventy-four per cent of those where the operator meets the customer face-to-face have at least one operator who lives in the area. In many other instances the operator once lived in the area and is well known to local people.

[10] Four places call themselves supermarkets but are actually very small operations. Three of them are run by local residents and extend the same favors to their customers as do other businesses.

[11] The exception, of course, occurs when strangers or persons from a different ethnic group enter the establishment.

And, if they pleased, the customers were allowed to swear a bit, wear their worst clothes, gossip with each other, or simply visit without buying anything.

This mixture of informality and business has become so stable in the area that many establishments have a fixed clientele that supports the business but on the other hand, makes commerce with strangers awkward. Since many of these businesses were established during the Italian hegemony over the area, it is among the Italians that street life and commercial exchanges come closest to merging. Along Harrison Street, where the Puerto Ricans have taken over, however, the process of merging street life and commercial life is still under way and several little grocery stores, record shops, cleaners, and barber shops have an off-and-on existence. Similarly, a number of Mexican-run businesses have cropped up and are following closely in the steps of their Italian predecessors. Ordinarily they are occupied and surrounded by several habitués who engage in a private and informal social life without having to buy anything. All these businesses grant favors to their customers,[12] and the license they extend goes so far as to include types of clothing, ribaldry, drinking, gambling, and rough-housing that would not be tolerated in a more impersonal establishment. In the Addams area, the customer is not always right, but he can also bring into question the one-price system as well as the authority of grades and labels.

Perhaps the following extract from my notes will give a taste of these informal business relationships.

Nina, a Greek lady of about forty-five, entered the grocery store where Nick (the Italian operator), Rosario (boy who worked in the store), and I were talking. Nina walked around a bit and then Nick yelled jovially, "Hey, Greek. What you want?"

Nina returned, "Goddammit, wait until I look around anyhow."

"Aw, come on Greek. Don't keep me waiting so long for just a nickel." Nick reached over and put a newspaper in her coat pocket. He always keeps a paper for her.

"Hey! Keep your hands off me, you bastard!"

"Hey!" said Nick drawing back and then threatening to approach again.

Nick and Nina completed some commercial transactions which were hardly noticeable. Nick began to write down her bill in her "book." Nina nudged me.

"What's that son of a bitch doing? I never know what my bill's gonna be."

"Why you swear so much, Nina? What if the priests hear you?" (Our Lady of Provins Cathedral is across the street. Sometimes the priests and nuns shop at the store.)

---

[12] E.g., cashing checks, giving credit, running children home to their parents, hanging up notices, saving some fresh eggs for a customer, etc.

"Oh, hell," said Nina, "whatta they care. Our priests can swear. Anyhow they ain't here."

"What about Summer[13] here. He's studying for the priesthood."

"If he ain't heard it, it won't hurt him. If you have, hell, be a Greek priest."

After a few other exchanges, "Nina, I heard your boy come home for Christmas," Nick said.

"Yea. He wants to get married. Can you imagine? Him only nineteen and in the Army like that."

"What's a matter," said Nick, "can't he keep it in his pants awhile? What's Elmira say?"[14]

"Same thing," said Nina, "What's the use of getting married now. He's just gonna go away. Wait, you'll wish you'd had your fun when you could. Get married and you'll have nothing but children."

"You know whattchu gotta do?" said Nick, balling up a fist and recommending its usage. Then he became nostalgic. "All these kids. They get married and then they regret it. Now if I'd a know'd it before I got married, you know." Nick nodded and insinuated the pleasures of bachelorhood.

Nina laughed. "Huh. You bastard. It's a good thing too. Somebody gotta look after you."

Nick laughed and grabbed at Nina as she left.

Between men and women in middle age and as safely married as Nick and Nina, this sort of ribald exchange is common. An older lady would probably have been treated with greater respect by asking her about her children, aches, and pains. A younger girl might have been teased more. But ribaldry is of even greater concern among male peers, as the following extract shows.

We were sitting in the X bar. The bar itself is quite small and L-shaped, and everybody was sitting with their backs to it in order to face one another. All were in their thirties and, except for myself, Italian.

"Hey Carmie," said Louie, "You know. I sent off two weeks ago for one of those hard-on books.[15] And they ain't sent it yet. Two weeks!"

"You want some of those books? Here." Carmie brought out a stack of books with pictures of half and fully naked girls.

"Hey!" Everybody went over to the stack of magazines. For a while there was bedlam.

"Look at those tits," said Louie patting the same location on his chest. "If my wife had tits like that I'd never get to work."

For a while we continued to dwell on the merits, measurements, and probable performances of the girls in the magazines. Shortly, however, they began to compare them with girls in the neighborhood. "You know Carmena. She's got big

---

[13] When I first entered the store Nick mistook my name as "Summer" and it stuck. Both Nina and Nick knew I didn't "have any religion."

[14] The mother of the potential bride. Notice that no one asked the bride's name. Everyone knew it.

[15] A pornographic book.

tits like that. And a big ass too!" said Tony, grabbing a handful of air as if it were Carmena's backside.

They went on to mention several other local girls who were equally endowed. There was no continuity, just a passing comment on each girl and her merits. "Now Tina, you know, that's real stuff," said someone. "Hell, if I could lay that, you couldn't beat me off."

"Say, you know," someone broke in, "there was a girl raped in the neighborhood. No kidding. Sommer's up on Polk. Yea. Some Shine, they say."[16]

"I heard some gal got raped up on Chicago (Ave.)," said Mike. "Yea, she's been up there ever since. Couldn't get layed anywhere else." There followed a short and humorous commentary on "rape-prone" girls.

The subject changed. "You know," said Louie, "after this I gotta get me a hand job this weekend. Maybe Saturday."

"What for?" said Carmie, "use your own. Whatchu think God give you two hands for?"

"It ain't the same," said Louie.

"What th' fuck's the difference?" said Carmie. "Ain't your hand as good as anybody's?"

There was a short and disjointed discussion of the advantages of being masturbated by a girl or doing it yourself. Then, the world series between the Cardinals and Yankees started on the TV set. We turned around to face the bar. In the meantime the conversation continued.

"Hey, Louie," said Carmie, "you wannanother (beer)?"

"Wait a while. I gotta watch for my healt(h). My old lady died o' sugar and I got the same trouble sez the doc." Louie went on. "Before my old lady died, you know, she always ate a lotta pasta and took her wine, you know. Then she had this sugar. We took her to the hospital to this sheeny doctor. They know their trade you know. He sez you can't tell. Like sometimes you got it and sometimes they ain't. It all depends. My old lady, she died. My old lady, I guess, was just too old. We put her in Mt. Carmel.[17] Whatta you gonna do? Anyhow she had the sugar. I gotta watch my healt(h)."

This sort of ribaldry and self-exposure reaches its peak in those establishments frequented by males of the same age. However, the women have their own establishments where they congregate and the "news" that leaks out from them is not far off the mark set by the men.

The appearance of local business places indicates the extent to which trade is attuned to an intimate group of habitués to the exclusion of outsiders. Twenty-one per cent of the businesses have no name at all. Locally they are simply referred to by the name of the owner. Apparently the assumption is that a separate name is unnecessary; everybody who might come in is supposed to know where it is and who runs it. Those businesses that possess a name often use that of the operator's family or a part of his

---

[16] So far as I know there was no rape. Rumors like this occasionally occur. When they have some basis in fact, everyone usually knows the names of those involved.

[17] One of the cemeteries that Italians in the Addams area favor. Addams area residents are as segregated after death as before.

name; for instance, "Al's," "Joe's," "Marge's." Even so, Addams area residents do not always respect the establishment's name and sometimes refer to it in a way that an outsider could not understand. For example, they call "Licensed Groceries" the operator's name and often they will simply refer to "the beef stand" or "the cleaners" although there are many such places in the area. However, they always seem to know which they are talking about and there is no confusion.

Advertising is almost non-existent except for one grocery store that puts circulars in the local mailboxes and posts prices in the windows. In most other stores, the prices of different items are seldom marked, either on the counters or the items themself. During the three years I was in the area, only one store ever had a "sale." "Specials," "price cuts," and changes of displays are almost unknown. With rare exception, there is no attempt to draw in new clients in addition to the old habitués.

Among the whites in the Addams area, the informal exchanges in these commercial establishments augment and extend those occurring on the streets. Because they are in public housing, the Negroes' section of the Addams area is restricted from commercial use. Except for a very few places, then, commercial exchanges among the Negroes do not extend the communication network of street life. The extent to which the Negroes have a personal knowledge of one another is correspondingly reduced. The most obvious result is a more constricted range of personal acquaintanceship and a greater degree of suspicion toward persons not intimately known. Also the Negroes are less thoroughly drawn into the area's provincialism and somewhat more adept at handling impersonal relations. These features are distinctive of the Negro section and will be considered in greater detail when each ethnic section is separately discussed.

Institutionalized Segregation of Sex and Age Groups

The most obvious consequence of these commercial establishments is that they help sustain the provincialism and ordered segmentation among the whites. As with street groups, establishment groups are relatively homogeneous on the basis of age, sex, ethnicity, and residence. Both of these groups parallel the "multicellular" structure of the neighborhood and insure each of its ethnic sections against major disruption as ethnic succession chews away at minor territorial units. Since business establishment and street groups do not wholly coincide in their membership, together they provide an extensive communication network in which personal information is freely revealed and can travel beyond the range of face-to-face relations.

The homogeneity of age and sex in Addams area street groups and establishment groups is reinforced by other institutional arrangements. A majority of the white children go to parochial schools, which insist that boys and girls as well as age grades be kept separate.[18] Once out of school most of the males enter blue-collar occupations in which they remain in all-male groups.[19]

This separation of age and sex groups continues in most places of recreation and entertainment. The local taverns are considered unfit for a respectable girl. In a few places where food is served, girls or women may come with their family or male friends. Occasionally, in a few taverns, there will be a single girl who hangs where her boyfriend works or spends his time. The rest of the men treat her with ribald familiarity, but their liberties do not involve sexual attentions. She is treated like another male member of the group; and, although not respectable in the eyes of the neighborhood, the men in the tavern ward off anyone who would try to "pick her up."

The distinctively male character of Addams area taverns becomes apparent when local males talk about where they can "put the make on a girl." In all, there is only one bar, a Negro nightclub on Roosevelt, that the males discuss as a realistic possibility. This is the only bar in the area that does not cater to a local clientele; it maintains a sophisticated decor, live entertainment, and does not serve food. Some of the local Negroes consider it a place for prowling males and virtueless girls. The whites see it as dangerous and never go there without a Negro escort.

The single pool hall in the Addams area is so thoroughly a male "hang-out" that a woman who entered for some purpose other than speaking to her brother or asking for her husband would be inviting sexual overtures.[20] Even more off-limits to women is the adult, male social athletic club ("SAC."). There are fourteen of these storefront clubs in the Addams area. Usually they are furnished with a bar, a television set, and some chairs. The men sit around gossiping, drinking, and playing cards. To my knowledge, not one of the older groups ever had a social or athletic event during the three years I was in the area. Mostly they gamble, drink, and talk.

Recreational places for youngsters are equally circumspect in separating

[18] Within the Addams area and adjacent neighborhoods the public schools are considered inferior to the parochial schools. While the Negroes do not voice this evaluation as often as the whites, they share it. Estimates based on a survey of boys ten to nineteen years of age, show that about 10% of the Negro boys attend parochial schools while 70% of the whites attend parochial schools.

[19] For some comments on the improprieties of all male occupational groups, see Donald Roy, "Banana Time: Job Satisfaction and Informal Interaction," *Human Organization*, 18 (Winter 1959–60): 158–68.

[20] There are two more such places on Madison Street, and Halsted. They are like the one in the Addams area, except that "hustlers" hang in them.

sex groups. Except for two playgrounds that have facilities for little girls,[21] all the others are set aside for male groups or games. Girls who invade the boys' playgrounds cast doubt on their character and invite sexual attention. Sometimes the older boys will have a social or athletic event to which they invite the girls. But the girls come and leave by themselves and seldom separate from their female companions except when on the dance floor. For the older girls, there is not a single place in the area they can call their own.

Next to the ethnic groups, spatial arrangements in the Addams area are most thorough at maintaining distance between the sexes. This segregation assures that most groups can openly discuss matters which would not be mentioned in "mixed company." It also lends to sexual roles and relationships a definition that is not typically American in the sense that they are not equalitarian and males are not expected to observe sexual restraint. Certainly Addams area males and females take an avid interest in one another. In fact, this interest is generally considered to be so strong that moral warnings are thought to be of little value and spatial segregation a necessity. Naturally, this does not mean that males and females in the area fail to see a good deal of each other. But their encounters take on the appearance of liaisons and become the source of gossip. Spatial segregation thus helps maintain a predatory definition of sexual relations; either girls remain to themselves, "in their place," or hazard their reputations.

Necessarily, then, most Addams area youths either spend their time in single sex groupings or manage their cross-sexual relations by stealth or bravado. Either way, their interaction falls outside the bounds of public appraisal and its consequent restraints. Among the males there is an almost Rabelaisian familiarity, involving name calling, "circle jerks," spitting contests, and a great deal of touching of one another. On the other hand, when males and females do get together, they have already set aside public morality to such an extent that further departures seem only a natural progression. Under these conditions, cross-sexual and unisexual relations simply increase the known range of personal shortcomings which get spread along the streets and in the establishments of the Addams area.

The Congestion of Domestic Life

In addition to the voluntary disclosures that Addams area residents willingly share on its streets and in its business places, there are a number of other personal matters that they might like to keep to themselves. Their

---

[21] Swings and seesaws. One is on the playground of a parochial school. The other is practically unused since is also has a basketball court and the mothers won't let their little girls go there because of "the big boys."

efforts here, however, are severely limited by the crowding and intimacy of domestic life.[22] Even where there is the strongest desire for privacy, girls must often dress, "make themselves up," run around in their slips, and sometimes use the bathroom in someone else's presence. Boys sleep in the same room as their older and more worldly brothers, wear each others' clothing, and perform their bodily functions in the same enclosures. Husbands and wives cannot keep their intimacies or arguments a private matter that others can at least pretend didn't happen. At times everyone may use the same towel, eat off the same plate, or indulge in a common obscenity. Fathers are seen in their underwear, mothers while in labor, sisters during their period, and boys when "beating their meat." Sometimes there are disclosures that could lead to serious consequences: abortions, incest, illegitimacy, adultery, and narcotics scars. More common, however, are those skeletons for which every family is supposed to have a closet: defecation, intercourse, parental arguments, and dressing.

As the evening draws to a close in the Addams area, people vacate its streets, and retreat to a homelife that allows for little privacy. Without privacy, the cultural rulings of modesty become impractical and shyness a personal fault. Within their own domicile, Addams area residents often abandon the rules of propriety and decorum because they seem so out of place. Sharing the same bathroom and bedroom congests relationships so that both affection and authority are not easily seen as situational proprieties. Relations become quite blunt since they cannot be ordered according to who has priority in a given space.[23] Inevitably, conflict over spatial usage results in a definition of personal power rather than situational rights.

Within the family circle, these conditions of enforced intimacy erode the impersonal social distance between family members and allow for further disclosures.[24] Despite the restriction of domestic life to near kin, these disclosures often leak out and become widely discussed on the streets. Partially this is because family members themselves divulge these matters to their street acquaintances. Further disclosures occur, however, because most residents cannot afford to place every family crisis in the hands of someone sworn to secrecy such as a doctor or lawyer. Instead, they are much more dependent upon the barter of favors that prevail among kinfolk, friends,

---

[22] According to the 1960 census, about 16% of Addams area homes had more than 1.01 persons per room. Excluding the projects, the percentage rises to 20%.

[23] The absences of firm enclosures to denote the priority of family members seems to be the basis for what many observers have called the spontaneous warmth and anger of lower-class families.

[24] For a more general discussion of how crowding affects family relations, see James M. Plant, *Personality and the Cultural Pattern* (New York: Commonwealth Fund, 1937).

and neighbors. Financial troubles, illegitimacies, separations, abortions, and other domestic difficulties often lay bare the innermost workings of a family, and the reliance on non-professionals in times of trouble tends to "give it away."

Families in the Addams area are further exposed by the occasional practice of "taking one's troubles to the street." Because the streets in the Addams area are so crowded, they furnish a kind of ideal "jury of one's peers." Where husbands and wives, friends, lovers, or street groups have come to the "end of their rope," they may appeal to this form of arbitration. For the older Mexican and Italian men, it is particularly humiliating to quarrel with a woman because men are supposed to give commands rather than submit to arguments. Thus, a woman who has been pushed to extremities may try to retrieve her situation by airing her complaints before the neighbors. Such displays are a staple for discussion among street groups.

Historical and Universal Social Environments

The enforced intimacy of family life and the homogeneity of most other groupings in the Addams area allows for a detailed and highly personal exchange of information. Since the various types of groups do not coincide in membership, they fit together to form a communication network that reaches throughout any ethnic section. Street groups are probably the most active link in this communication network because they are the most open to inspection and the casual acceptance of new members.

Because of the intimate and unguarded nature of street life and its contributing sources, the facts that residents know of one another are drawn from a long history of gossip and private disclosures. With so much information at hand on one another's personal histories, general morality is neither a dependable blueprint for action nor an appropriate way of treating people with whom the residents have shared so many intimacies. Where possible, then, each individual is evaluated against his own historical precedents. In turn, sanctions are exercised primarily when someone deviates from what others feel to be his "true self;" it is then that people become "phonies," "finks," or "jive."

The social order produced by these individual expectations is not aptly described by the concepts "role" or "norm." These concepts apply most appropriately to entire categories of people who can be defined without knowledge of their past performance: e.g., neighbors, pedestrians, motorists, and peers. In the Addams area a knowledge of personal reputation far outweighs these categoric considerations. It simply becomes inappropriate to refer to norms that are not tailored to each individual's identity.

This historical and individuated social order has both advantages and disadvantages for the residents. Usually the residents do have a firm notion of what to expect from one another. Moreover, an exact knowledge of one another's personal character is often quite reassuring when compared to the apprehensions inspired by their social statuses. Jointly compromised by common disclosures, the residents enter a pact assuring one another's safety.

This social order, however, is distinctly limited by the number of people one can know through such private sources. Addams area residents must literally memorize the personal character of one another without the benefit of general rules that would apply to whole categories of people. This is not too great a disadvantage since each ethnic-territorial section within the area is relatively small. The restriction of associations beyond one's age, sex, and territory further limits the range of knowledge that is required. It is also advantageous for Addams area residents not to extend their loyalties or become too dependent beyond a narrow territory surrounding their own home. Small sections of the inner city are regularly displaced through the processes of ethnic succession, urban renewal, and rezoning. The narrow reach of each resident's associations and trust assures that he will not be too disturbed by these excisions.

Part 3

Ethnic Solidarity

Introduction

Despite the unity outsiders attribute to the Addams area, the residents know themselves to be badly divided. Broadly speaking, these internal divisions follow ethnic and territorial lines. Within each territorial-ethnic section there are certain variations, some of them due to ethnic traditions and others resulting directly from population size or minor ecological differences.

By far the most striking contrast is between the Negro and the Italian sections. For instance, almost all the Negroes live in public housing while, on the other hand, the Italians usually control both their households and commercial establishments. Unlike the Negroes who have very similar incomes and almost no political power, there is some internal differentiation of income and political power among the Italians. Such differences draw the Italians and Negroes apart and generate radically different styles of life. For purposes of contrast these two ethnic sections are discussed in greater detail than are those of the Puerto Ricans and Mexicans.

In most ways the Puerto Rican section is the least complex of those in the Addams area. There are no more than 1100 Puerto Ricans in their section and, within broad age ranges, most of them know one another on a "personal basis." The Puerto Rican section is notable for the extent to which personal relations suffice, and until 1965 no named groups had emerged among them.

The Mexicans are more numerous, and several named groups have developed among the teenagers. Unlike the Italians, however, similar Mexican groups have not survived into adulthood, although there are indications that this may eventually occur. The Mexicans seem to have much in common with the Italians, and frequently their relationship is congenial. What gives the Mexicans pause, however, is the occasional necessity to divide their loyalties between the Italians and the Negroes.

The chapters that follow concern both the various ethnic groups and the sections they control. The actual pattern of residence is less distinct than are these ethnic sections but it is only within each section that ethnicity places its characteristic stamp on social life.

Although it would be misleading to overemphasize the extent of differences between these ethnic sections, such differences as do occur loom large in the Addams area. The residents are actively looking for differences among themselves. Awareness of their common lower class standing does not provide these differences and, in any case, may arouse only suspicion and distrust. The ethnic sections in the area, however, constitute basic guidelines from which the residents of each section can anticipate certain forms of reciprocity and the alternative dangers that may be in store elsewhere.

6

The Park and the Italians

The Spirit of Omerta

The portion of the Addams area now controlled by the Italians is only a residue from the encroachments of the other three ethnic groups. In total land space, however, it is the largest of any controlled by a single ethnic group. In population, however, it is not exceptionally large; and throughout this section an unusually high proportion of Mexicans have been accepted by the Italians as neighbors. What the Italians lack in numbers, however, is often made up for by an extraordinary reputation for the use of sheer force and for easy access to "influence" or "connections." It is said, for example, that many of the Italians are "Outfit people" and that many more could rely on "mobsters" if they needed help. Also, it is the general view that the Italians control both the vice and patronage of the First Ward, a political unit that includes the spoils of the Loop.

This conception of the Italians in the Addams area, although exaggerated, is not without foundation. There are some very famous Italians in the Addams area, and they frequently get a "spread" in the city newspapers.[1] There are many others not nearly so prominent but whose personal history is still known in the neighborhood. At least five Italian policemen live in the area, and a few more who grew up there are assigned to the local district. The other ethnic groups have not a single resident or ex-resident policeman among them. Most of the precinct captains are also Italian; and, outside the projects, the Italians dominate those jobs provided by

---

[1] Including: (1) the purported head of the Chicago "Syndicate;" (2) a vice-president of the most prominent bank in town; (3) the Democratic committeeman of the First Ward; (4) a legislator to the Illinois House of Representatives; (5) a "bookie" who controls many of the "joints" in the Loop; (6) the man who represents the Seventh District in the House of Representatives in Washington; (7) the chief "gunsul" for the "Syndicate"; (8) a number of minor "hoods" who have no recognized specialty but are still well known; and (9), until recently, the alderman of the First Ward.

Not all these people live in the Addams area at the present time. However, their repute and notoriety linger on through family names and frequent references to their common birthplace.

public funds.[2] There are a number of Italian businessmen, each of whom controls a few jobs. However, it is also widely believed that they can "sponsor" a person into many of the industries of the city; for instance, the newsstands in the Loop, the city parks, the beauty culture industry, a large printing company, and a number of clothing firms.

While there is some substance to this belief in Italian power and influence, it is actually quite exaggerated. Many of the Italian political figures, for instance, seem to have little more than the privilege of announcing decisions that have been made elsewhere. In most of the recent political actions that have affected the area, for example, they have remained mute and docile. When the Medical Center was built and then extended, they said nothing. The Congress and the Dan Ryan Expressways were constructed with the local politicians hardly taking notice. Finally, when the University of Illinois was located at Congress Circle, the politicians, mobsters, and, indeed, all the male residents conceded to it without even a show of resistance. In fact, it was only a group of Italian and Mexican housewives who, at this point, took up arms and sought to save some remnant of the neighborhood. In some circles this ineffectuality was explained by the insinuation that the "right people" had been "paid off." A more common view was that these same "people" had bought up land in the hope that it would be purchased for the expressways. This failing, they invited the university into the area to take the property off their hands. Residents who share either outlook often add that the local politicians had little to lose since the Negroes would eventually take over the area and they would be out of office in the near future. The local Italian politicians, however, did not even "put on a show" of opposition or encourage alternative measures (e.g., urban renewal) that might have saved their constituency. It appears, then, that they did not even try to extend to the utmost their stay in office.[3] Among themselves, the Italians sometimes acknowledge this and dismiss their local politicians and city employees as lackeys of the Irish.[4]

---

[2] E.g., city parks, sanitation, etc. Italians speak of this as "city work" and seldom refer to the job title. It is common throughout the area for the residents to refer to the industry rather than someone's job title except in the case of priests, policemen, school teachers, doctors, and lawyers. In the immediate neighborhood, the practice of identifying one's industry is often more informative, since it indicates one's likely "connections" rather than specific job skills. The latter may be a matter of indifference, but the former are something to take seriously.

[3] Already they have lost two positions: alderman of the First Ward and legislator to the Illinois House of Representatives.

[4] Specifically, they are called "Irish Dagos." The Italians still hold to the view that the Irish "run the city." There is some basis for this; but, as in the case of their own mystique of power and influence, it is probably an exaggeration derived mostly from public appearances.

The Italians' notoriety for being in the rackets and having recourse to "strong-arm" methods is also a considerable exaggeration, or at least a misinterpretation. The majority of the local Italians are perfectly respectable people and gain nothing from organized crime. However, many of the common family names of the area have been sullied by some flagrant past episode. In the area, family histories remain a basis for judging individual members and are extended to include all persons who share the same name. In another neighborhood this information might be lost or ignored as improper. In the Addams area, however, it is almost impossible to keep family secrets; and, once betrayed, they are kept alive in the constant round of rumor and gossip.

The local Italians themselves contribute to their shady reputation because there are many occasions when they find it advantageous to intimate their connections with the "Outfit." Outsiders, for example, are often quite flattered to think that they are being brought into the confidence of someone who knows the underworld. The Italians find this attention equally flattering and often oblige by elaboration and invention when they are at a loss for facts. Also, it is far more prestigious to have other people believe that one's background is buried in crime and violence than in public welfare.[5] In America, organized crime has always received a certain respect, even when this respect had to be coerced. A recipient of public welfare is simply dismissed as unimportant. Thus, some of the local Italians prefer to be mistaken as "hoods" than to be disclosed as recipients of public welfare.

In addition, some of the Italians feel that a reputation of being in with the "right people" can in some circumstances, insure them against victimization. They often intimate "connections" with the "Outfit" when facing the members of another ethnic group under uncertain odds. The Italians also make vague hints about their "connections" when in an argument among themselves.

Within the circle of friends and relatives, the Italians often complain bitterly of how they are maligned by the press and by their neighbors. Nevertheless, they still remain cautious in their dealings with one another; and probably, more than anyone else, the Italians are intimidated by a half-myth of their own creation. Indirectly, this myth gives them considerable cohesion and a certain autonomy from the judgments and actions of the wider society. It is almost impossible to persuade one of them to make a

---

[5] During the depression many of the Italians went on welfare, and at one time they made up a large proportion of those in public housing. Today, the Negroes are the biggest recipients of public aid and housing. The Italians are loath to admit they were once in the same position.

complaint to the police; indeed, they shun all public sources of social control. They handle grievances, contracts, and exchanges in a very informal manner, usually limited to the immediate parties. If in need, they exact aid in the form of favors and generally ignore sources available to the general public. As a result, the Italians have been able to sustain among themselves the image of an independent, powerful, and self-confident people.

The cohesion and solidarity of the Italians, however, is very limited. It is based primarily on the suspicion that social arrangements are best made by private settlements. This suspicion, in turn, is based on the assumption that recourse to public means can do little more than excite retaliation and vengeance. These same suspicions and doubts, however, undermine the possibilities of a unified and explicit stance by the Italians toward the wider community and political organization. First, very few of them believe that the others will "go along" in joint efforts unless it is to their personal advantage or they are under some dire threat. Second, the Italians simply fear that a united public stand will elicit a similar posture on the part of their adversaries and eliminate the opportunity for private negotiations. Accordingly the Italians either shun public confrontations or slowly draw away, once so engaged. For example, in the 1920's a number of local Republican insurgents in the Addams area made no headway against their Democratic and Irish masters, and eventually they were brought back into the fold of the West Side Bloc. In the 1930's the "White Hand" made an industrious attempt to organize in the neighborhood, but after what seemed an auspicious beginning, people began to draw back and after a few years the movement died.[6] The recent uprising of the women in league with Mrs. Scala initially made a strong start at preserving the neighborhood but then failed to gain popular support. In retrospect, then, the spirit of *omerta* seems ineffectual when it confronts the explicit efforts of the wider community.[7]

The inability of the Italians to accept or engage in public appeals leaves them somewhat bewildered by the Negroes' civil rights movement. By their standards, the Negroes are making a "federal case" out of something that should be handled by private agreement. Indeed, even those who accept the justice of the Negroes' cause remain perplexed by the Negroes' failure to

---

[6] See Landesco, *Organized Crime*, pp. 935–75.

[7] Literally, *omerta* means a conspiracy between thieves. However, the Italians use it to mean any private agreement that cannot be safely broached before the general public. The point is that (1) their common cause cannot be laid openly before the general public with any hope of a solution that is favorable to one side without damning both sides, and (2) each side assumes that the other cannot fully enjoy the prospect of publicly "finking" on his adversary.

approach them in some informal manner. Throughout the summer of 1964, when demonstrators were most active, the Italians always seemed aggrieved and surprised that the Negroes would "pull such a trick" without warning. The Negroes took this as a "sham" and felt that the Italians had ample reason to anticipate their demands. However, to the Italians this was not the point. Of course, they knew that the Negroes had many long-standing demands and desires. In fact, a good number of them were convinced that the Negroes wanted to take over the entire neighborhood. What struck the Italians as unfair about the Negroes' demonstrations was their tactics: a sudden public confrontation without any chance for either side to retreat or compromise with grace.

Ultimately, both the Italians and Negroes did take their differences behind closed doors, and each settled for something less than their public demands. The main bone of contention was a local swimming pool dominated by the Italians and their Mexican guests. It was already late summer when the Negroes and Italians "got off the street" and began to discuss how they would share the pool. Once both sides had reached an understanding, the Negroes managed to swim in the pool on only two or three occasions. Each time their privileges were granted by *ad hoc* arrangements, and no permanent commitments were made. The fears of the Italians were always assuaged by an informal arrangement with the police to guard against the violence they expected from the Negroes. By Labor Day the issue was dead because the swimming pool closed and the civil rights movement disbanded into its own private world of planning for the next summer. Thus, the Italians seem to have won a battle—or delaying action—if not a war.

In the background, of course, was the oppressive belief that the benefits of social life make up a fixed quantity and were already being used to the maximum.[8] Thus, even the most liberal Italians assume that any gain to the Negroes must be their loss. On their own part, the Negroes make the same assumption and see no reason why the Italians should give way without a fight. Thus whatever good intentions exist on either side are overruled by the seeming impracticality or lack of realism.

The Ethics of "Natural Man"

The Italians' career in the Addams area has been shaped by a traditional world view which relies heavily on a belief in "natural man." For example, it is said to be "natural" for men to be sexual predators; for mothers to

---

[8] This fallacy has a long and difficult history in economics. Perhaps the best general discussion is in Joseph A. Schumpeter, *History of Economic Analysis* (New York: Oxford University Press, 1954), pp. 335–406 and 605–87.

love their children, regardless of what they do; for girls to connive at marriage; for boys to hate school; for girls not to fight; for children to be mischievous; for a businessman to cheat strangers; and for anyone to choose pleasure in preference to discipline and duty. Implicit in the concept of natural man is the conviction that moral restraints and ideal standards of behavior have little real power in a situation in which they contradict man's natural impulses. Innumerable laws can be passed, a formal hierarchy created, and the entire environment changed; but such external measures cannot alter the nature of human beings. Civilization, then, is a mere gloss or clever facade to hide man's true nature.[9]

Often, although not always, man's natural impulses are at odds with his moral standards. Indeed, otherwise there would be no need for the church, the police, the government, and all other bodies of social control. However, it is not always possible for these external bodies of social control to keep track of what people are doing. Inevitably, then, there will be occasions when persons are free to choose between acting naturally and acting morally. On their own part, the Italians may have considerable conviction in their personal preference for morality. In their dealings with other people, however, they have little faith in this thin thread of individual morality. Correspondingly, their own personal morality becomes utterly impractical and is replaced by whatever amoral expedient seems necessary for self-defense.[10]

The general outcome seems to be an overwhelming mistrust of impersonal or "voluntary" relationships. The other side of the coin, however, is an equally strong tendency to fall back on those relationships and identities where one's own welfare is guaranteed by "natural inclinations." For the most part these are kin relations, close friendship, common regional origins (*paesani*), joint residential unity, and sacred pledges.[11] Thus the Italians in the Addams area have tended to turn in upon themselves and become a provincial moral world.

---

[9] As might be expected, certain Italian writers have given this point of view its fullest expression. See for example, Niccolo Machiavelli, *The Prince and the Discourses* (New York: Modern Library, 1940); Velfredo Pareto, *The Mind and Society*, (New York: Harcourt, Brace, 1942); and Benedetto Croce, *Politics and Morals* (New York: Philosophical Library, 1945).

[10] Edward C. Banfield, *The Moral Basis of a Backward Society* [Glencoe, Ill.: Free Press, 1958]) has made somewhat the same observation on southern Italians. His concept of "amoral familists" (*Ibid.*, p. 85), however, seems overly narrow because it does not include many relationships in which mutual trust (1) is not based on kinship alone (e.g., age and sex categories), (2) is contingent on public exposure (e.g., "*civile*"), and (3) includes the possibility that two unrelated individuals may find in one another a "common nature" (*campanilismo*).

[11] E.g., marriage, godparenthood, etc.

Reformulations of Cultural Traditions

Actually, many of the Italians are quite "americanized." Frequently, however, these people lead something of a double life. During the daytime they leave the neighborhood and do their work without much thought of their ethnicity. When they come home in the evening, however, they are obliged to reassume their old world identity. This need not be so much a matter of taste as necessity. Other people are likely to already know their ethnicity, and evasions are apt to be interpreted as acts of snobbery or attempts at deception. Moreover, members of the other three ethnic groups refuse to accept one's americanization, no matter how much it is stressed. To the others, an attempt to minimize one's ethnicity is only a sly maneuver to escape responsibility for past wrongs or to gain admission into their own confidence. Finally, there are still many "old-timers" in the neighborhood, and it would be very ill-mannered to parade one's americanism before them. Thus, within the bounds of the local neighborhood, an Italian who "plays" at being an American runs the risk of being taken as a snob, phony, opportunist, coward, or fink.

In the Addams area the informational content that perpetuates different ethnic identities is kept alive by an intricate communication network. Some of the channels in this communication system are gossip, slander, invective, and confidentiality. Moreover, there is also the constant exchange of accusations between ethnic groups. Ethnic jokes and insults serve somewhat the same function. Even the local business places are outfitted and decorated in such a way that one is constantly reminded of the details of each ethnic identity. Within this sort of communication system, it is nearly impossible for someone to evade his ethnicity, no matter how imperfect his familial socialization.

Among the Italians themselves, notions of ethnicity are particularly well-elaborated. For the most part, these internal subdivisions are based on regional origins in Italy.[12] By contrast, the other ethnic groups have very little internal differentiation. The Negroes, for example, make only a vague distinction between those raised in the South and those raised in the North. Among the former, Mississippians are sometimes singled out for special contempt. However, none of these divisions lead to cohesive social unities.

---

[12] Each *paesani* and province has its stereotype: e.g., Calabrians are said to be stubborn and mulish; Basilicatians, slow, dull, and undependable; people from Bari, sly, deceitful, and clever. Certainly no one would claim that these stereotypes invariably fit the people coming from those regions. Nonetheless, each stereotype remains an important fixture in the cultural apparatus with which a person's behavior is assessed. Thus, a generous and easygoing Calabrian is judged quite differently from a Neapolitan who acts in exactly the same way.

Among the Italians, however, their *paesani* takes on great importance, and it remains the first perimeter beyond the family within which they look for aid or feel themselves in safe hands.[13] Most *paesani* continue to hold their annual summer picnic and winter dance. Some of them have grown into full-scale organizations with elected officers, insurance plans, burial funds, and regular poker sessions.

Of all the ethnic groups in the Addams area, the Italians still have the richest ceremonial life, despite their many years in this country. Aside from the annual *paesani* dances and picnics, there are parades, *feste*, and several other occasions. In the summer, their church, Our Lady of Vesuvio, holds a carnival that duplicates much of the Italian *feste*.[14] On Columbus Day there is a great parade in the Loop which is exceeded in grandeur only by the one held by the Irish on St. Patrick's Day. During Lent there are several special religious events and afterwards a round of dances, parties, and feasts. Throughout the summer a local brass band periodically marches through the streets playing arias from Puccini and Verdi. Sidewalk vendors sell Italian lemonade, sausages, and beef sandwiches. Horsedrawn carts go about selling grapes during the fall winemaking season, tomatoes when they are ready to be turned to paste, and fruit and vegetables at almost any time of the year.

Among the Italians, even weddings, communions, funerals, and wakes maintain some of their communal nature. Weddings held at Our Lady of Vesuvio are usually known of beforehand and often attract a number of onlookers as well as those invited. Afterwards the couple and their friends drive around the neighborhood in decorated cars, honking their horns at each other and whomever they recognize on the streets. Parochial school children usually receive first communion as a group and attract a good deal of attention. Wakes are also open to almost anyone, and funeral processions often tour a portion of the neighborhood. On these sort of occasions,

[13] In all probability, the *paesani* has been more important in this country than it ever was in Italy. On reflection, this seems reasonable because in Italy a person's *paesani* would include practically everyone with whom he came into day-to-day contact. Thus, it would be useless as a basis for selecting those one could trust or first approach for help. In this country, however, a fellow *paesani* is certainly more trusted than a complete stranger. Accordingly, such relations have probably been cultivated so that by now they have been embellished with many added expectations that were never possible or necessary in Italy.

[14] I am told that in the 1920's and 30's each *paesani* held its own feast and the entire summer was punctuated by their celebrations. Today, however, all these occasions have dissolved into a single occasion. Some might take this as evidence for the Italians' loss of their cultural forms and progressive Americanization. However, I would suggest that it only demonstrates the extent to which their territorial unity has brought them together and given birth to a single dramatic ceremony to celebrate their unity. In this sense, their sole carnival is only a final recognition that they form one *paesani* in Chicago rather than several in Italy.

the Mexicans follow much the same practice, although they lack full control of a local church where they can carry out these affairs to the same extent as the Italians. Among the Negroes and Puerto Ricans, however, weddings, funerals, and religious events tend to be quite private affairs, open through invitation alone.

The Italians are also favored by the relatively long period over which many of them have been able to know each other and to decide upon whom they can or cannot trust. Over time, a considerable amount of information has been accumulated on many persons, and this circulates in such a way as to be available to even a fairly recent resident. Moreover, the intertwining of social relations has become so extensive that contact with one person often opens passage to many others. In this sense, "getting acquainted" is almost unavoidable for a new resident.

Named Groups

The local forms of social organization in the Italian section are far more extensive and complicated than those of the other ethnic groups. At the top are two groups, the "West Side Bloc" and the "Outfit," which share membership and whose participants are not all from the Addams area (see table 4). The West Side Bloc is a group of Italian politicians whose constituency is much larger than the Addams area but which includes a definite wing that is local to the area. Generally its members are assumed to belong to or to have connections with the "Outfit." A good deal of power is attributed to them within the local neighborhood, city, state, and nation. The "Outfit," more widely known as the Syndicate,[15] includes many more people, but it is also assumed to reach beyond the Addams area itself. Locally, it is usually taken to include almost anyone who runs a tavern or a liquor store, or who relies on state licensing or city employment. A few other businessmen and local toughs are accredited with membership because of their notorious immunity to law enforcement or their reputed control of "favors."

Indirectly, the "Outfit" extends to a number of adult social-athletic clubs (SAC's). These clubs invariably have a storefront where the members spend their time in casual conversation, drink, or play cards. A few of their members belong to the "Outfit," and a couple of these clubs are said to have a "regular game" for "big stakes." Each group is fairly homogeneous in age

---

[15] Although, at first, I thought them to be the same, Outfit, Syndicate, and Mafia are not synonymous terms. In the case of Outfit, one can speak of the St. Louis Outfit, the Milwaukee Outfit, and the Chicago Outfit. The Syndicate includes all of them and the Outfits in other cities as well. Syndicate has no plural form. Mafia is used to refer to Italians only, and it also has no plural. Thus, the Outfit seems to indicate the local syndicate, including both Italians and non-Italian members.

TABLE 4
NAMED GROUPS LOCATED IN THE ITALIAN SECTION

	West Side Bloc				The Outfit	
Local adult males involved in wider society.						
Adult SAC's	Law SAC	U.S. Pals	Fashions	Barons of Burgundy	Privateers	Dee Gees
Young Men's SAC's	*Chapeaus (Chap O's)	Hut *Dukes	*Eminents Heirs of Taylor	Garabaldis Suave Gallants		*Hallmarks
Street Corner Groups Oldest	*Contenders	M and T's	May Dukes		Mexican	
	*Jr. Contenders	*Duchesnes	Tayhommes		Barracudas	
	*Meteors	*Celestials	*Cosmopolitans (Schenleys)			
	*Jr. Meteors	*Jr. Suave Gallants				
Youngest	*Midget Meteors					

( ) Indicates subsequent name change or variant of name.
* All names preceded by the term "Taylor".
|| Explicit Alliance.

composition, but the groups collectively range between the late twenties up to the late sixties.

Below these adult SAC's are a number of other SAC's which also have a club house, but whose members are much younger males. As a rule, they are somewhat beyond school age; but only a few are married, and practically none of them have children. To some degree, they are still involved in the extra-familial life that occupies teenagers. Occasionally they have dances, socials, and impromptu parties. On weekends they still roam around together, attending "socials" sponsored by other groups, looking for girls or for some kind of "action." Within each young man's SAC, the members' ages cover a narrow range. Together, all the groups range between about nineteen and the late twenties. They form a distinct and well-recognized age grade in the neighborhood because of their continuing involvement in those cross-sexual and recreational activities open to unmarried males.

Nevertheless, these young men's SAC's are somewhat outside the full round of activities that throw teenagers together. A good portion of their time is spent inside their clubhouse out of sight from their rivals or most bodies of social control. Most members are in their twenties and are able to enjoy openly the routine forms of entertainment or excitement that the wider community provides and accepts. When they have a dance or party, it is usually restricted to those whom they invite. Being out of school, they are not forced each day to confront persons from beyond their neighborhood. Since many of them have cars, they need not trespass too much on someone else's domain.

These SAC's are not assumed to have any active role in the "Outfit." At most, it is expected that they might be able to gain a few exemptions from law enforcement and an occasional "favor."[16] It is assumed that they could solicit help from the "Outfit" if they got into trouble with another group, but very rarely are they drawn into this type of conflict. Almost invariably their opponent is a much younger "street group" which has encroached on what the SAC considers its "rights."[17] Even at these times, however, their actions seem designed to do little more than rid themselves of a temporary nuisance. Once rid of their tormentors, they usually do not pursue the issue further, and for good reason. To charter such a club requires three cosigners, and these people may withdraw their support if the group becomes too rowdy. Also, they have a landlord to contend with,

---

[16] E.g., a job, a chance to run an illegal errand, a small loan, someone to sign for their clubhouse charter (this is required by law), and the purchase of stolen goods or of anything else the boys happen to have on hand.

[17] E.g., tried to "crash" one of their parties, insulted them on the streets, made noise nearby, or marked up their clubhouse.

and he can throw them out for the same reason. Finally, they cannot afford to make too many enemies; they have a piece of property, and it would be only too easy for their adversaries "to get back at them." Unlike all the groups described in the other three sections, they have a stake in maintaining something like law and order.

All the remaining Italian groups shown in table 4 include members who are of high-school age. While they too call themselves "SAC's," none of them have a storefront. All of them do have an established "hangout," and they correspond to the usual image of a street corner group. Among these groups age-grading is a prominent feature, and five different age levels are recognized. The correspondence between groups at the same level, however, is not exact; the boys tend to tell their ages by tracing them through the age hierarchy. The Junior Contenders, for example, are judged to be about the same age as the Duchesnes because both groups are next in age to the three eldest groups (Contenders, M and T's, and May Dukes) who are said to be about the same age. Within certain chronological limits, then, age grades provide only an ordinal ranking.

These street corner groups include two alliance structures that are expressed in the names they share. While these alliances include only a minority of the groups, they seem to spell out the entire sequence of age grades to which the other groups must fit themselves. Also it might be emphasized that the group generally accepted as the strongest in the Italian section was The Contenders, whose primacy is corroborated by both their seniority and their junior following.

While the street groups in this section of the area often express admiration for the adult SAC's, they seldom develop in an unbroken sequence into a full-fledged adult SAC. Usually when they grow old enough to rent a storefront they change their name, acquire new members from groups that have been their rivals, and lose a few of their long-term members. Some groups disband entirely, and their members are redistributed among the newly formed SAC's. Of the twelve young men's and adult SAC's, only one of them is said to have maintained the same name from the time it was a street corner group. Even in this case some members have been added and others lost. Together, then, the Italian street corner groups make up the population from which future young men's SAC's are drawn, but only a few street corner groups form the nucleus of an SAC.

Conceptually, however, the Italian street groups and the older SAC's form a single unity. In the eyes of the boys, they are somewhat like the steps between grammar school and college. While there may be dropouts, discrete breaks, and amalgamations, they still make up a series of steps through which one can advance with increasing age. Thus, each street group tends to see the adult SAC's as essentially an older and more perfect version of itself. What may be just as important, however, is their equally strong sense of history. Locally, many of the members in the street groups can trace their group's genealogy back through the Taylor Dukes, 40 gang, Genna Brothers, and the Capone mob. Actually there is no clear idea of the exact order of this descent line; some persons include groups that others leave out. Moreover, there is no widespread agreement on which specific group is the current successor to this lineage. Nonetheless, there is wide-spread agreement that the groups on Taylor Street have illustrious progeni-tors. On some occasions this heritage may be something of a burden, and on others a source of pride. In any case, it is unavoidable, and usually the Italian street group preface their own name with the term "Taylor." Among the younger groups this appellation is omitted only when their name is an amalgam made up from a specific street corner or block. Only the adult SAC's regularly fail to acknowledge in their name the immediate territory within which they are located.

Since they see themselves in a direct line of succession to groups reputed to be associated with the "Outfit," these street corner groups might be expected to have a strong criminal orientation.[18] In the Addams area, how-ever, the Italian groups are best known for their fighting prowess, and their official police records show no concentration in the more utilitarian forms of crime.[19] Like the other adolescent groups in the area, however, the Italian boys are not really free to choose their own goals and identities. Territorial arrangements juxtapose them against similar groups manned by Negro and Mexican boys. If the Italian street corner groups fail to define themselves as fighting groups, their peers in the other ethnic groups are certainly going to assume as much.[20]

There is also considerable rivalry between Italian street corner groups of roughly the same age. Commonly they suspect each other of using force to establish their precedence. In turn, each group seems to think it must at least put on a "tough" exterior to avoid being "pushed around." Privately there is a great deal of talk among them about the "Outfit" and about criminal activities, but it is academic in the sense that there is no strong evidence that their behavior follows suit.

It is interesting that the adult SAC's who actually have members in the rackets avoid any conspicuous claims about their criminal activities or

[18] Richard A. Cloward and Lloyd E. Ohlin, *Delinquency and Opportunity* (Glencoe, Ill.: Free Press, 1960), pp. 161–86.

[19] See Chapter 11.

[20] Before the Negroes and Mexicans moved into the area, the situation was much the same; only at that time they were juxtaposed against the Negroes below Roosevelt, the Slavs on Eighteenth Street, and the Italians on Western.

fighting abilities. Their names, for example, are quite tame, while those of the street groups tend to be rather menacing. Also, their dances, leisure-time activities, and interrelationships are quite private and unpretentious. Unlike the street groups, they never wear clothing that identifies their group membership. The older males in the SAC's make no apparent attempt to establish a publicly known hierarchy among themselves. Other people occasionally attribute more respect to one than another of them, but there seems to be little consensus on this. On their own part, the older groups seem to pay little attention to their relative standing and to be on fairly good terms. During my three years in the area, I never heard of them fighting among themselves.

Cross-Sex Relations

Unlike the Negro and Mexican ethnic sections, there are no female counterparts to the named Italian street corner groups.[21] A very few Italian girls belong to two Mexican girls' groups that "hung" in the Mexican section. This, in itself, was exceptional; almost always the minority members in a street group are from a lower ranking ethnic group.[22] The Italian girls, however, are under certain constraints that may be lacking for those in the other ethnic groups. Naturally, their parents disapprove of such a blatant display of feminine unity.[23] But this is true in all the local ethnic groups. The Italian parents, of course, may gain stature by their power and precedence in comparison to the Negro and Mexican adults. Yet, what seems far more significant is the general form that boy-girl relationships take among the Italians. On either side, the slightest hint of interest in the other sex is likely to be taken in the most serious way; as either a rank insult or a final commitment. Thus, any explicit alliance between a boys' and girls' group can be interpreted in only one of two ways: (1) all the girls are "laying" for the boys or (2) they are seriously attached to one another. Neither side seems quite willing to betray so much and, thus, they avoid such explicit alliances.

This dilemma was quite evident on many occasions while observing the Italian boys and girls. For example, the girls seemed extraordinarily coy

[21] Of course, the Italian girls, like everyone else, tend to cling together in small groups along the sidewalk. None of them, however, have acquired a name.

[22] Aside from the Italian girls, there was only one other exception to this. A small number of very young Mexican and Puerto Rican boys who lived in the projects belonged to Negro groups. This, however, tended to be a temporary situation. As soon as the whites became fourteen or fifteen years old, they joined groups of their own ethnicity or became altogether unaffiliated.

[23] There seems to be far less adult disapproval of male groupings, especially among the Italians. Of course, many of the men belong or have belonged to such groups.

when they were in a "safe"[24] position. However, when alone and on their own they became equally cautious and noncommittal. On public occasions, the boys seemed almost to ignore the girls and even to snub them. On Taylor Street, for instance, an Italian boys' group and an Italian girls' group used to "hang" about ten feet from one another. Almost invariably they would stand with their backs to one another, although there were many furtive glances back and forth. During almost two years of observation, I never saw them talk to one another. Later, I was somewhat surprised to learn that everyone in each group was quite well known to the other. For either of them to have acknowledged the other's presence openly, however, would have been too forward. The boys are quite aware of this dilemma and complain that the girls are not free enough to be convenient companions. This, they say, is one reason why they have to go elsewhere to "date." At the same time, however, they perpetuate the old system by automatically assuming that the slightest sign of interest by a girl makes her fair game, even when she may be assuming his good intentions. Out of self-defense, then, the girls are compelled to keep their distance. On private occasions, of course, there are many Italian boys and girls who sneak off to enjoy what others might consider an entirely conventional boy-girl relationship (petting, necking). In public, however, they studiously ignore one another. Throughout my time in the area I never saw a young Italian couple hold hands or walk together on the sidewalk.[25]

The Barracudas and the Park

The groups arranged in table 4 form a single line of succession between age grades with marked rivalry among groups within the younger age grades. A few groups in the Italian section did not fit this scheme, the most obvious being the Barracudas.

The Barracudas were the first Mexican street corner group to emerge in the Italian section. About the same age as the Junior Contenders, they first became a named group in the spring of 1964. All members were Mexican.

Once established, the Barracudas installed themselves in the northwest corner of Sheridan Park (see map 6). The significance of this location can be appreciated only if one understands the role of this park within the Italian section. Practically every Italian street group in the area makes use of this park, and several of them have their hangout there. Other people in

[24] E.g., with their parents, in church, etc.
[25] Such activities are not common among the Negroes, Mexicans, and Puerto Ricans; but at least they do occur.

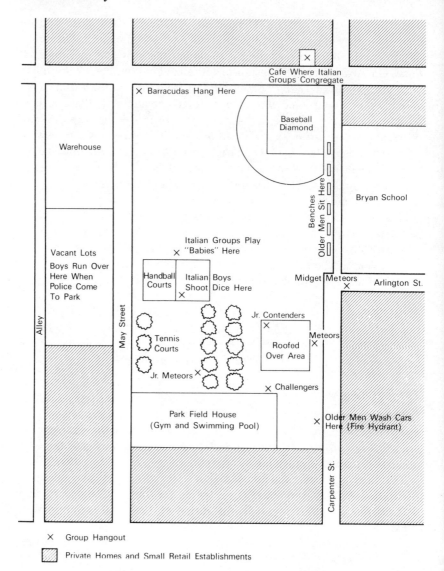

MAP 6. Sheridan Park and Surrounding Area

turn refer to the Italian groups collectively as the guys from the Park.[26] Sometimes, the entire Italian community is spoken of as the "people over by the Park." The park itself is partitioned into a finely graduated series of more or less private enclosures, with the most private hangout going to the reigning group and the least private to the weakest group. The northwest corner of the park is the most exposed of any portion, and this is where the Barracudas installed themselves. Even in this lowly spot, however, they were much resented by the other groups. To the Italians, the Park was almost a sacred charge and the Mexicans' intrusion was a ritual pollution rather than a mere loss of space and facilities. The Barracudas were harassed, ridiculed, and insulted. On their own part, they became belligerent and vaunted all sorts of outrageous claims about themselves.[27] Soon the situation deteriorated, and the Italian groups became extremely harsh with the Barracudas. Since the Barracudas were no match for even some of the younger Italian groups, they removed themselves to one member's house near Racine and Harrison.

Their new hangout placed them in an extraordinarily anomalous position. Ethnically they were identified as a Mexican group. As a group, however, they were located in a part of the area which had been conceded to the Puerto Ricans. Individually, most of them continued to reside in the Italian section. The general result seems to have been to isolate the Barracudas from any of the other group hierarchies and to place them in opposition to every group in the area. Within a year, every white group was their enemy, and the Negroes were not their friends. The Barracudas responded in kind and became even more truculent and boastful. More than any group in the area, they openly embraced the stance of a fighting group. They continued to write their name all over the neighborhood and even on some of the other groups' hangouts.[28] In the meantime, they made a clubhouse out of a "lean-to" adjacent to a building on Harrison Street. Inside they

[26] This is not to be confused with "Peanut Park." As its nickname indicates, Vernon Park is relatively unimportant in the neighborhood. This is not due to its size, because Vernon Park and Sheridan Park occupy about the same acreage. However, Sheridan Park includes a number of buildings and other facilities, including the only local swimming pool. These are valued resources and worth fighting for. However, even these benefits do not seem to be directly responsible for the Italians' tenacious hold on the park. The facilities of the park do not seem to be valued so much for their recreational value as for the privacy they provide. Certainly, this is the way they are allocated among the Italian groups.

[27] For example, they wrote their name on the streets, buildings, and walls all over the area. Also, they had "calling cards" printed which introduced them as the "Fabulous Taylor Barracudas." Many of the Mexican and Italian groups have such cards printed, but the term "fabulous" included on the Barracudas' card is exceptionally pretentious.

[28] Most groups paint their names on a street or wall near their hangout. It is a rank insult to do the same near someone else's hangout.

installed a shield on which they wrote "hate," "kill," and several other violent phrases. "Packing" a weapon became almost routine with them, and eventually they collected a small arsenal. In time they had several small-scale fights with both the Italians from the Park and the Mexicans around Polk and Laflin. In due course, they acquired so many enemies that they could hardly risk leaving the immediate area of their hangout. At the same time, some of them began to go to Eighteenth Street, where they had "connections."[29] However, this only brought them into conflict with other groups in this neighborhood. By the summer of 1965 the Barracudas were as isolated and resentful as ever.

The Incognitos and the Pica People

Two other groups in the Italian section, the Pica People and the Incognitos, are excluded from table 4 for contrasting reasons. The groups' names are themselves an expression of their isolation from the others. The Incognitos self-consciously avoided comparison with the other groups; they did not hang in the Park, hold "socials," or become involved in any of the local sidewalk confrontations. About the same age as the Contenders, the Incognitos were notably different in their exclusion from the local round of kudos and recriminations.

The "Pica People" is a derisive appellation meant as an insult for five young men about nineteen to twenty-five years of age. Although these five individuals associate regularly, they claim no group identity and become angry when called the "Pica People." Unlike the Incognitos, the Pica People are well-known and often accused of some predatory display. They do not fight for group honor, but there is friction between them and all the street corner groups in the Addams area.

It was impossible to determine how these two groups came into existence.[30] What is known of their composition, however, may throw some light on why they were excluded from the structure including the other groups. All informants described the Incognitos as "good guys," still in school and no trouble to anyone. They were not considered college boys but, if asked, most informants said they thought some of them might go to college. Local youth agencies made no attempt to work with them, and the entire neighborhood seemed to feel they were not dangerous. Other street corner groups

[29] The boys used the term here to refer to relatives. This usage is common throughout the Addams area.

[30] I talked only twice with the Incognitos, who simply said they "grew up together." Local people started calling the Pica People by that name after a movie in which the "Pica People" were sub-humans. I knew some of the members of this group, but they became so angry at any mention of the name that I could not discuss it with them.

in the Italian section did not look down on them, but they did exempt them from the ambitions that brought other groups into opposition.

The Pica People were just the opposite. All members were boastful of their "Outfit" connections and their ability to intimidate other people. Connections with the "Outfit" are certainly not a source of stigma in the area; however, the Pica People were unable to capitalize upon these connections. The members possessed so many personal flaws that they were rather useless to the "Outfit." One member was slightly claustrophobic. Another was so weak that even much younger boys pushed him around. A third had an exceedingly unfortunate appearance. Under the circumstances their pretensions became laughable.

The Incognitos and the Pica People seem to represent the extremes of a range in which the street corner group is considered the normal adolescent gathering. Modest and well-behaved youngsters are excluded as exceptions, as are criminally inclined but unsuccessful young men. Both of these groups fell outside the range considered normal by the local residents and were thereby disassociated from the total group hierarchy.

The Basis of Adult Power

As will be apparent in the next two chapters, the social context of the Italian street groups is somewhat different than that of the street groups in the other three ethnic sections. Among the Italians, the major share of coercive power still remains in adult hands. The wider community may not be very pleased with the form their power takes, but it is the only case where the corporate power of the adolescents is tempered by that of the adults. Also, since many of the same adults have an active role in distributing some of the benefits that are held in store by the wider community, their power is further augmented. Perhaps the most obvious result of the adults' ascendency is that the adolescents do not simply dismiss them or adulthood as unimportant. A more immediate consequence, however, is to give many of the adults the prerogative of exacting considerable obedience from the local adolescents. It is not at all uncommon to see an Italian adult upbraid and humble one of the local youths. Not all adults have this privilege; but many do, and their example provides a distinct contrast to the other ethnic groups where similar efforts would be a futile gesture.

In the long term, of course, the effectiveness of these coercive controls among the Italians may do little more than confirm their convictions that, outside of natural tendencies, there is no guarantee to moral conduct except economic and numerical strength. Within their own little world, however, such coercive measures constitute a fairly viable system of social control.

Personal privacy and anonymity are almost impossible. In turn, each person's known or assumed "connections" dampen most chances at exploitation because of the fear of unknown consequences. Thus, the opportunities for immorality presented by transient relations and "fair game" are fairly rare. Within these limits, such an authoritarian system of social control will work. Outside their own section, of course, these conditions do not hold; and the Italian boys find themselves free to seize whatever advantages or opportunities present themself. What is worse, they can only assume that others are just as free to take an equally predatory course. Who will take the first step depends only on who is favored by immediate circumstances. Thus, the behavior of the Italian boys tends to contrast sharply between the times they are among other Italians in their own section and the times they are elsewhere. Among themselves, they are usually only a rowdy and boisterous crowd. With strangers or in other parts of the Addams area, however, they become particularly arrogant and unscrupulous.

With these qualifications in mind, it appears that well-established adolescent street corner groups are quite compatible with strong adult authority and influence. In fact, judging from the Italian section, these adolescent street corner groups seem to be the building blocks out of which the older and more powerful groups have originated. The younger groups continue to replenish the older ones and help maintain the structure within which adults are shown deference.

Moreover, the total age-graded structure of groups in the Italian section relates youngsters to the wider society both instrumentally and conceptually. The Italian street groups see themselves as replacements in an age structure that becomes progressively less provincial. At the upper age level, groups even stop prefacing their name with the term "Taylor;" and a few of their members have a place in the wider society through the "Outfit" and West Side Bloc. The relationship between these age grades also provides a ladder down which favors and opportunities are distributed. The wider community may hesitate at accepting the legitimacy of these transactions, but they are mostly of a conventional form. The "Outfit" and the "West Side Bloc" have a strong interest in maintaining a degree of social order, and the sorts of wanton violence associated with gangs do not at all fit their taste. To fully appreciate the role of these groups in the neighborhood, however, it is necessary to contrast the Italian section with the remaining ethnic sections.

7

The Projects and the Negroes

The Heritage of Political Arrangements

In relative numbers, the Negroes make up only about 14–17% of the total population in the Addams area. They achieve their importance, however, more by what they portend than what they are. On the West Side the proportion of Negroes has been steadily increasing for a long time. All the other ethnic groups have retreated from them, and the general assumption is that they will eventually "take over."[1] Oddly enough, it is the lowly status of the Negroes that makes them such a portentous enemy. Because of the universal fear of stigma in being associated with them, it is assumed that no group in the area can halt their invasion. Thus even this small group of Negroes is considered a far more serious contender than any combination of other ethnic groups.

To understand how the Negroes fit into the Addams area, it is necessary to locate them in the context of both past and present political arrangements. For several years the Italians have held a near monopoly on all political power and patronage. The other ethnic groups have been propitiated by a variety of "favors" on condition they support the Italians. Until recently, however, there has been no serious contender to the Italians' right to represent the area and to dispense whatever favors they could command. The Italians have been content with the privilege of distributing patronage even if they did not receive the lion's share. In the present case, the benefits of this position have been considerable. Since the Addams area is in the First Ward, its influence penetrates the "Loop," the main business section of the city. In turn, a variety of legitimate businesses and vice interests have found it convenient to accommodate the Italians by giving them somewhat more than their share of the exemptions, goods, and privileges that can be distributed through political means.

---

[1] Both the First Ward and the Seventh Congressional District include sections that are outside the Near West Side; however, control of these political units has always been lodged in the hands of Near West Side residents.

Alongside the many concrete benefits that accrue because of the Italians' political monopoly, historical precedent confirms their misgivings over any intruder. Before the Italians gained political control, they served a long apprenticeship under the Irish. By the 1920's the Italians had almost entirely replaced the Irish as residents in the various political units that include the Addams area. Still, the Irish held on to political control by every conceivable method. Eventually, however, the Italians openly challenged the Irish. At first, the Irish used bribery, extending to the Italians many additional favors. Then they resorted to intimidation and finally to outright force.[2] The entire issue was ultimately dramatized in 1921 by the killing of an Italian candidate for alderman, Anthony D'Andrea. His death was attributed to John Powers, an Irishman and the incumbent alderman. For the moment, the Italians could do little more than give D'Andrea a sumptuous funeral. In subsequent years, however, they almost completely displaced their Irish overlords.

These precedents have left a heritage of institutional and moral arrangements. Their most important outcome is the pervasive belief that political power is not something that another ethnic group would willingly share. The Italians simply assume that any opponent will never be satisfied with less than total usurpation. Thus, like their Irish predecessors, they hesitate to yield an inch lest their opponents take a mile.[3] Consequently, they believe that every gain by the Negroes is necessarily a loss to the Italians. The ultimate outcome, then, is a political struggle carried out with the understanding that "winner takes all."[4]

Recently the Italians' suspicions and fears have been corroborated by still other events. Ever since the Negroes took over the Jane Addams Projects, many of the Italians have recognized the importance of federal funds as an omen of Negro invasion. Thus, portions of the urban renewal

---

[2] The general progression is documented in John Landesco, *Organized Crime in Chicago* (Chicago: Illinois Crime Commission, 1929), pp. 935–54.

[3] Some of the Italians recognize this dilemma and will go so far as to say that it is "fair" to give the Negroes some measure of political representation. What gives them pause, however, is the more general belief that the Negroes would never be satisfied by such halfway measures.

[4] In the language of game theory, this means that both parties are playing a "zero-sum game," whereas they need not do so. Seemingly, there is nothing in the political situation itself which warrants so narrow a division of benefits. In fact, a good deal of both the public and private facilities and services of Chicago are either underused or allocated with considerable inefficiency simply because they are restricted to a single ethnic group. In the Addams area a prominent example immediately comes to mind. Many of the Negroes in the Jane Addams Projects do their shopping over on Halsted Street at the cost of some added time, effort, and trouble. In the meantime several nearby business places are slowly declining because they will not accede to anything other than an Italian clientele.

program and even the University of Illinois are often referred to as "something for the niggers."[5]

It would be quite misleading to suggest that very many of the adults and even a few of the adolescents are aware of the area's political history or the likely consequence of the University and urban renewal program. Of course, a few do have this knowledge and pass it on to others. Most generally, however, it is expressed in the abbreviated form, "The niggers want everything," without further explanation. In fact, a verbal transmission of the historical particulars is really unnecessary. Throughout the area the visible effects of history are encoded in the current arrangements that obtain for almost every facility in the area. The streets, the businesses, the parks, and the schools are all marked off as the exclusive domain of one or another ethnic group. Most often, the symbolic paraphernalia[6] that decorate an establishment are also ethnic-linked. Thus the "collective memory" of the local people need not always be transmitted in verbal form. Instead it is codified in the objective effects and practices that function as continuing reminders of long-forgotten historical origins. All that seems to differentiate the various groups is the points on which they focus attention. The Italian boys are concerned over who shall take control of the streets, the schools, and a wide variety of local hangouts. Their parents may share some of the same apprehensions, but they are also worried over the future state of their homes, jobs, and business places. The Negroes are equally convinced that the Italians will never voluntarily yield any of the benefits vested in the Addams area. Thus, by their suspicions and distrust of each other, both groups are caught in a struggle from which they can rest only after total victory or total defeat.[7]

In their struggle with the Italians, the Negroes are burdened by a number of other circumstances. First, the Negroes are almost wholly confined in public housing. In Chicago public housing, ADC recipients are especially favored, and the general view is that all the residents of the projects are

---

[5] Sometimes this conviction is admitted with such simplicity that it is easy to overlook its significance. One Italian informant told me with well-meaning candor that, "I'm sure glad they built the University for the niggers. They need it!"

[6] Posters, displays, products, pictures, newspapers, names, radio programs, graffiti, etc.

[7] E. W. Burgess, *Urban Areas of Chicago: An Experiment in Social Science Research*, ed. T. V. Smith and J. D. White [Chicago: University of Chicago Press, 1929]), emphasized this sort of competition structure between ethnic groups. He seems to have assumed, however, that a strict zero-sum type of strategy was the only possible competitive structure. In fact there are many other alternatives; but, like Burgess, Addams area residents do not consider them. Basically, the problem seems to be that anything other than "winner takes all" strategy requires some measure of trust on the part of both ethnic groups; i.e., a rule of the form "we'll let you use x if you'll let us use y." Apparently this level of trust simply does not exist between ethnic groups in the inner city.

"public wards."[8] Moreover, the standardization and restrictive rulings that govern the projects almost totally eliminate all those overt signs that families customarily depend on to present themselves to the outer world. The Jane Addams Projects are a drab and uniform continuity. Undoubtedly the apartments are fairly clean and roomy. However, they entirely lack most of the ordinary external embellishments, adornments, and decorations that families use to notify others of their tastes, beliefs, income, practices, and background. Thus, the first line of family impression management is lost, and an outsider can only surmise that all the residents are alike.[9]

Second, project living is one of the most permanent and inflexible forms of absentee landlordship. In the history of most ethnic groups, there has been a constant alteration and accommodation of existing facilities to their own uses. Today the same progression goes on among the Italians, Mexicans, and Puerto Ricans in the Addams area. The lower floor of a residence is turned into a business place. Family members, relatives, and friends are drawn in as "sweat labor." Sometimes, by great frugality, a building is purchased and cut up into additional "flats" which can be squeezed for every cent they will produce. At every turn, personal labor supplants that which requires hard cash. In the eyes of the wider community these ventures are "abuses" or, at best, result in an eyesore on the face of the city.[10] For the local residents, however, such ventures are the first rungs on the social ladder that reaches up to where such judgments can be passed.

Among those who live in the projects, however, all these minor entrepreneurial ventures are totally out of reach. This has the obvious effect of eliminating several of the more devious pathways of upward mobility and social differentiation that have been so important in the career of various ethnic groups.[11] As a result, the Negroes are reduced to the most abject and menial "hustles" that are left: pimping, casual prostitution, shoplifting, "policy," and occasional traffic in "reefers." All of this, however, must be managed under the oppressive suspicion that the CHA (Chicago Housing

---

[8] Actually, only about 20% of the families in the Jane Addams Projects are on ADC or Welfare.

[9] This problem has been discussed at greater length in a separate paper by the author, "Public Housing and The Problem of Family Impression Management" (unpublished paper presented at the Illinois Academy of Criminology, Chicago, Ill., 1964).

[10] The general pattern is outlined by Daniel Bell, "The Breakup of Family Capitalism" in *The End Of Ideology* (New York: Collier Books, 1961), pp. 39–45, and George Orwell, *The Road to Wigan Pier* (New York: Harcourt Brace 1963).

[11] Daniel Bell, "Crime as an American Way of Life: A Queer Ladder of Social Mobility" in *The End of Ideology*, pp. 127–50.

Authority) has planted "finks" on every floor to spy on them.[12] The residents are thereby further estranged from one another, and whatever level of trust might already exist is undermined.

In the long term, however, the most important consequence of project living may be the way it restricts most opportunities to achieve a stake in the prospects of the local community and to develop the kind of leadership and social differentiation that is so critical in forming a stable moral community. In the Jane Addams Projects the Negroes can never alter the buildings to their own use, and all that keeps them there are a few friends and an income too small to rent better housing. If they become more affluent, they leave. Even this decision is outside the realm of personal choice. According to the rules of the CHA, anyone who earns beyond a certain income level is obliged to leave.[13] The result is an overwhelming homogeneity in which differences of income, education, political influence, and occupation are so lacking as to fail to designate potential leaders and spokesmen. The Negroes often resort to several formalized community organizations, small groups that are usually engendered by some of the local welfare agencies. These groups are usually short-lived and transient in their membership. Leadership within them tends to be rather artificial, since the elected officers seldom have any social credentials aside from rare instances of personal acclaim. Otherwise there is a dearth of leadership and a tendency to take lightly the pretentions of those who get pressed into leadership positions by some of the welfare agencies.

In addition to the oppressive homogeneity, there are a plethora of other problems involved in project living: the inability of friends and relatives to settle near one another and create a little moral world exempt from the

[12] This belief has some basis. The police do occasionally use plainclothesmen to make investigations in the projects. From their point of view these measures are only necessary: the vertical plan, enclosed courtyards, warren-like passageways, and uncertain boundaries between dwelling units make it nearly impossible for a policeman in a squad car or on the beat to provide adequate surveillance or to isolate one dwelling unit from another.

[13] The rules are adjusted for family size.

INCOME UNITS FOR FEDERALLY AIDED DEVELOPMENTS (1964)

No. of Persons	Admission ($)	Continued Occupancy ($)
2	4200	5125
3	4400	5500
4	4600	5750
5	4800	6240
6	5000	6500
7 or more	5200	6760

These are maximum incomes and not average incomes, which, of course, are lower.

insinuations of the wider community; a fear of accumulating "immovable" property lest it be taken as a sign of excessive income; the inability to "put up" a relative or friend for an extended period of hardship; a special police force created to watch over them; the myth that any effective political organization among project dwellers will be subverted by transfers and evictions; a series of rather strict rules that constrain high decibel parties and other forms of socializing; some rather restrictive measures on the ownership of telephones and television sets.

The project residents do not always hold each other responsible for their lowly position. Quite often, they will explain that the other people in the projects are there because of circumstances they could not avoid. However, this explanation provides them no comfort at all. Whether a person has been reduced to an abject position by his own efforts or by those of some-one else, he is still outside the realm of easy trust and companionship. A desperate man is still a desperate man no matter who is responsible for his predicament.

Style of Life

In large part the conditions of project living seem only to extenuate patterns that already have their historical precursors. A certain level of transiency is implicit in the housing regulations that remove people after they have gone beyond a given income range. The inability to settle around kinsmen and long-term friends is perhaps greater in the projects than in private housing. In any case the projects do not increase the conditions for stable relations, and the ultimate result seems to be a highly fluid population in which acquaintances are temporary or, at least, expected to be temporary.

In the Jane Addams Projects these conditions of impermanence seem to elicit a variety of novel social signs that function to introduce people to one another. Greetings, conversations, and clothing are highly subject to fads and fashions. Considered in the context in which they occur, all of these novelties and "exoticisms" seem to serve a very necessary communicative function.

Negroes living on the West Side and in public housing face every sort of misgiving, suspicion, and fear. To become eligible for an orderly social relationship they must either try to assuage these fears and doubts or take up such an awesome appearance of power that they are guaranteed "free passage." In either case, they must exaggerate the available signs that let others know what they "really are." The most direct means of doing this is simply to extend, emphasize, and elaborate existing styles of clothing, manners of speech, walk, stance, and demeanor. Colors become extremely loud or entirely lacking, styles advance to the very forefront of the period, and mannerisms become "way out."

In the Jane Addams Projects there is a constant round of fads, novelties, and extemporaneous feats. Dances, speech, clothing, gestures, and even sex practices undergo a continual change, elaboration, and attrition. There seems to be an unending search for the signs that will surely identify those worthy of merit, trust, or power. These signs, however, seem to be always imperfect, since the search goes on and on.

Concurrently, there is also a strong undercurrent of uneasiness and skepticism about what people "really are." Sometimes this is evident in the extremely effusive greetings that seem to be necessary to assure one of friendship although both parties may have seen each other only the day before.[14] Upon meeting, a handshake is an essential start, especially with whites. Throughout the remainder of the encounter other bits of physical contact regularly punctuate the general flow of interaction.[15] An extraordinary repertoire of "insults" and instances of license provide intermittent guarantees that they can afford such liberties. "Signifying," "mommy-rapping," or "jiving" seem only the more stylized of these.

At the same time, there is steady appeal to force where familiarity and exceptional signs of trustworthiness or power do not furnish a clear indication of one's future safety. Acts of violence without material gain, for example, reach their apex among the Negroes in the area.[16] The extent of "gun-packing" may be exaggerated, but still it is an omnipresent threat. Less drastic but more common are bluffing contests in which both parties

---

[14] The storefront church offers a great opportunity for these social presentations. In contrast, the more sedate denominational churches are defined as cold, distant, and uncertain. In the latter, a relatively poor Negro can never know exactly where he stands.

[15] This often takes the form of a stylized "hand-tapping." One person offers his hand, palm upwards. The other lightly taps it. Generally this ceremony follows a verbal exchange where one party has "won a point." It is the latter who has the option of offering up his hand.

[16] For information on this point, see chapter 11. This observation seems to apply to Negroes in general as well as to those in the Addams area. For example, arrest rates for assault and carrying weapons are from eight to ten times as high among Negroes as among whites. The ratio between rates of robbery is appreciably lower, but still high; about 5.5 to 1 (Harry E. Barnes and Nagley K. Teeters, *New Horizons in Criminology* [Englewood Cliffs, N.J.: Prentice Hall, 1959], p. 173). In the latter case, however, I suspect that whites make up a much larger proportion of the victims, and even these discrepancies do not indicate the full extent to which Negroes must use force among themselves to gain little more than their own *sense* of safety. Thus, the hypothesis is that Negroes use force for material gain more or less as opportunity strikes, while they use force without material gain mostly among themselves to insure their own safety. On this point it might be noted that Wolfgang's results certainly show much higher rates of victim-precipitated homicides among Negroes ("Victim-Precipitated Criminal Homicide," *Journal of Criminal Law, Criminology and Police Science* 48 [June, 1957]: 1–11).

search for an end to the indeterminancy that overshadows their relationship. Boys cow one another by "stare-downs," denigrate each other by the term "boy," and sometimes become so vociferous and threatening that they are said to be "woofing."[17] Often, of course, these efforts end in a draw and can be settled only if verbal threats and promises are recast in the heat of physical combat. Afterwards the combatants do not necessarily become permanent enemies. Somehow, the ambiguities of their past have been settled by gaining sure knowledge of where they stand.

The same problem is evident in the project residents' perpetual apprehension of deception, "con-artists," or "phonies." Apparently no one is willing to accept another at face value, and extreme proofs of one's identity and sincerity are required. Effusive greetings, name-dropping, "woofing," "rapping," and other verbal trials are only some of the more direct ways of doing this. Dress, grooming, decorum, stance, and even one's way of walking can be enlisted to eliminate doubts and suspicion. Among the Negroes in the Addams area, the major identities that have to be avoided are those denoted by the labels "country," "savage," "nigger," and "Uncle Tom." Thus, to show their sophistication, some girls go to school in high heels, "fix" their hair into fantastic shapes, and in recent months have shortened their skirts to a perilous level.

In contrast to the girls, the Negro boys in the Jane Addams Projects face a somewhat more ambiguous dilemma. If the boys completely repudiate the image of an "Uncle Tom," they risk being mistaken for a "savage." In this Scylla and Charybdis, two alternatives are open. On the one hand he can become a "gauster," by wearing the "rag," "shaping" his hair, belonging to a gang, adopting the "pimp's walk," and wearing a belted coat and baggy trousers. On the other hand, he can become "Ivy" by wearing a button-down collar, tight pants, and always keeping himself in immaculate order. The "gauster," however, runs the risk of being considered a "savage," while the "Ivy" may be suspected of being "sissy."[18] In either case, "keeping cool" may preserve a questionable identity when others would be discountenanced.

From a distance, these seem to be what often strike outsiders as so

---

[17] The term "boy" is used with much the same meaning it has in the South. Also, it is delivered with the same blank expression and lack of tonal change that it has in that region. Girls often follow the same practice in using the term "girl."

"Woofing" is a form of bluffing that is particularly vociferous, but there is uncertainty as to how seriously it should be taken. The "woofer" preserves the opportunity to retreat by pleading, "I was just jiving you, man."

[18] Here "sissy" means a homosexual, not a preadolescent boy who acts like a preadolescent girl.

"crude" and "vulgar" about the dress of Negroes as well as many other minority groups. In the perspective of polite society all this is far too "obvious" and, for that reason, "vulgar." However, in the eyes of the Negroes in the Addams area, the obviousness of these signs is their central virtue. Only in this way can they be sure of alerting other people that they are a safe associate or too acute and powerful to be treated as "fair game." Thus, much of this "vulgarity" seems only an *amplification of the signs* that presage most social relations.

A particular illustration of this point is what the Negro boys call "wearing the rag." Originally the "rag" was a bandana used to protect "processed hair."[19] Whites, however, seem to have mistaken it as a sign of gang membership or individual truculence. In contrast, Negroes often considered it a mark of effeminacy or a concession to white standards of beauty. Over time, however, the whites' definition seems to have won out. Today, many Negro boys "wear the rag," without processing their hair, to convey gang membership. Often they wear it only when they are going into another neighborhood, under the assumption that others will take it to mean gang membership and leave them alone. Among their own friends, they may abandon it. In some sections west of the Addams area, however, the "rag" is a customary item in the uniform of certain street groups.

Somewhat similar historical sketches might be traced for most of the other local "exoticisms" that deviate from prevailing standards or anticipate oncoming styles.[20] The black leather jacket, "gauster" and "ivy" uniforms, "soul food," "pimp's walk," "process," and the "rag" all have a part to play in this mute dialogue. Sometimes they evince a certain sophistication (being "hip") and protect the bearer from being taken as a dupe ("square," "trick"). At other times, they bespeak a kind of naked power (being "big") and ward off the supposition they are fair game (a "punk," "patsy"). Also, they may invite sociability (the "sport") where fear and avoidance ("playing dead") might otherwise occur. Indeed, there are a multitude of social identities (the "stud," "fox," "cat," "dude," "clown," etc.) and corresponding relationships which can be signalled or initiated by these "exoticisms" of dress or behavior.

As with the "rag," however, all of these novel signs are often

---

[19] Hair that has been straightened and marcelled. The bandana that protects this coiffure is arranged much like that of "Aunt Jemina" who decorates the pancake flour box. When worn by a male, the bandana makes him look like a pirate straight out of *Treasure Island.*

[20] For example, see Walter Miller's account of the diffusion of jazz. W. Kvaraceus and Walter Miller, *Delinquent Behavior: Culture and The Individual* (Washington, D.C.: National Education Association, 1959).

misunderstood by the white ethnic groups and redefined to suit their own beliefs. A Negro in the Jane Addams Projects, for example, would rarely mistake a janitor who owns a Cadillac, a Brooks Brothers suit, and a Dobbs hat for a "phony." He is a real "sport" who doesn't bury his money and is game for any kind of "action."

By turning such items to different uses, however, the Negroes upset the other ethnic groups' apple cart of order, that is, the assumption that public signs are inalterably connected to psychic states, social backgrounds, and future courses of action. Without this assumption, everyone becomes a potential impostor, and the dependable world of order turns to chaos. In their lowly position, the Negroes in the Jane Addams Projects flaunt this assumption and the other ethnic groups retrieve their composure by tracing a circuitous route between these novel social signs and stereotyped psychic states and social circumstances. The Italians are especially prone to these reinterpretive accounts because the Negroes' style of self-presentation is so different from their own. Since they are drawn so tightly into their own local world, the Italians are especially unresponsive to the fads and fashions of the wider society. Sometimes the Italians see the Negroes as deliberately rejecting all the signs that indicate sobriety, family loyalties, and neighborliness. Indeed, one way the Italians indicate their care for the neighborhood is by a studied indifference to the wider community.

Sometimes the Italians also take Negroes' style of self-presentation as a calculated insult to themselves. The Negroes are said to be "showing off," "parading themselves," or "just trying to be different." Of course, there are times when some Negroes try to "jive" (mislead), "put on," or "turn on" the local Italians. For this purpose, however, the Negroes appeal to a rather self-conscious technique: a mixture of insults and a show of familiarity so ambiguous that the Italians do not know quite how to take it. Occasions of this sort are rare, since the Negroes live mostly among themselves.

A more immediate problem for the Negroes is to select other Negroes who are respectable, dangerous, powerful, trustworthy, or simply friendly. In this endeavor ordinary public signs are almost useless. Practically all the Negroes are poor, and this alone is enough to suggest a certain desperation. Also, there is the standing belief that nearly all project dwellers are on ADC and are either lazy, licentious, or the resentful victims of unhappy circumstances. An unknown number of others are said to be "dope fiends" and totally out of control of their faculties. Some—no one knows quite who they are—are said to be "finks" for the police, CHA or FBI. The project residents make a groping effort to sort out the "hoods," "sports," "hipsters," or "soul-brothers." Occasionally they fear that a few people among them are nothing better than "niggers."[21] Thus, it is not so much their own inferiority that upsets the Negroes as that of their neighbor.

Despite all the attempts by the Negroes to find a set of signs that will define each other's intentions, their accomplishments seldom last for long before they become outdated. In part, this may be due to the inability of the Negroes to control and standardize the meanings attached to each stylistic version. The misunderstandings of whites—and, in the Addams area, of the Italians—constantly intercede to redefine each form. Eventually, as in the case of the "rag," the whites' definition seems to win out, and the Negroes are forced to find a replacement.

The transient nature of these stylistic forms, however, is largely due to their usage in the Negro section. As with fads in general, they are serviceable only so long as they distinguish a select group of people and testify to their moral character, intentions, and familiarity with current standards. Once such stylistic forms have become commonplace, they no longer denote so select a group.

For this reason many of the stylistic forms observed in Jane Addams Projects lasted only a year or so before they disappeared. The dances were especially short-lived, lasting no more than a few months. One year the "rag" was a sign of the "sissy"; the next it was an indication of gang membership. When I first came to the area the general term of approbrium was "mellow"; when I left it was replaced by the term "boss." The necessity to keep abreast of these changes in order to assure my informants that I was "in" and worthy of confidence made me especially aware of their function in the Jane Addams Projects.

Certainly these stylistic forms have not been invented by the Negroes in the Addams area, nor are they unique to them. In this study of middle class Negroes, Frazier gathers together some of the same material under the caption the "gaudy carnival" which he explains as a public denial of private feelings of inferiority and insecurity.[22] In day-to-day circumstances, however, this gaudy carnival may serve an altogether public and social function. Where persons are firmly entrenched in public statuses that are respected, trustworthy, or powerful, they can afford the art of understatement, subtlety, and modesty. With so many virtues it is easy to wait for someone else to point them out. Addams area Negroes are not so well placed.

---

[21] Sometimes the term is used by Negroes among very good friends in a joking relation. But it is also used to condemn someone who fulfills portions of the white man's stereotype.

[22] E. Franklin Frazier, *Black Bourgeoisie* (New York: Collier Books, 1962), pp. 166–67.

Whether they live in the Jane Addams Projects or in Bronzeville, however, Negroes occupy a place in American social structure that engenders certain suspicions and misgivings. In either case an appeal to the briefest of stylistic forms singles them out as an exception and informs others of their worth as a predictable companion. No doubt the suspicions that attend residing in the Jane Addams Projects are more forbidding than those that cast a shadow over the residents of Bronzeville. In turn the residents of the Jane Addams Projects seize upon the extremes of this "gaudy carnival" with a higher frequency than those in Bronzeville. Perhaps their status is similar to poor Negroes throughout the city who live in private housing. The point is that the uniformity of the housing projects do little to redress the oppressive homogeneity that faces them, and thus they must grasp at whatever novel and ever-changing stylistic forms may help allay this distrust and homogeneity.

Mixed Blessings

While the Jane Addams Projects are not an unmixed blessing, the Negroes there are quick to point up some of the advantages. Compared to most other housing projects, these projects make up a relatively small unit. Thus, many of the residents know each other rather well, and an even higher proportion can recognize one another by face. In a situation where anonymity may foretell unknown dangers or provide an opportunity for predation exempt from retaliation, it is very comforting to be surrounded by familiar faces. At the same time, however, people are often so well "cast" in the minds of local residents that any attempt at personal change meets a stone wall of doubt. In this context it is nearly impossible for someone to "turn over a new leaf," even when everyone agrees it would be for the better.

Secondly, the Jane Addams Projects are a "low rise" development that never reaches beyond four stories. In local circumstances this conveys several assurances missing in a "high rise." For instance, there is the recognition that the police might actually be able to provide some measure of surveillance and protection. Correspondingly, the necessity of taking similar coercive measures into their own hands is somewhat less pressing than in the "high rise." Moreover, each entrance into the Jane Addams Projects is used by only four to eight families. Among such a small number of people, facial recognition is easy, and a stranger is especially obvious. By contrast, those who live in the "high rise" must face from five to seven hundred people without knowing for certain why they are there. Similarly, many of the trouble spots and minor "no-man's-lands" of the "high rises" do not occur when a project is no more than four stories high. There are no elevators, the roofs are not altogether outside ground level observation, and the stairwells do not extend into regions where one can achieve almost total anonymity.

A third advantage to the Jane Addams Projects is that they were built in 1936 when the amount of space considered necessary to a family was less than it is today. Thus, most of the apartments have only a few rooms, and with adjustments to present standards, there is a tendency for them to be occupied by small families. The ratio of dependents to adults is rather low compared to most projects, and while most of the adults are unaware of their favored position, in relation to the rest of the city, they can still appreciate each particular situation in which they outnumber the adolescents.[23] Like most persons, the adults in the projects assume that young people have not reached the age where they "know what's good for them." Sometimes they will cross the street rather than confront a group of young boys lounging on the sidewalk. Occasionally, these same adults may resort to such blatant defensive maneuvers that the adolescents are left without any honorable line of retreat. In either case, little is accomplished except to estrange further the young and the old. To the advantage of the adults in the Jane Addams Projects, situations of this kind are less frequent than they are for those who live in projects with apartments for families with many more children.

A fourth condition that affects the Negroes in the Addams area, but which is somewhat difficult to appreciate, is the fact that along with all the other groups in the area they are in the minority. Within the entire neighborhood, there is fairly sure knowledge that no group could muster a clear quorum and that each must hesitate before it goes too far. As a rule, then, they equivocate by engaging in numerous minor skirmishes but back off from a full-scale confrontation. Actually this may multiply the incidence of minor displays of force, but it also keeps in abeyance anything that might reach the dimensions of a riot.[24]

Named Groups

Unlike the Italian section, there are no named local groups among the adult male Negroes in the Jane Addams Projects. There are, of course, some groups devoted to "community organization," but these are short-lived, transient in their membership, and include people from outside the

[23] On the average there are 3.2 minors per family in all Chicago public housing. In the Jane Addams Projects there is an average of only 1.5 minors per family.

[24] Allen D. Grimshaw suggests, with some doubt, that this may have been one reason certain ecological areas were free of racial riots during their heyday. ("Urban Racial Violence in the United States: Changing Ecological Considerations," *American Journal of Sociology*, 66 [September, 1960]: 109–19).

Addams area. Typically these groups are created *de novo* by welfare agencies, and their existence is unknown to most of the residents.

The absence of adult groups comparable to those among the Italian males can be attributed to the Negroes' living quarters. Within the projects there are no storefronts to be rented, and the buildings around them remain unavailable to the Negroes. However, the Negroes are also a relatively new population, and so far only a few of the street corner groups that have developed in this section have reached manhood. So far none of them have persisted into adulthood, and only the Negro youngsters have thoroughly local named groups. However, as will be pointed out below, even these groups seem susceptible to some sources of instability not present in the other ethnic sections.

When I first arrived in the area, the general pattern of group relations was as summarized in table 5. There were eight groups arrayed in three age grades, each group being exclusively of one sex. Between two of the groups there was one explicit alliance denoted by the group names.

TABLE 5

NEGRO STREET CORNER GROUPS (1963)

Oldest Groups (16–19)	Magnificent Gallants ‖	Bon Ton Fillettes♂ (Enraptured Misses) (Prima Donnas)	Patricians
(13–15)	Midget Gallants	Rapids	
Youngest Groups (10–12)	Choir Boys	Etruscans	Vultures

(   ) Indicates subsequent name change.
‖ Indicates explicit alliance.
♂ Girl's group.

By 1964, however, the situation had changed to that outlined in table 6. Broadly speaking, there seems to have been two reasons for these alterations. First, during this time some of the Magnificent Gallants and the Patricians were weaned away from their groups and drawn into the civil rights movement. Others got married or went into the service, a few had to leave home because of project rules,[25] and a small number received fairly long jail terms. At the same time, however, neither of these groups were replaced by other groups who had now reached the appropriate age (the Midget Gallants and Rapids). This break in the continuity of the older

[25] Due to the restrictions on income levels, it is often necessary for an older boy to leave home once he gets a job.

TABLE 6
NEGRO STREET CORNER GROUPS (1964)

Oldest Groups	Prima Donnas*♀		Enraptured Misses*♀
	Gutter Guys = Gutter Gals♀ (Choir Boys)		Etruscans
Youngest Groups	Jaybirds	Hawks	Stags

* Both girls' groups were previously joined in the Bon Ton Fillettes.
(   ) Indicates previous names.
= Indicates explicit alliance.
♀ Girls' group.

structure seems almost entirely the result of the Chicago Youth Development Project and the Negroes' responsiveness to its program. First, there was considerable success in forming several adult groups that became involved in the civil rights movement and local civic affairs. Second, many of the older adolescents were drawn into comparable groups for their age level or a number of *ad hoc* athletic teams that had no existence outside the local Boys' Club. Thus, in the eyes of the surrounding adults there was no well-identified (named) gang among the older boys. Of course, there remained many small groupings of older boys who hung around on the sidewalks; but the lack of a name seems to have exempted them from the constant suspicion that they might form the nucleus of a much larger and predatory gang.[26] In fact, by 1965 the most prominent street group in this section was the "Gutter Guys." All of the members were quite young (fourteen to fifteen) and unable to be much of a challenge to the older groups in the other sections.

The relative decline of street groups in this section brought with it two other unexpected results. First, the Italian groups to the northwest seem to have taken it as sure evidence that the Negroes were relatively defenseless. In due course, they became particularly blatant in the indignities they thought necessary to keep the Negroes "in their place." On their own part the Negro boys chafed at the rein even while many of them had freely imbibed the doctrine of non-violence. A second problem was a dislocation within the Negro community itself. By taking part in the civil rights movement and in a number of local civic affairs, the Negro boys in the projects received a certain acclaim and respect. In turn, their traditional rivals in

[26] For example, it was always assumed that the Magnificent Gallants and the Patricians could "recruit" an untold number of collaborators. Since their demise, no group has been accredited with such power.

the "Village," below Roosevelt, took offense and did their best to restore a previous order in which they had somewhat overshadowed the boys in the Jane Addams Projects.[27] Their efforts in this case took two different courses. They first made an unsolicited effort to "horn in" on the peaceful demonstrations being carried out by those in the Addams area. Momentarily, when the demonstrators were rebuffed, it appeared that the interlopers from the "Village" might seize both leadership and notoriety by a more aggressive policy. However, as the peaceful demonstrations gained more momentum and success, the boys from the "Village" fell into the background.

As the summer drew to a close and the civil rights movement relaxed over the winter,[28] the boys from the "Village" tried another alternative. Since the Addams area had been stripped of its protective forces, the Village Boys felt free to sample the pleasures, girls, and "action" available in it. At the same time, they also took the liberty of "starting something" with the local Italians and Mexicans, even when the Negro boys in the Jane Addams Projects stood "to take the rap."

This last invasion by the Village Boys seems to have reached its peak in late 1964 during a dance that took place in the dead of winter. It started with an "open dance"[29] held by the Italians at the local Boys' Club. Since this club was usually conceded to the Negroes, this was a venturesome act in its own right, and there were many premonitions of what would occur. Some thought the Italians were simply looking for trouble. Others felt the club was being taken advantage of because the Italians had never extended similar privileges to the Negroes. On their own part, the Italians had also come with the apprehension that they might have to resort to force. In the course of the dance several guns, knives, and other weapons were "noted" in one way or another.[30] Moreover, once this information made the circuit of the local grapevine, the projected number of weapons became astronomical.

[27] The number of persons below twenty-one in the "Village" far exceeds that in the Jane Addams Projects; about 7000 to 1500.

[28] It must be remembered that civil rights leaders had earmarked this season as a "long hot summer."

[29] There are four kinds of dances or socials: "Quarter parties," which are held in someone's home with the entrance price of twenty-five cents; basement parties, which are family affairs that draw in a few close friends; "closed socials," which are open only to those who have been invited by the group who sponsors the affair; and "open dances" that can be attended by anyone who can afford the entrance fee. It is the latter which generally arouses the greatest concern because this draws the largest and most unpredictable crowd. The Italian dance was of this last type.

[30] At such dances, boys are often "frisked" if they are suspected. This usually does little more than amplify the impression that serious trouble is on the way. The weapons are easily smuggled in via the girls' purses.

The dance was given on extremely short notice, and both Mexican and Negro boys were uncertain about whether or not they were welcome.[31] Still, both were sufficiently cautious that they kept their distance from the dance. Some of the boys from the group called the "Village Deacons" freely walked around the periphery of the dance, but they did not enter. When the fight broke out among the Italians, however, a number of Negro and Mexican boys came to watch them fight among themselves. One of the "Village Deacons" was particularly forward and went up to where he could get a good look. An Italian boy said something to him, and both of them began to fight. From that point on the Italians and Negroes fell upon one another, and a five minute melee resulted. During the entire incident there were many points of obvious interest,[32] but what is important here is the leading role taken by the boys from the "Village." Not only did one of their members take the first step in a situation ripe for conflict, but the first Negro boy to join him was also from the "Village." After this, the Negroes from the Addams area and the Italians at the dance had little alternative but to "take sides." The minor fracas that took place lasted no more than five or ten minutes, but just after it ended, more than fifty boys from the "Village" rounded the corner and ran toward the club. The police, who got there at about the same time, headed them off, and they scattered into the Projects. Both before and after this melee, the Village boys continued to "lord it over" those in the Addams area and threatened to take in hand the problem of dealing with the Italians to the northeast. In fact, by early 1965 some of the Negro boys from the "Village" had made a tenuous pact with some of the Mexican boys in the Addams area.[33] Each was to aid the other in case of trouble with the Italians. On their own part, the Negro boys

[31] A successful "open dance" is an extremely complicated undertaking. Within the limits of this study, it is impossible even to list the necessary steps. One important tactic, however, is to "let the word out" about who should or should not be there. This is usually done in a very subtle way through the local grapevine, and it takes considerable time: the dance has to be properly labeled by the name of the sponsoring group; the occasion for the dance has to be announced; street workers have to be forewarned whether or not "their boys" are welcome; youth officers and policemen must be alerted in a very casual manner—otherwise they will panic and either bring so much "heat" on the dance that it "flops" or help create the firm conviction that trouble is brewing. All of this takes time and, in the present case, was left undone.

[32] For example, (1) the boys limited their attacks to each other and did not harm any of the Negro or white adults who stopped the fight; (2) none of the girls participated but only stood by; (3) the Mexican boys who were at the dance joined the Italians, while those not at the dance ran into an adjacent office and they "sat it out"; and (4) many of the Italians knew the Negro boys they were fighting rather well, but many of those who fought alongside the Italians were utter strangers.

[33] Nominally the pact was between the Village Deacons and the Stylists. However, either of them could have recruited a large number of other boys of the same ethnicity within their respective territories.

in the Addams area became quite restive; and there was some question of how long they would exchange the prestige and honor of belonging to formal and legitimate groupings for the prospect of using force to "put down" the Italians.

After the inroads of the Village boys and the melee at the dance, it became clear that the Negro gangs were serving a useful social function for their section. They were its guardians and had excluded a wide variety of people whom all the local Negroes feared. Here, the Negro gangs operate much like those among the Italians and Mexicans. Indeed there are strong parallels between the Negro section and the other three sections in the Addams area. In this chapter, differences rather than similarities have been highlighted to point up the Negroes' unique placement in the Addams area.

To a large extent, the peculiarities of the Negro section can be understood by its historical placement relative to the other sections in the neighborhood. Some Italians are especially apprehensive of the Negroes and think that they may eventually take political control of the area. Since the Negroes are almost totally in public housing, they are excluded from most entrepreneural enterprise and subject to a good deal of involuntary transiency. The uniformity of their living quarters and a lack of income or occupational variations create an oppressive homogeneity in which fads or gaudy paraphernalia are used to amplify one's social claims and intentions. More than any other group in the area, the Negroes are under the caretaking of social welfare agents and fearful of being betrayed by their own neighbors.

Taken together, all of these conditions produce a distinctive style of life. Whether it is a unique culture shared by the Negroes alone or an amalgam of Americanisms seems beside the point. All cultures are an amalgamation of elements stolen, borrowed, or inherited from diverse sources. Like most people, the Negroes in the Addams area have borrowed widely and innovated where possible. What is distinctive about the Negroes in the Jane Addams Housing Projects is the way they piece together these cultural elements to fit their own purposes. Undeniably this creates a style of life that makes it difficult for them to enjoy easy commerce with some of the other ethnic groups who are less responsive to current social movements, fashions, and fads. Still, within the Negro section itself these elements contribute toward an essential order.

Undoubtedly certain things are missing in the Negro section which, if present, would better fit the Negroes to their environs. Unlike the Italians, they lack any named groups among the adult males. In part this may be due to their recent arrival in the area and general economic conditions that make it difficult for Negro gang boys to stay together once they become adults. The Negroes are excluded from organized crime because the Italians already possess a monopoly on it. For the same reason they lack any notable form of local political power.

The Negro section is also a partial exception to the segmental and provincial character of all the other ethnic sections. In several important ways the Negroes are dependent on the adjacent areas to do their shopping, to carry out their religious preferences, and to seek some of their recreations. If the adjacent areas were torn down, it would seriously change their daily habits. All the other ethnic groups could at least maintain an impaired provincialism.

In the absence of so many of the basic grounds that people use to select their associates or anticipate one another's behavior, it is surprising how well the Negroes in the Jane Addams projects can manage with a variety of stylistic and expressive forms. Seen from a distance, their continual attempts to keep abreast of recent expressive innovation may seem wearing and frantic. This would be a mistaken view. The Negroes in the Jane Addams Projects pursue these expressive forms with every bit as much zest as more respectable people grasp at the more permanent signs that mark their own station in life.

8

The Puerto Ricans and the Mexicans

Polk and Laflin: The Mexicans

The westernmost part of the Addams area, excepting Ashland Avenue (see map 2), is a center of Mexican settlement and invasion. This is the least distinct of all the ethnic areas in the neighborhood. In a rather vague way it is referred to by the metaphors, "the guys over on Polk and Laflin," "the guys over on Fillmore and Loomis," or simply as "over where the Mexicans live." The designation of these terms or phrases as metaphors is justified on the grounds that any Mexican from this section shown on the map can be indicated this way. In turn, as metaphors, these phrases not only *denote* an objective collection of people, but *connote* a variety of other less obvious characteristics. In the view of the other residents it is assumed that the Mexicans in this section will "stick together" and "take sides" against anyone else. Also, it is generally expected that the Mexicans will eventually displace the remaining Italians. There is the standing suspicion that Puerto Ricans, Italians, and Negroes cannot move freely in this section.

Despite the manifest expectations, suspicions, and fears that surround it, this section of the Addams area is a particularly vague entity. The Mexicans constitute only a little more than 50% of the population, while the Italians make up most of the remainder. Moreover, the Italians still manage a large portion of the businesses (see table 7). The section is labelled Mexican primarily because of their role in its street life. The only named street groups in the section are Mexican groups, and together they seem to have firmly discouraged the Italians from any claim to the section. First, the Italian boys dissociate themselves from the section because of the practical problem of how they would arrange their relationships with all the Mexican groups. Second, there is the more general problem of how an Italian group in this section would manage the external stigma and suspicions that would attach to their location. As one Italian boy who lived there put it, "Look, if we hang over there [on Laflin], you know, how we gonna get along with the Mexicans, and what are the rest of the guys

TABLE 7

PROPRIETORSHIP AND LOCATION OF COMMERCIAL ESTABLISHMENTS

RESIDENTIAL AREA	ITALIAN					MEXICAN				
PROPRIETORSHIP	ITALIAN	MEXICAN	NEGRO	PUERTO RICAN	OTHER	ITALIAN	MEXICAN	NEGRO	PUERTO RICAN	OTHER
Grocery store	29	2	1			5	5	1		1
Fruits and veg.	2									
Fish market	2					1				
Sausage store	2									
Tortilla store		1								
Meat store	3				1					
Cheese store	3									
Bakery	7	1				2				
Shoe repair	5									
Shoe store	2									
Clothing store	2				1		1			
Tailor	3									
Dressmaker										
Lemonade stand	7					1				
Hot dog stand	5									
Beef stand	5					1	1			
Ice cream stand	1		1							
Cafe	5					1				
Restaurant	2						1			
Tavern	10					3	1			
Liquor store	1									
Night club										
Currency exchange	1									
Lawyer	3									
Notary Public	2									
Income tax service	2									
Real estate and mortgage	2					1				
Dentist	1									
Clinic										
Optometrist	2									
Doctor	1									
Hospital	1									
Laundry	1				2		1			
Cleaners	4					2	1			
Service St.	2									
Auto Repairs	2				1					
House Repair	1									
General Rep.	1									
Welding Shop										
Barber Shop	9					3	1			
Beauty Shop	5					3	1			
Furniture Store	1									
Upholster	1									
Hardware Store	2					1	1			
Elec. Repair	3									
Other*	12					3	1			
SUBTOTALS	155	4	2	0	5	28	15	1	0	1
%	93%	2%	1%	0	3%	62%	33%	2%	0	2%
TOTALS	166					45				

* Above this group all establishments are grouped together if their services overlap. In this last group the services do not overlap. Includes florist, travel service, music store, dance school, funeral home, record shop, drug store, gift store, candy store, cigar store.

TABLE 7—continued

NEGRO					PUERTO RICAN					TOTAL AREA				
ITALIAN	MEXICAN	NEGRO	PUERTO RICAN	OTHER	ITALIAN	MEXICAN	NEGRO	PUERTO RICAN	OTHER	ITALIAN	MEXICAN	NEGRO	PUERTO RICAN	OTHER
	1			1	2			8		36	8	2	8	2
										2				
										3				
										2				
											1			
										3				1
										3				
								1		9	1		1	1
										5				
				1						2				1
				1						2	1			2
		1		1						3		1		1
										8				
										5				
										6	1			
										1		1		
				1				1		6			1	1
					1					3	1			
	1				3	1		1		16	3		1	
		1			2					3			1	
					1					2				
										3				
										2				
										2				
								1		3			1	
									1	1				1
				1										1
										2				
		1						1		1		1	1	
										1				
				1	1					2	1			3
				1	1			1		7	1		1	1
							1		1	2			1	1
				2				1		2			1	3
										1				
										1				
								1					1	
		1			1					13	1	1		
					1					9	1			
				2						1				2
										2				
										3	1			
										3				
					3	1		2		18	2		2	
0	2	4	0	12	16	2	0	19	2	199	23	7	19	20
0	11%	22%	0	66%	41%	5%	0	49%	5%	74%	9%	3%	7%	7%
		18					39					268		

[Italians] gonna think? We'll get bum rapped for everything along with the Mexicans."

Faced with this dilemma, the Italians seem to have given up any further claim to this section; and only a few vestiges of their past dominance remain. There are three storefront SAC's that are maintained by adult Italians, but the members seldom "hang" on the streets any more.[1] There are a few casual cliques of younger Italian boys who occasionally hang in the area; but none of them have a name, and often they go further east for their street life. As indicated in table 7, quite a few Italian business places still exist in the section but most of them have been "compromised" to one of the patterns outlined in chapter 3.

Internal Boundaries

Since the Mexicans' chief claim to this part of the Addams area is their place in its street life, its boundary remains the most fluid and uncertain. Passage along its streets, in its shops, and through its alleys is still fairly easy, except for the Puerto Ricans who live on Harrison and Ashland. However, it is rather common in the afternoon or early evening to see Negroes and Italians walking through the area in twos or threes. Many Italians, of course, live there and remain around their housefronts for most of the free hours of the day. Generally, the Negroes are in transit.

This freedom of passage is probably extended more fully to adults than to adolescents. Since the Mexicans' control over the section is registered primarily by their adolescent street corner groups, it is others of the same age who stand as the major contestants. The adults are assumed to want little more than free passage and the usage of local stores and homes. Adolescents from another section are suspected of more serious designs.

However, even the younger Mexican males seem to benefit from the rather fluid status of this section.[2] At present, they can move about with a fair degree of freedom and manage to associate with a number of people from outside their own little world. One problem, however, is that Taylor Street runs squarely through the lower half of the section and divides the Mexicans into two separate wings. Taylor Street is a main thoroughfare that starts in the Loop and extends almost to the limits of the inner city. Within the Addams area itself, it is not an impersonal domain because all the adjacent businesses are ethnic-linked and tailored to a local clientele. Still, the street is a major artery for transportation, and the residents have

[1] Two of these SAC's closed in early 1964.

[2] This is probably a temporary situation which will end once the Mexicans have gained full control or the University of Illinois and the Urban Renewal Program remove both the Italians and Mexicans.

been inured to the sight of outsiders catching their buses and making deliveries. Within the limits of Addams area ideology, this marks off both an obstruction and area of license. Practically anyone has the right to go there to shop or sightsee. At the same time, its facilities are so complete that there is little cause for a resident's going beyond it. In addition, a willingness to expose oneself to the hazards of such "mixed company" seems also to be a sign of the "adventurer." Thus, the boys who live on one side of Taylor and cross over to the other arouse a variety of suspicions about what they are "up to."

Despite the importance of Taylor Street as a boundary within this section of the area, there are many friendships and other affiliations that bridge both sides. Some boys have lived on both sides, and others have relatives in both places. Apparently these relations are still so numerous that they explain most of the cross-traffic.

Before the clearance for the university in 1963 there were two Mexican sections, and territorial divisions between them were much more significant. The triangle formed by Blue Island, Taylor, and Halsted (see map 1) constituted the second Mexican section. It was dominated by several Mexican street corner groups, the best remembered being the Toltecs. The Toltecs were said to have achieved great notoriety and to have gathered around themselves a hierarchy of younger groups similar to those in the Italian section.

When the neighborhood was still intact, the Mexican groups in that section were strongly opposed to those in the western section of the Addams area. Even today some of the older Mexican boys can recount fights between groups from these two sections. In their remembrance, it was dangerous for boys living in one section to walk into the other. Some boys said they had more trouble with the other Mexicans in this eastern section than with the adjacent Puerto Ricans, Negroes, and Italians.

The prior existence of two opposing Mexican sections within the Addams area indicates how ethnicity alone is not a sufficient basis for the unity of each section. Whenever boundaries intervene, opposition seems to form despite common ethnic origins.

It is also worth observing how the segmental and relatively independent character of these ethnic sections makes them impervious to so many of the forces that affect a "zone of transition." If, as often happens, one territorial segment is excised, the remaining ones can still exist without serious impairment. Thus, the Addams area and its adjacent neighborhoods are like a multicellular animal whose separate members can be severed without major loss to the survivors.

A People in the Middle

The Mexican section abuts the sections of all the other ethnic groups. Moreover, a large number of Italians still reside within it. These conditions give the Mexicans a number of problems that are not equally pressing for the other ethnic groups.

The Italians who remain in this section are surrounded by an aura of mystery and unabashed power. Rumor has it that many of them are "Outfit" people and that several more have "connections." This rumor may be false more often than true; but the Mexicans in this section do not have a measured knowledge of the Italians' affiliations, and even a vague rumor is an improvement over total ignorance. The Mexicans are not cowed by the Italians, but when certain other considerations are taken into account, the Mexicans hesitate to make enemies of them.

Many of the Mexicans live in the Italian section and are so assimilated that they are often taken for Italians. Those who live in the Italian section are often faced with the problem of taking sides, particularly when the Italians and the Negroes come to grips. Having kinfolk and friends in the Mexican section, they press for restraint.

The Mexican section, however, shares a long boundary line with the Negro section. A few Mexicans live in the projects, and the Mexicans are not so numerous that they can afford to ignore the Negroes. As a result the Mexicans tend to "sit out" the disputes of the Italians and Negroes.

The general practice became quite clear on two occasions. When in the summer of 1964 the Negroes began a "swim in" at Sheridan Park, the Mexicans refused to take sides. During the "swim in" they became indignant when some whites from outside the Addams area insisted they state their position. Prior to this incident the Mexicans had gained entrance to the same swimming pool by "going in through the back door"; that is by accompanying an Italian friend, making themselves inconspicuous, and propitiating the "right people." At no time had they explicitly demanded or received an unequivocal right to use the swimming pool. Even today they take the role of "guests," although there seems to be little doubt about the continuity of their privileges.

The same problem was apparent during and after the "race riot" between the Negroes and the Italians at the local Boys' Club. As the two groups began to exchange blows, a few Mexican boys who were looking on ran into an adjacent office where they waited out the fight. As one Mexican boy ducked into the office he explained, "This ain't got nothing to do with us."[3]

---

[3] I was standing at the doorway letting the Mexicans in the office. The boy who made the statement was one of the more prominent members of the most important group in the Mexican section.

Throughout the remainder of the fracas, only one of these boys took an active part. He helped drag one Negro boy into the office after the latter had fallen to the floor and was being kicked by two or three Italian boys.

The Negroes seem to appreciate the difficulty of the Mexicans' position. In their altercations with the Italians they do not explicitly ask the Mexicans to side with them, and there does not seem to be much open rancor when the Mexicans fail to do so. Those civil rights leaders who insisted that the Mexicans support or oppose the Negroes' entrance into the swimming pool at Sheridan Park were not residents and had little idea of the local understandings between ethnic sections.

The difficulties arising from the inability of the Mexicans in this section to ignore their Negro and Italian neighbors are accentuated by the Mexican's obvious lack of autonomy. Their control of this section dates back no more than five or six years. So far, they have not been able to develop or capture many of the establishments that are necessary to either their practical or their ceremonial life (see table 7). Unlike the Puerto Ricans, the Mexicans make many of their day-to-day purchases from Italian businesses within the section or elsewhere in the area. There is no other Mexican business center nearby, except the one on Eighteenth Street. However, the Mexicans in the Addams area and those on Eighteenth Street have serious misgivings about one another. The latter are generally considered to be the most vainglorious of all their ethnic group on the West Side. In contrast, those in the Addams area are adjudged "squares" or, what is worse, "tools" for the Italians. For the most part, then, the local Mexicans resort to places within the area itself.

For their ceremonial life the Mexicans often go out of their own section. To commemorate Our Lady of Guadalupe they must go over to St. Assisi, where at least the sacred elements of this ceremony are still carried out. This event takes place in the dead of the Chicago winter, and all the secular accompaniments have been eliminated. To make amends, Our Lady of Provins has recently innovated an out-of-season fiesta to honor their favorite saint. The situation is a little awkward, however, with all the local Italians looking on.

On the date of their national independence, the Mexicans must go to Halsted Street, where a parade commemorates this holiday. At one time, this portion of Halsted was part of a Mexican community that extended all the way to Eighteenth Street. Today, however, the clearance for the university has left most of the street lined with rubble, and the Negroes have occupied nearly all that is left. Thus, the parade has the incongruous aspect of being half in a wasteland, half in a Negro community. On reflection, this parade seems a true representation of the Mexicans' dilemma.

Named Groups

Within this section there are a number of named street corner groups, and there is a constant apprehension that personal disputes cannot be kept among the initial protagonists. This is a problem chiefly among the adolescent males, because they are immediately involved. The general pattern of group relations in this section is outlined in table 8. In all, three principles seem sufficient to give a full account of the structure. First, the groups are bisected into two territorial segments that stand in mutual opposition. This primary distinction, of course, is only a replication of others that have already been mentioned. Second, age grades are respected within each of these segments. A third principle of organization is a series of explicit alliances expressed by group names. All of these principles have been found to apply in both the Italian and Negro sections.

TABLE 8

MEXICAN STREET CORNER GROUPS

AGE GRADES	"HANG" BELOW TAYLOR STREET		"HANG" ABOVE TAYLOR STREET
Oldest	Regents = Regenettes ‖ Jr. Regents Cardinals	Jr. Princes Privateers	Erls* = Erlettes ‖ Jr. Erls Stylists (Domiciles) ‖ Miniature Stylists
	Etruscans = Etruscanettes Marprinces = Marqueens ‖ Jr. Etruscans		

Note: All names preceded by the term "Taylor."
(   ) Indicates subsequent name change.
= Indicates explicit alliance.
* When informed they had misspelled their name (Earls), this group insisted on maintaining the same spelling.

Like the Negroes, but unlike the Italians, the Mexicans have girls' groups (four of them). The Mexican girls' groups, however, are different from those of the Negroes in that they are invariably allied with a boy's group. The boys call them "broads" and make light of their virtue. Still, it is doubted that others from outside the group have the same license.

The major break between these Mexican groups is the wedge that Taylor Street drives between them. As indicated already, the Mexicans cannot cross this internal boundary without raising the question of what they are up to. This creates a division between the Mexican groups, and age grades in either part view their counterparts with suspicion. As with the adults, however, the Mexican boys in these two sections share many kinfolk and friends. Usually they find these connections to be sufficient to excuse each other's passage across Taylor Street.

The opposition among groups in this section is probably better described as rivalry than outright antagonism. There have been almost no fights among them, and only a few rumors have developed around a possible confrontation. As a rule, their opposition is expressed only in the form of verbal jousing, a tendency to act irresponsibly at each other's "socials," and an avoidance of those places where their opponents "hang." By far the most serious antagonism was that between the Stylists and the Etruscans. At one time there was considerable talk of a "jam" between the two groups, but this came to nothing aside from a few sidewalk scuffles between isolated individuals. Nevertheless, this gave both groups a good deal of publicity and seems to have established them as the "successors" in each territorial segment.

In 1965 the Erls and the Regents attempted to establish a young men's SAC, modeled after those of the Italians. By then the boys in these groups had become eighteen or more years of age, and both groups rented a storefront for a club. After a brief time they had trouble raising the rental fees among themselves. Both groups recruited new dues-paying members and held "open socials." Each attempt to acquire funds proved to be disruptive and to attract police attention. In a few weeks the two groups abandoned their storefronts. Afterwards both groups broke up into several unnamed cliques that went their separate ways.

The disappearance of the Erls and Regents brought consequences for all the other groups, illustrating their previous interdependence. The Etruscans and the Stylists immediately assumed leadership in their respective sections, and there was new talk of a fight between them. The Junior Erls, the Erlettes, and the Regenettes disbanded. The Junior Stylists, not wanting any part of the seniors' antagonism with the Etruscans, made their intentions clear by renaming themselves the Domiciles.

With the inability of the Regents and Erls to establish a young men's SAC, it appeared unlikely that authority could be shifted to the hands of Mexican adults as in the Italian section. The immediate difficulty they faced was insufficient funds. Oddly enough, only a few of the boys could not afford their dues. Even so, these few undermined the others' faith in their clubhouse, since each member refused to pay his dues until all others had.

As a result, the major share of coercive power within the Mexican section remains in the hands of adolescents. The adults frequently acknowledge this by avoiding them and by their expressions of fear. Still, the situation is not so dire as in the Negro section. Some of the Mexican men are gathered in small friendship groups, and a few of them are known to be connected with the "Outfit" through their Italian friends. They are not easily intimidated by the adolescent Mexican groups.

A return visit in 1967 showed there were still no named adult groups in the Mexican section. By then, however, most of the Mexicans had been displaced by the urban renewal program. With residential stability and better employment opportunities, there seems no insurmountable barrier to the development of adult groups among the Mexicans. Indeed, before I came to the area, two such groups had emerged in the triangle east of Blue Island. Their storefronts were still extant, although the members had been scattered. While the character of the Mexican section can be described as a compromise between that of the Negroes and the Italians, its internal development seems to lean toward that of the Italians.

Harrison Street: The Puerto Ricans

Newcomers

The Puerto Ricans are among the most recent invaders of the Addams area. There are only about 1700 of them in the Addams area, and approximately 1100 live on Harrison and Ashland Streets. Numerically the Puerto Ricans dominate both of these streets, and the area adjoining them has been thoroughly ceded to them. Because of their small number and placement at the periphery of the neighborhood, however, the internal differentiation within this section is far less developed than in any of the others.

In this ethnic section the Puerto Ricans have taken over almost all the business places and provide most of the street life. These are the signs that the local residents take to indicate an area's ownership. Their importance is illustrated by two very small places on Harrison Street which are still operated by Italians and remain a center for their street life.

Locally, Harrison Street is so thoroughly identified with the Puerto Ricans that the name is a circumlocution for the members of that ethnic group. To the other residents there is good reason for this. In all, there are thirty-four business places on the street. All but two of them are attuned to Puerto Rican trade. Most of these have their "hangers-on," women or men on the inside, young boys or girls at the doorway. A combined record shop and cleaners has a loudspeaker that plays their popular music. In the summertime the men gather in front of this establishment, set up a table, and play cards. Nearby, tambourine and guitar music sometimes drifts out of a storefront church. Old men sell different flavored "ices" from portable stands. Young boys and girls hang around these moving businesses. Down the street, out of view of the crowd and beyond the grocery store and record shop, are several abandoned buildings. At night the doorways serve the older boys and girls as a "lovers' lane."

It is fairly easy to see why the Puerto Ricans (and, before them, the Mexicans) were able to first establish themselves on Harrison and Ashland.

Along Harrison the buildings are probably the most deteriorated of any in the area and have long been blighted by the area's heaviest concentration of industry. The east side of Ashland is flanked by a line of old mansions that are inappropriate to the income level of local people. These mansions have been divided and subdivided into numerous flats. At the same time, both the mansions on Ashland and the apartment houses on Harrison are so huge that they are outside the range of local ownership. Thus, a lack of local ownership and a scarcity of other renters opened them to the Puerto Ricans.

Institutional Shortcomings

The Puerto Ricans have been halted from extending their invasion beyond its present range. On the adjoining streets the buildings are much smaller and are not so threatened by industry or destruction. As a result, the Puerto Ricans are stranded in an area that is lacking in some of the institutions necessary to their day-to-day life (see table 7). They have no Catholic church of their own, no liquor store, and no place to buy clothing. Either they must share the facilities of the other ethnic groups or go north along Ashland where there are several small Puerto Rican business places and some large chain stores.

These movements outside the neighborhood seem to have two consequences for the Puerto Ricans in this section. First, those who leave the area become withdrawn from many of the concerns, antagonisms, and issues that occupy the remainder of the residents. Second, Puerto Ricans either remain the most thoroughly contained within their own ethnic group or, once they step out of these bounds, they sample a less ethnic-linked slice of American culture than that found in the Addams area alone. To a greater extent than some of the other ethnic groups, then, they seem to face the dilemma of being either thoroughly Puerto Rican or simply "American."

These traffic and commercial patterns leave a distinctive stamp on the Puerto Rican section. The small businesses and doorways that line its streets are extremely intimate and private worlds. The casual groupings gathered around these storefronts are especially gregarious and noisy but fall into an awkward silence when someone from another ethnic group tries to join them. Children and adults alike gather on the streets to play dominoes, eat, and listen to records. Conversations shift back and forth between English and Spanish. In their informal street life, there is no doubt of the section's distinctive Puerto Rican character.

In this section, however, there are practically no formal or ceremonial occasions that are distinctively Puerto Rican. The two storefront churches seem entirely "American" in their services. Weddings and funerals are not held locally and are very private affairs. The weekends bring no dances or parties to the section, and there is no public recognition of church holidays.

Compared to the Mexican and Italian sections, the flow of Puerto Rican street life is unbroken by ceremonial reminders of their traditional culture. Except for the sporadic use of Spanish, and for some songs and games, there are few signs of their traditional culture; and the Puerto Ricans do not especially protect these as their own. Alone among the groups in the area, they have nearly abandoned their special foods and their preparations.

As a result, much of the cultural content of the Puerto Ricans' ethnic identity is being lost. This does not mean that the local Puerto Ricans are simply merging into the surrounding population. They remain a very distinct group, but their ethnic identity consists largely of the negative and stereotypic versions cast in their direction by the Mexicans and Italians. The Puerto Ricans do not agree with these stereotypes, but they have been able to salvage so little of their traditional culture that they cannot effectively contradict these allegations.

The basic reason for these cultural losses is the absence of any ceremonial establishment within the Puerto Rican section. Their weddings, funerals, and christenings, for example, must be carried out elsewhere. Since there is no nearby Puerto Rican neighborhood that has the necessary facilities, they must share those of another ethnic group, where they abandon their own cultural forms. The two storefront churches encourage rather than retard these cultural losses. An increasing proportion of the Puerto Ricans are being converted to a denomination discontinuous with their past.

The Privileges of Powerlessness

Because they comprise such a small, well-contained group and are so uniformly the outcasts, the Puerto Ricans are likely to be overlooked in the residents' constant search for "who's to blame." So far as most of the other residents are concerned, the Puerto Ricans are simply too small a group to "start something," whether it be a gang fight or a burglary. Indeed, rumor has it that they are afraid to leave their own section and "can't bother anyone." Thus, to an unusual extent, the Puerto Ricans escape the constant labeling and minute determination of responsibility that are pursued by the other ethnic groups.

This special exemption from standing loyalties and conflicts seems less the result of action by the Puerto Ricans themselves than of inaction by those around them. A little less than two blocks away, north along Van Buren and Ashland, their fellow nationals practice the same segmentary system of social combinations as the other ethnic groups in the Addams area. Also, on a few occasions, the Puerto Rican boys on Harrison Street did take up a series of names, but these generally lasted for only a day or two. Their momentary claims were never given permanence by the fears, accusations, suspicions, and insinuations of the adjacent Mexicans and Italians.

The absence of named groups among the Puerto Ricans does not reduce the amount of conflict and deviance among them. The Puerto Rican youngsters make up about 10% of the area's juvenile population, and they contribute about the same percentage of its known delinquencies. Among these youngsters, conflict and opportunism seem to be more individualistic and unplanned than among those of the other ethnic groups. Fully 60% of their known juvenile offenses between 1963 and 1965 consisted of "strong-arming" another youngster.

Observation of the adults in the Puerto Rican section also disclosed similar instances of conflict. Typically these were fights between drinking partners, close friends, or persons who were intimates. Ordinarily, other people did not "jump into" these altercations, but at the same time they did not report them to the police. The lack of named groups among the Puerto Ricans seems to have left them free to indulge in purely personal animosities. Nonetheless, the Puerto Ricans make up so small a group that personal acquaintances usually pave the way to safe associations.

The Harrison Street Boys

Before 1965, the Puerto Ricans were known by only two labels. As a whole, they were referred to as Puerto Ricans, "P.R.s," "Riccapoles," or "Porkeys." However, the transient members of the adolescent male groupings that appear on the streets were combined under the appellation "The Harrison Street Boys." This is not a term that the Puerto Ricans invented, and it is used mostly by the other ethnic groups to designate any congregation of Puerto Rican boys who happen to be visible at the moment. Among themselves, the Puerto Rican boys adopted many different names, but none of them have "stuck."[4]

The label "Harrison Street Boys" carries with it the assumption that all of the boys will act in unison and are mutually loyal. The boys do not accept this name, however, and for almost three years not a single fight among the Puerto Ricans was labelled as a "gang fight."

In early 1965, the first named adolescent group arose in the Puerto Rican section. It was called the Hispanic Caballeros and endured well past the end of this study, six months later. Its origins could be traced directly to

---

[4] In early 1965, less than a week after the Chicago television premiere of "The Young Savages," one group of Puerto Rican boys began calling themselves the "Thunderbirds." It is interesting that they chose the name of the Italian gang rather than of the opposing Puerto Rican gang.

conditions affecting the entire Puerto Rican section. The members of the Hispanic Caballeros were boys between thirteen and fifteen who frequently went to a YMCA in the "Puerto Rican Strip" because they were unwelcome at the recreational centers controlled by the other ethnic groups in the Addams area.

The "Puerto Rican Strip" is controlled by several adolescent groups, the most notorious being the Van Buren Royals. The Royals took offense at the invasion of the Hispanic Caballeros; and wher the latter made known their identity, the Royals threatened to "whip their ass." The Hispanic Caballeros gained some notoriety through this threat and remained in existence, whereas many previous attempts by the Puerto Rican boys had fallen on deaf ears.

The Puerto Ricans, however, remain a very small population, and so long as they stay in their own ethnic section, personal relations seem adequate to handle most daily contacts. First names and family names are so widely known that people need not refer to one another by group names. In this respect the Puerto Ricans seem to lie at the low point of a scale of population size which extends through the Mexican section to the Italian section at the upper end. In both of the latter sections the population is simply too great for most people to know one another personally. The degree of internal differentiation among the Mexicans and the Italians seems to proceed along the same scale, being most elaborate in the most populous group.

The problem of anonymity in the Negro section is not directly comparable to that in the Puerto Rican section. Certainly the Negroes are more numerous, but they also live in public housing. Unlike the Puerto Ricans, the Negroes cannot meet any of their commercial and religious needs without relying heavily upon the other ethnic sections. The Negroes, then, must frequently manage relations outside their own section. The Puerto Ricans, as illustrated by the Hispanic Caballeros, face the same problem, but to a lesser extent. Their section remains largely an ethnic island like that of the Italians and Mexicans.

Part 4

The Boys' World

Introduction

The broad structure laid down by the ordered segmentation of territorial, age, ethnic, and sex groupings provides the skeletal outlines within which young males in the Addams area can define their own relations. Generally, Addams area youngsters observe closely the structural precedents which they share with the adults. Their groups are made up of members who share the same territory, ethnicity, age, and sex. Opposition between groups drawn from each of these segments is a common feature and within these groups personal identities are well elaborated. The boys' world is largely a duplicate of that of the adults.

Despite the importance attributed to each of these segments, no more than half the boys in the Addams area belong to a named gang. This is an important consideration because it suggests the specialized functions the gangs perform. In the Addams area the street-corner group is the keeper of its ethnic boundaries; however, not all the local boys are needed to perform this task. These groups also diminish the degree of anonymity in each ethnic section. Once again, however, their own actions decrease the necessity for adding the remaining boys to their ranks.

The boys also follow the other residents in their subscription to a set of private understandings often unknown to outsiders. The street-corner group seems the most provincial of the many provincial worlds that radiate from each group to include the entire Addams area. Within the street-corner group, grudges, friendships, and alignments are so private that the boys' actions sometimes seem inexplicable to the other residents. This does not mean that the street-corner group is complying with the prescriptions of the adult world, but rather that its structure duplicates that world.

The structural principles of age, residence, and territoriality create their own problems because they are subject to change. The boys' groups are continually faced with these changes, and they are the grounds for alteration within each group. Outside their groups, the boys must manage their relations across ethnic sections and cope with representatives of the wider community, such as the police. Each of these forces brings into play a variety of situations over which the boys can exercise only limited control.

The findings on these street-corner groups in the Addams area are remarkably similar to those compiled by Thrasher thirty years ago.[1] Both this study and his show the continuing importance of age, sex, ethnicity, and territoriality as selective principles for composing the street corner group. Thrasher occasionally tempers the importance of age-grading, ethnicity, and territoriality, arguing that they may be ethnic survivals and not essential to the street corner group. But thirty years after his survey, they seem equally important in the Addams area.

[1] Frederic M. Thrasher, *The Gang* (Chicago: The University of Chicago Press, 1927; rev. ed., 1963).

9

The Composition of Local Street Corner Groups

In the Addams area there are thirty-two named boys' street corner groups. By a reasonable estimate, these groups will include only about half the boys in the area during some portion of their adolescence. Some form of selection must exist to exclude so many boys. At first glance no such principle seems evident because the criteria for membership are so general to the adolescent population. The named street corner group, however, seems to perform a relatively specialized function that does not require the efforts of all the boys in the neighborhood. It is above all a way of easing the problem of anonymity where personal knowledge cannot extend to so large a number of people. In the Addams area, although an individual's personal acquaintances may extend very far, they still cannot include everyone he encounters. The street corner group seems a way of simplifying this problem.

Sex

This chapter concerns mostly the adolescent male groupings in the Addams area. Between 1962 and 1965, however, there were six girls' groups in the area, more than Thrasher found in the entire city in 1927.[1] Other female street corner groups have been reported from different parts of the city, and their emergence may reflect the general emancipation of females that has occurred since Thrasher's time. All the girls' groups in the Addams area, however, occur among the Negroes and Mexicans. Neither the Negroes nor the Mexicans were numerous during the period Thrasher did his study; and the Italians, who were very much present in the 1920's, still maintain a strict male monopoly on their street-corner groups.

With one exception, the remaining groups are wholly male in their composition. For a short time the Rapids had a girl member who was a sister to one of the male members. She attended their meetings as a "secretary"

[1] Frederic M. Thrasher, *The Gang* (Chicago: University of Chicago Press, 1927; rev. ed., 1963).

and would "hang with the guys." Otherwise she played no further part in their joint activities, and she soon dropped out of the group.[2]

This definite break between the sexes is common throughout the Addams area. It is perhaps the first and most serious cleavage in the neighborhood. Boys and girls rarely "couple off" except by stealth. Men hang with other men, and women with other women. All but one tavern is a man's world. The home is equally a woman's world.

Dating in the strict sense is practically unknown.[3] At most local dances and occasions for entertainment, the boys come with other boys, the girls with other girls. Once there, boys and girls may dance or talk for a few minutes, but then they usually part and go back to their separate cluster of friends. Holding hands, embracing, or walking alone with one another in public is so rare that it is a source of comment and speculation. After a dance, some boys may walk a few girls home on the pretext that it is not safe for them to walk home alone. But, here again, a group of boys accompanies a group of girls with no definite pairing off.

Often a boy will say that he has "a girl," and she will acknowledge his claims. This admission carries with it very few mutual obligations, and the girl continues to attend most local affairs with her girlfriends. She also pays her own way to any socials or movies and remains quite independent of her boyfriend. Meetings between boyfriends and girlfriends are, as a rule, casual encounters that appear unintended. They meet at a local beefstand, hamburger grill, or street corner. Generally these meetings are not prearranged, but are the result of a mutual understanding of each other's daily routine. Even on these occasions, both the boy and the girl are likely to be in the company of their friends.

Rarely, a boy or girl may speak of having a date. This, however, tends to be almost like the casual encounters mentioned above, except that there is some prior arrangement for the meeting. An example from my field notes may help illustrate this type of dating.

While I was driving down Grenshaw, E, a Mexican girl, flagged me down and asked for a ride to her boyfriend's house. She explained that she had a date. Since she was dressed in "peddle pushers" and had her hair up in curlers, I was curious about her "date." Besides this was the first date I had heard of after more than eight months in the area.

---

[2] None of the girls' groups included a male member. Locally there were two social clubs that were "coed." However, they met in a local agency and definitely were not street groups. Like the Rapids, they were Negro groups. As I shall point out later, the Negro boys seem far more amenable to cross-sex relations and more at ease around girls.

[3] I.e., where a boy (1) picks up the girl at her own home with the knowledge of her parents, (2) pays her way to some entertainment, (3) remains with her throughout the occasion, and (4) takes her home.

We arrived at her boyfriend G's home and found him sitting in front of the house with a number of his male friends and two girls. We sat down and talked for about thirty minutes. It was only after this time that I realized that this was her "date"!

I left and drove by an hour or so later. They were still there, the girls sitting quietly while the boys talked among themselves.

Even such "dates" are not common, and they are about as far as either sex goes in what could be called "dating relations." Thus, there is little tendency for couples to pair off, even when they acknowledge each other as "my girl" or "my guy." It is more common for the boys to speak of "our girls" than "my girl."

Once the boys are no longer in school, at age eighteen or nineteen, there are some changes in the direction of more serious dating. At this age the boys may actually start "hanging" regularly with a girlfriend and go with her to quite a few social events. However, this seldom includes picking the girl up at her home and need not involve paying her way. Most often it means necking in one of the many "lovers' lanes." A few boys may spend a great deal of their spare time at their girl's home. This situation is more similar to courtship than dating. Also, by this age, the street corner group is beginning to break up and disappear.

All of these statements need to be qualified by one important exception. Although the Negro boys seldom "date" in the fullest sense of the word, they are far more likely to engage girls openly in conversation and casual relations. It is fairly common to see a Negro group on the sidewalk that includes both a number of males and females. They are not paired off, but still they are involved in a single conversation. "Rapping"[4] with one's girl friend is also a frequent activity. At local dances the Negro boys are eager to be expert performers. Unlike the dances for whites, there are no large clusters of male "wall flowers," and very few female couples dance together.[5] Boys and girls often touch each other but this is seldom an explicit sign of affection.

Among the Italian boys, the situation is almost the reverse. They are reticent at dances, seldom "hang" with girls, and almost never touch a girl in public, except to dance. When they do confront one another, they remain

[4] Rapping can mean "signifying." Between boys and girls, however, it usually means a kind of rough kidding or teasing contest.

[5] In the early stages of a white dance, almost all the dancers are female. Later, as the lights get darker, the floor crowded, and the music deafening, some of the boys join them. However, there are always a number of male wall flowers and some females dancing with one another. The Negro boys, on the other hand, will sometimes dance with one another rather than miss a dance. Occasionally two or three boys will dance with the same girl at the same time. In both cases this is possible because the current dances do not require body contact.

guarded or simply noncommital. Sometimes they are almost rude to one another. As already pointed out, there are no named Italian girls' groups in the area.

The Mexican boys seem to occupy an intermediate position between the Negroes and Italians. Frequently a group of boys will allow a group of girls to "hang" nearby, and occasionally a boy and a girl will sit together in public. Such relationships, however, are confined to a single group of girls, and the boys usually refer to them as "our girls."[6] The Mexican boys are especially likely to be aligned with a local girls' group. Like the Italian boys, however, they are backward at dances, seldom pair off into couples, and remain guarded in most circumstances in the presence of girls.

This cleavage between sex groups might be interpreted as an indication of the boys' uncertainty and doubt of their masculinity. The boys are afraid of girls because they question their own ability with them. Certainly this does not represent the residents' own outlook. If Addams area residents are convinced of anything, it is of each other's sexuality. To them sex is a biological fact, and no amount of moralizing and indoctrination can thwart such natural tendencies. Girls are weak and ready victims. Boys are predatory and strong. Thus, each sex is dangerous to the other, and the only way to insure their safety and morality is segregation or surveillance. Girls stay in the company of girls, even when they are going to meet boys. The first step in dating is ruled out by the parents' insistence that their daughters be accompanied by other girls. Mixed groups are viewed with suspicion and dislike.

Certainly the boys are not hesitant about asserting their masculinity when a girl's caution or social surveillance are lacking. As in most lower class neighborhoods, premarital sexual relations are common for males. The girls are far more "careful," but locally a few are known to "put out" and the boys make full use of them.[7] "Gang bangs" are infrequent, but do occur. Adventuring into another neighborhood to look for girls is routine, especially for the older Italian boys. On these occasions they are anything but "backward." Thus, one can hardly take the boys' reticence in their own neighborhood as a sign of their sexual uncertainty when they abandon it so readily elsewhere. In any case, the local girls certainly do not doubt the boys' sexual competence.

Actually, in the Addams area the kind of polite social interchange we call dating is lacking. Such a relationship embodies the implicit assumption that either party can be trusted to exercise sufficient self-control to protect

---

[6] Among the Negro boys, almost any local girl is eligible for such a relationship.

[7] There are about a half dozen such girls. Locally they are viewed with contempt and much abused. A couple have nicknames that describe their place in the neighborhood; e.g., Angela "the Whore."

the other's moral status. Addams area residents regard this as desirable and morally correct. At the same time, however, they doubt that one's sexual urges can be so easily domesticated. Thus, instead of being uncertain about their sexual identity, they are probably more sure of it than almost anything else.[8]

Size

In the Addams area, street corner groups seldom included more than twenty members at any one time and averaged from twelve to fifteen members. There is, however, some transiency in any group, and their number will vary slightly from time to time. A group with twenty members may have included as many as twenty-five to thirty during its total lifetime. There are also a few "hangers-on" in addition to the regular members. It is not that the definition of membership is unclear but that, occasionally, another boy or two are considered safe or worthwhile associates. To the boys, there does not seem to be much ambiguity in this relationship, and they easily distinguish it from full membership.

The figures in table 9 include all members who belonged to the indicated groups over a one- to three-year period. Groups are included only if the ages of all or almost all the boys were known. A good number of the Italian boys are omitted; their birth dates were rather secret, and the other residents, along with several street workers, were unable to obtain them. However, the table includes a majority of all the groups in the area, and estimates obtained on the size of the remaining groups indicate they would fall within the same range.

At any one time, the number of members would almost never be as high as those given in table 9. If all groups had been studied for the same amount of time, these numbers might still reflect the relative size of each group. However, some of the data were gathered over a three-year period and some over a one- or two-year period.[9] Taking these difficulties into consideration, one may still make some observations.

[8] There is some tendency for social scientists to redefine the signs of masculinity to consist of such things as succeeding in school, sports, and work. In turn, fighting, fornication, and aggression are interpreted as "over-compensation," a sign of immaturity or latent homosexuality. It is interesting that gang boys make the counter-accusation that "headshrinkers" must be "fags" because of their polite and indirect manner.

The conflict between these two vocabularies of motives is clearly reported in Alfred C. Kinsey, *et al.*, *Sexual Behavior in the Human Male* (Philadelphia: W. B. Saunders, 1949), pp. 384–85.

[9] I found it completely impossible to take a census of each group at comparable age levels. Some groups did not exist during the entire period, and others were already older than any common age level I could select. Also, it took much longer to obtain the membership in some groups than in others.

TABLE 9

SIZE OF 21 STREET CORNER GROUPS

AGE GRADE	NAME OF GROUP	NUMBER OF MEMBERS OVER A ONE- TO THREE-YEAR PERIOD
Oldest (16–18)	Erls	29
	Jr. Princes	19
	Regents	25
	Magnificent Gallants	26
	Patricians	8
	Jr. Contenders	26
Intermediate (14–16)	Jr. Erls	13
	Stylists	18
	Etruscans	25
	Barracudas	17
	Pirates	18
	Cardinals	10
	Rapids	12
	Midget Gallants	15
	Meteors	21
Youngest (11–14)	Caballeros	8
	Miniature Stylists	14
	Roman Dukes	16
	Gutter Guys	19
	Etruscans	16
	Jr. Meteors	10

First, the range of group sizes is comparable to that of most of the groups reported by Thrasher.[10] None of the rare but extremely large groups with hundreds of members found by Thrasher are now present in the Addams area. While two such groups are said to exist in other parts of the city, they still seem to be rare.

Second, the largest group always seems to be one of the oldest groups within each ethnic territory. The Magnificent Gallants, Junior Contenders, and Erls are respectively the largest in each ethnic hierarchy. There are other groups in the same age level which are much smaller, but the largest group always seems to occur at this upper age range. The three largest groups also happen to be the three which were the most prominent and mutually antagonistic. Throughout 1963 and 1964 they were juxtaposed in a fairly well-defined opposition as the leading groups in their respective ethnic section.

Age

The age range for several groups is given in table 10 as a yearly deviation around the modal age of each group. The age range itself is fairly narrow

[10] Thrasher, *The Gang*, pp. 72–76.

TABLE 10

AGE DISTRIBUTION AMONG 21 STREET CORNER GROUPS*

ETHNIC IDENTITY OF GROUP	NUMBER BELOW AGE MODE			NUMBER AT GROUP AGE MODE	NUMBER ABOVE AGE MODE			UN-KNOWN
	3 OR MORE YEARS	2	1		1	2	3 OR MORE YEARS	
Mexican	3	12	35	80	47	25	3	6
Negro	1	7	24	36	16	5	3	4
Italian		1	10	24	14	3	3	2
Totals	4	20	69	140	77	33	9	12
Sub-total of "others"†		1	8	18	14	3	1	1

* For list of groups included, see table 9.
† All boys not of the same ethnicity as the majority of the boys in their group.

with about 79% of the members falling within a three-year range. Only about four per cent of the boys deviate from the modal age by three or more years. All this seems to follow the local view that "little boys" and "big boys" are dangerous to one another or unlikely to share any common interest.

In most groups the age distribution seems to be skewed slightly toward the upper rather than the lower age ranges. Thirty-five per cent of the boys fall above the modal age while 25% fall below it. Also, within each group, the boys who do not belong to the dominant ethnic group are either very close to the modal age or somewhat older; of forty-six boys, only five are more than one year from the modal age and four of these are above the mode. Thus, while the boys adhere rather closely to the modal age, there may be some preference for older boys, especially when they are not from the dominant ethnic group.

These findings again show the continuing importance given to age by those living in the Addams area. Like most of the groups studied by Thrasher, boys gravitate towards others of the same age.[11] This does not mean that the residents assign an outright, positive value to associations within a fairly narrow age range, but something like its reciprocal. Associations between boys of disparate ages are disapproved of because the older ones may "run over" the younger ones or "get them in trouble." Thus, it is probably because of their caution and concern for their children that many local parents perceive the peer group as the only alternative for association.

[11] *Ibid.*, pp. 72–76.

Ethnicity

The ethnic composition of each group is given in table 11. The ethnic identity of each group is always determined by the majority of its members. The Negro groups are entirely Negro, and of course this is the way they are identified in the neighborhood. In all the remaining groups, at least 50% of the members are from the ethnic group with which the group is identified.

TABLE 11

ETHNIC COMPOSITION OF 21 STREET CORNER GROUPS

ETHNIC IDENTITY OF GROUP	COMPOSITION				
	MEXICAN	ITALIAN	NEGRO	PUERTO RICAN	OTHER
Mexican	84% (179)	3% (6)	...	3% (7)	9% (20)
Italian	18% (10)	77% (44)	...	...	5% (3)
Negro	...	...	100% (96)	...	...
TOTAL	189	50	96	7	23

Together, the Mexican and Italian groups include forty-six boys from another ethnic group. Seven of these are Puerto Rican boys who belong to Mexican groups. Twenty-three are boys who are not from any of the four local ethnic groups: southern whites, Poles, and one Gypsy. The Puerto Ricans and "others" have no local groups of their own and must belong to one of the others if they belong to a group at all.

Ten Mexican and six Italian boys "cross over" to join groups identified with another ethnic group. These sixteen boys represent less than 5% of the area's street group membership, demonstrating that ethnic cleavages are indeed great. It is also apparent that boys tend to join upwards in terms of ethnic prestige. Whites never join a Negro group, and Puerto Ricans tend to join Mexican groups. Mexican boys occasionally join an Italian group, but Italian boys almost never join a Mexican group.

In most cases the accepted ethnic idenity of a group totally dominates its relations with groups from another ethnic section The minority members in each group are either overlooked or assumed to be like those of the majority. This seems largely due to the confinement of each group to its respective ethnic section and the residents' assumption that its membership is composed of the section's dominate group. The Barracudas, for example, were entirely Mexican, and this was well known to the Italian boys around Sheridan Park. Once they removed themselves from the park to the Puerto Rican section, however, many of the boys from the Mexican section thought they were Puerto Ricans.

Internally, however, differences of ethnicity can be a serious problem to a group. The Cardinals, a Mexican group, included three Italian boys whose parents strongly objected to their belonging to a Mexican group. After a short time, the Italian boys dropped out of the Cardinals.[12]

Residence

Unlike age, sex, and ethnicity, a boy's residence is subject to sudden and unanticipated shifts. Thus, these first three criteria can be used as stable principles of organization, but residence is less dependable. Still, it is fairly clear from table 12 that boys in the Addams area manage to preserve a considerable degree of territorial unity. About half (57%) of the members in the Mexican groups reside in the Mexican section. Almost all (93%) of the members in the Italian groups live in the Italian section. Nearly as many (87%) of the Negro boys live within their section.

The strong territorial unity of the Italian groups can be regarded as a result of their exclusivism. As the ranking ethnic group, they are in a good position to choose who can join them. The territorial unity of the Negroes, however, is more likely the result of their exclusion and overwhelming restriction to the Negro section. The Mexican boys, like their parents, are a "people in the middle" and are unable to take so exclusive a stand as the Italians. They accept many (23%) of their members from other sections in the Addams area. However, even they almost never accept a non-Mexican who lives in his own ethnic section. They have no Puerto Rican members who live in the Puerto Rican section, and only one of their six Italian members lives in his own section. Since the "others" do not have a local section of their own, their residency is not a matter of great concern to their host group.

In all the groups there are some members (17% to 4%) who do not live in the Addams area. In the few cases where complete information was available, these tended to be boys who (1) had once lived in the area or (2) were related by kinship to one of the other members in his group.

---

[12] The Gutter Guys included one boy whose mother was Negro and whose father was Mexican. In the group he "passed" as Negro and is included in that category in table 9. His brother, on the other hand, "passed" as Mexican and belonged to a Mexican group, the Barracudas. He is labeled as Mexican in table 8.

Although there are no whites in the Negro groups included in table 8, before 1962 two whites did belong to one very young Negro group (Hawks). However, as this group advanced in age, the white boys dropped out.

TABLE 12

RESIDENCE OF MEMBERS OF 21 STREET CORNER GROUPS

| ETHNIC IDENTITY OF GROUP | ETHNIC IDENTITY OF MEMBERS | ETHNIC SECTION OF RESIDENCE | | | | | | TOTALS |
		ITALIAN	MEXICAN	NEGRO	PUERTO RICAN	OUT OF AREA	UN-KNOWN	
Mexican	Mexican	15% (26)	58% (103)	4% (8)	5% (9)	15% (26)	4% (7)	100% (179)
	Puerto Rican	14% (1)	57% (4)			29% (2)		100% (7)
	Italian	17% (1)	50% (3)	17% (1)	17% (1)			100% (6)
	Other		55% (11)	5% (1)	5% (1)	35% (7)		100% (20)
Italian	Mexican	83% (10)				17% (2)		100% (12)
	Italian	100% (32)						100% (32)
	Other	100% (3)						100% (3)
Negro	Negro		1% (1)	88% (84)	1% (1)	10% (10)		100% (96)

In almost all groups, the number of members who live outside the neighborhood is quite small. In the Rapids, however, they made up almost half the group. Actually this was a rather odd group. First of all it had one female member. Also, the older groups (Gallants and Patricians) seemed to have regarded them with suspicion and disfavor, although they were too young to be rivals. Eventually two of the outsiders left the group and joined groups below Roosevelt Road. After an existence of about a year they disbanded altogether. Apparently their composition was simply too heterogeneous to produce a cohesive group. All the other groups lasted two or more years.

Among the Mexican groups, the Barracudas also stand out because of their residential location. Most of them live within a section which belongs to the Italians rather than the Mexicans. As indicated earlier, the Barracudas first installed themselves in the northwest corner of Sheridan Park but moved to the Puerto Rican section after relations with the local Italian groups became difficult. Since they had no comparable groups, the Puerto Ricans were unable to expel the Barracudas. By virtue of their residential location, they were unacceptable to the other Mexican groups. Having openly identified themselves as a Mexican group, they remained on equally bad terms with the Italians. Thus, the Barracudas were stranded with no friends and many enemies. In due course, they became extremely aggressive and openly embraced the values of fighting, destruction, and "toughness."[13] Yet, there was little they could actually do, since they were so surrounded by enemies. Their aggressive stance, however, seems to have arisen out of the incongruities between their residence, the place where they "hung," and their ethnic identity. Otherwise they were like most of the boys in the other groups—friendly and even protective once they knew you. Perhaps the best description of their situation was rendered by a phrase the boys would write on the walls around their hangout: "In Barracudas We Trust."

Despite the tendency of each group to form a residential unity, there is probably less uniformity here than in their sexual, chronological, and ethnic composition. Except for one member, all are males. Eighty-eight per cent of all the boys in table 12 belong to a group identified with their own ethnic group. Seventy-nine per cent are within about a year of the modal age. However, 60% live within the same local ethnic section to which their group belongs.[14] To a considerable degree, this is probably due to geographic mobility. Most of the groups appear to start with a membership that is highly localized. The data in table 13 seem to bear this out: the proportion of members who do not live in the local neighborhood increases as one advances up the age levels.

Since Addams area residents assume that persons who live in the same area will stick together, residential moves seriously affect group loyalties. The most common reason for a boy leaving his group seems to be a change of residence. Of thirty-four boys who were definitely known to have quit the groups listed in table 9, fourteen did so because they moved from the area. The remainder left for various reasons: seven went into military service; two left town for federal retraining programs; four got married; five got regular employment; one went to jail; and one quit simply because he did not want to belong to his group.

Except for the boy who quit on his own initiative, none of these thirty-four boys aroused any resistance when they left their group. This boy encountered a great deal of resentment among the other boys and the threat of a serious fight. The fight was averted by a local street worker, but only

---

[13] The boys made a coat of arms on which they wrote "Hate," "Kill," and similar directives. They also referred to the area around their hangout as a "turf." The term was never used by the other groups.

[14] However, about 88% of all members reside in the Addams area. It should be remembered here as elsewhere, that this is a very small area covering about a third of a square mile. The four ethnic sections within it make up much smaller areas.

TABLE 13

NUMBER AND PERCENTAGE OF MEMBERS WHO LIVE
OUTSIDE THE NEIGHBORHOOD FOR EACH AGE GRADE

| | RESIDENCE | | |
AGE GRADE	WITHIN ADDAMS AREA	OUTSIDE ADDAMS AREA	TOTALS
Oldest (16–18)	80% (107)	20% (26)	133
Intermediate (14–16)	88% (131)	12% (18)	149
Youngest (11–14)	100% (83)	... ...	83
Total	(321)	(44)	365

one of the boys in the group would later speak to the ex-member. Residential moves, however, always seem to be an acceptable reason for severing relations.

Residential changes are a serious problem to all members of a street corner group. Such changes force them to acknowledge the impermanence of their associations and their group life. They also present the possibility of divided loyalties and the necessity of constantly replenishing their membership. All of these are shared problems and affect equally those who have moved and those who have not.

Conclusion

In the Addams area, sex, age, ethnicity, and residence achieve an extraordinary importance in the eyes of the local boys. At one and the same time they mark off both the major cleavages between groups and the residual limits within which associations and trust are possible. These cleavages are based on such shared tenets as: girls should not be left alone with boys; "big boys" are too tough or a bad influence on younger ones; lower status ethnic groups are rightfully resentful and thus dangerous; other people are apt to look at the stranger as "fair game." Thus, both the residents' ideal morality and their realism tend to restrict stable associations to the local, single sex, ethnically homogeneous peer group.

In this sense, the street corner group is not a new invention but arises out of a very ancient moral tradition. Far more novel are the middle class practices of having children spend a great deal of time within their house-hold and of encouraging early cross-sex relations.[15]

If the distinctions of age, sex, residence, and ethnicity are sufficient to generate fairly cohesive and identifiable street corner groupings, there remains the question of why many Addams area boys never become affiliated with them. Of course, many—if not all—of the unaffiliated boys have a small clique of friends who regularly hang together. By most standards, however, they would not constitute a "gang." Within the Addams area, the thirty-two named street corner groups could accommodate only about half the local boys, assuming there is a 20% turnover of membership each year.

To give a tentative explanation of this disparity, it is necessary to retrace some of the critical problems in interpersonal relations in the Addams area. By most accounts, the lower class status of Addams area residents brings to them a certain humiliation because outsiders look down on them. This, however, is a debatable point,[16] and what seems to be most evident among them is a concern about each other's poverty, minority group status, poor education, ignorance, and lack of opportunity. Poverty, they are convinced, breeds amoral opportunism. Differential status on the basis of ethnicity is unjustified and sufficient to make anyone resentful and vindictive. A lack of education indicates an equal lack of self-discipline and ambition. Those whose opportunities are limited are sure to harbor anger and vengeance against those who have them. In deciphering each of these separate signs of lower class status, Addams area residents do not differ much from those in more affluent circumstances. As with most middle class people, it is easier to get them to accept everyone's theoretical equality than it is to get them to walk through a strange slum neighborhood after dark.

The central meaning attached to their slum residence, then, is a distrust,

[15] Throughout the works of Cohen (*Delinquent Boys* [Glencoe, Ill.: Free Press, 1955]) and Ohlin and Cloward (*Delinquency and Opportunity* [Glencoe, Ill.: Free Press, 1960]), one is never quite sure whether they are trying to account for the origin of the street corner group itself or of its "delinquent values." If these writers are attempting to account for the emergence of "delinquent values" among adolescent street corner groups, then these values may have developed in an altogether different type of group (for instance, adult criminal groups) and subsequently diffused to the adolescent street corner group. The street corner group itself seems to develop quite logically out of a heavy emphasis on age-grading, avoidance between the sexes, territorial unity, and ethnic solidarity.

[16] Otis D. Duncan ("A Critical Evaluation of Warner's Work in Community Stratification," *American Sociological Review* 15 [April, 1950], pp. 205–15), has argued quite reasonably that in our culture the separate characteristics of lower class status are not combined to produce a uniform definition of a whole category of people. He suggests that each of these characteristics (e.g., income, education) should be treated as logically independent because they are treated that way in our society. This, of course, does not deny that they may have a statistical or functional relationship.

fear, and uncertainty among people so long as they rely upon public signs to establish their expectations. The first and most obvious line of development is to search out those personal signs that indicate trustworthy associates. In most cases, this means establishing a personal relation in which there is a massive exchange of information and the creation of a private morality that binds them together. When large numbers of people are involved, however, this is not a practical solution.

Another alternative is to develop special or novel "markers" which set aside several persons and assign a determinate set of expectations to them as a group. Thus, instead of having to obtain personal information about each other one at a time, the residents can progress group by group. In this way, a fairly large number of people can be "known," some individually and some as representatives of a group. Whether these expectations indicate a course of trust or avoidance, they at least remove some of the indeterminacy in the neighborhood.

The named street corner group provides one of the ways in which the residents can be grouped together to reduce this problem of indeterminacy. It is not necessary, however, for all boys to belong to such groupings. Once a certain number of them have been placed in these groupings, the remainder will be small enough to allow management of their relations on a personal basis. Suppose, for example, that it is possible for an adolescent in the Addams area to recognize and know about 150 adolescents in that part of his neighborhood where most of his time is spent. At the same time, assume that there are about 2000 people who live in this area. About half of them will be females who are harmless by most people's standards. Another portion of the remainder, say two-thirds, will be too young or too old to be a danger for adolescents. By these calculations this still leaves about 330 male adolescents at the same age level who come into regular contact with each other. This is about 180 more than any one adolescent can know sufficiently well to negotiate within a fairly safe and determinate social world. If, however, about 190 of these adolescents are combined into ten named street-corner groups, it is again possible to "know everybody."[17] Thus, only about 190 boys within this age grade would need to belong to a named street corner group. The remainder could handle their relations on a personal basis.

The manner in which a particular boy becomes a member of a named street corner group then, may be almost entirely a stochastic process in which boys continue to form such groups until there is no one left in their area of routine movement of whom they do not have knowledge. Certainly

[17] Assuming that it is as easy to know one group of nineteen boys as it is to know personally a single boy.

this does not mean that the boys will set out, self-consciously, to settle the problem of anonymity by joining a street corner group. What is far more likely is that a boy will find himself among a fairly large number of others whom he does not know and whose behavior is uncertain. As a result, he restricts his movement and associations to a small group of boys whom he knows personally and who live close by. This alone will create several highly localized groups of boys who are identified with a special street location. Also, since it is impossible to identify all of the separate members of these groups, their street locations will often become convenient labels for identification. In the cross-fire of accusations and suspicions, some of these labels will be taken up by the boys themselves as well as by their opponents.

This process would continue until all the remaining boys outside such groups could be known personally and referred to by their individual names. From that point on, further group labeling would be redundant and unnecessary. Within this process, however, certain groups of boys would be more or less likely to acquire a label. Some might "hang" in a more conspicuous place than others. Several might live in the area for only a very short period and move before they could be incorporated in the local groups. In some cases, a boy's residence, ethnicity, and age may be so incongruous with that of the local groups that he is excluded from membership.[18] Occasionally parents may confine their children so near the household that they do not have peer friends.

Certainly the fact that such identities are often imposed from the outside does not mean that boys would not take pride in their group identity once established. Like almost any public identity, it becomes a sensitive issue, something that cannot be denied, and may need defending. Also, once established, such a series of group identities can become a reference for emulation and envy. For those who gain a name and "reputation" there is always the possibility that they will go on to merit it and thus become "heroes"; people whose claims to be above the limitations of ordinary humanity are proven. No doubt others will follow, attempting to fill the footsteps of their predecessors.

Within the Addams area, many younger boys were eager claimants to the public identity that a named group provided. In their casual street groupings they often proposed to each other different names for their group and some went so far as to tell others "who" they were. The ambitions of these younger boys, however, were regarded as only a sort of pretension so long as others were acquainted with them as individuals. Thus, many a street group's claim to a common identity simply was not acknowledged by

---

[18] For example, a relatively young Mexican boy living in the Italian section.

others and instead led to a good deal of ribbing; for example, "Shit, they ain't got no club. That's just Bobo, Macy, his brother, and . . . etc." After being made fun of for a week or so, almost all of the younger boys would stop bringing up their claim to a group identity. By contrast, even the most impermanent congregation of boys who were unknown could become the source of serious speculation; for instance, "Hey, did you see those guys? Are they from over on California (Avenue)? The Mighty C's?"

There are many difficulties with this argument and it is at best speculative. First, there is no reliable way of estimating the number of boys one person can know sufficiently well to have some definite expectations about them. Second, it is possible for boys to solve the problem by restricting the area and population within which they circulate. This solution has definite limits, however, because most very small areas (for instance, a single block) would not include a full complement of the institutions necessary to adolescent life. Third, there is no way of establishing the age range within which boys are considered sufficiently dangerous to each other that anonymity is a serious problem to them. The information needed is (1) the age a boy has to be before other boys consider him dangerous and (2) the age beyond which males are assumed to know better than to hurt wantonly other people.

Finally, by most standards the named street corner gang seems a poor solution to the problems of anonymity and distrust. If there is a serious indeterminancy in the expectations shared by adolescents, then it would seem more desirable to mark off "peaceful" rather than "dangerous" groupings. This, however, is a serious misconception about how street-corner groups are regarded by the residents. Within the inner city the members of the white SAC's and the Negro social clubs are hardly the unruly and unreachable youths that we are led to expect. Often they are the best-known and most popular boys in the neighborhood. They sponsor almost all the local dances and parties. Nearly always they form the local league of ball teams. They provide much of the excitement of street life and dominate most of the local youth agencies. Adults cheer on their ball teams, and girls eagerly attend their dances. In general, people find it flattering to know them. They may be tough, but that is hardly a fault in the inner city.[19]

Each of these points is only *ad hoc* repair work on an argument that was speculative at the start. The argument has a certain credibility, however, in view of the most obvious characteristics of street corner groups. Almost all

[19] It might be pointed out that in W. F. Whytes' *Street Corner Society* (Chicago: University of Chicago Press, 1955), pp. 194–252, Doc eventually decided to run for public office. His popularity and general respect are hard to understand unless acquired as leader of the "Norton Street gang."

of their names include a reference to the location where they "hang." In no case do they seem to include more than a portion of the adolescents in a particular neighborhood. Alternatively, no study has been able to show any dramatic differences between gang and non-gang boys from the same area.[20]

This entire approach to gang formation reaches back to an earlier one which emphasized transiency, population density, ethnic succession, uncertain property values, and so on.[21] In this study, however, these conditions are not simply regarded as corollaries to a process of population selection or deeper pyschological problems. Instead they are taken to play a direct role in the casual matrix of delinquency and gang behavior. Transiency among slum residents creates anonymity in which knowing other people is often felt to be the only guarantee to one's safety. It affects the transient and the nontransient alike, and either of them may resort to coercion and opportunism if their suspicions seem to warrant it. Similarly, population density can be so great that the majority of residents cannot know each other, even if some of them happen to have comfortable and roomy homes. Population shifts and ethnic succession cast into doubt all the little assumptions that people have been able to make about the usage of local parks, their rights to specific locations, and the importance of certain boundaries. In the breach, the street corner group emerges as one of the more obvious social groupings whose behavior can be anticipated.

The function of the named street corner group in counteracting anonymity where personal acquaintance is out of reach points up the importance of personal knowledge whenever it is practicable. Addams area residents often know a wide arc of people personally and appeal to group identities only as a last resort. This practice places great emphasis upon individual identities, intimate personal disclosures, and a close adherence to those personal precedents that have been laid down. The local street corner groups are private worlds in which personal precedents can become known and binding. The street corner groups not only make their members known to the remainder of the neighborhood, but create a network of personal acquaintances that augment those already in existence.

[20] James F. Short, *et al.*, "Perceived Opportunities, Gang Membership, and Delinquency," *American Sociological Review*, 30 (February, 1965): 56–57.

[21] Clifford Shaw and Henry McKay, *Juvenile Delinquency and Urban Areas* (Chicago: University of Chicago Press, 1942).

10

Primary Groups
and Personal Identities

In most ways the adolescent street corner group is like any other primary group in which personal loyalties exist alongside several general rules and public demands.[1] Military units, work groups, fraternities, and even families follow this pattern. There are, however, certain critical differences between street-corner groups and other primary groups. Military units and other primary groups are embedded in a larger framework of formal relations in which they are regularly called upon to give an accounting of themselves. Moreover, they have an internal formal structure of their own that is approved by the wider society.

According to some authorities, the street corner group also possesses an explicit set of norms comparable to those of any other group. Others go further to suggest that the street corner group is embedded in a larger matrix of lower class values and roles which serve as a positive incentive for their behavior. Either viewpoint leaves the impression that the street corner group is a kind of mirror image of conventional groups. This is quite misleading if taken to represent the boys' own outlook. The boys see their groups as a series of individual histories, each of which is linked to some of the others. Relations with the wider community are often hostile since most of the directives they receive from the wider community take the form of proscriptions rather than prescriptions.

Norms and Uniformity of Behavior

In the Addams area it is extremely rare for a boy to mention anti-social behavior as the avowed purpose of his group, whether the inquiry is made in the boy's confidence or in a public situation. Also, the term "gang" is almost never used as a label for their *own* group even in private conversations

[1] George Homans, *The Human Group* (New York: Harcourt, Brace and Co., 1950); E. A. Shils, "Primary Groups in the American Army," in *Continuities in Social Research: Studies in the Scope and Method of "The American Soldier*," ed. R. K. Merton and P. F. Lazarsfeld (Glencoe, Ill.: Free Press, 1950), pp. 16–39.

among themselves. Among the whites, a named street-corner group is almost invariably called a "SAC" (Social Athletic Club), while among the Negroes, the term "Social Club" is equally common. Neither of these labels are meant to convey an anti-social purpose, but emphasize the boys' interests in sports, dances, parties, and mutual association.

Few of the local groups have even a rudimentary set of explicit rules which a member is expected to obey whether or not they meet his personal inclinations. By and large, the boys view their group as the happy coincidence of their individual inclinations. When they cannot assume this sort of spontaneous cohesion, the group tends either to split up into cliques that go their own way or to lapse into indecision and inactivity. This, of course, does not mean that the boys can never assume a set of common purposes. Their unity of action is limited to those occasions when they feel they can depend upon each other's personal character rather than on mere compliance with social rules. In fact, the boys usually doubt each other's willingness or ability to obey such rules. For example, it was nearly impossible for most street workers to get the boys to contribute to a common treasury because they had no faith that the other members would contribute to it. Even when the boys concede the necessity of such a fund, the street worker usually found himself the only person trusted with their joint savings.

Similarly, it was exceedingly difficult to get most groups to decide on issues by voting on them. This was especially true of the Italian and Mexican groups; the Junior Contenders, Junior Regents, Meteors, and Erls all dismissed such decision-making techniques as "bullshit." The Negro boys seemed more amenable to such methods, and a few groups went so far as to make an attempt at following "Robert's Rules of Order." Once their street worker was gone, however, they also seemed to lose any faith in each other's willingness to obey such rules.

The selection of officers in each group met with similar difficulties. At one time or another almost every group acquired its "social worker"[2] and was faced with the request to elect "officers": a president, vice-president, and treasurer.[3] Among the Italian boys this was often a fruitless gesture, and they usually resisted open definitions of their place in the group. The white boys had almost no explicit internal differentiation in the form of roles and rules that were binding despite differences in opinion. Officers, when acknowledged at all, were always imposed from the outside. In most Negro groups, there was usually someone designated as their "president," and

---

[2] The term "social worker" is used almost exclusively by the Negro boys. Both the Negro and white boys speak of their "sponsor."

[3] Among the Negro boys, they sometimes elect two more officers: a secretary and sergeant-at-arms.

for a short time, one group had a "war counselor." In either case the process of selection was obscure. According to the boys, they simply picked the "right guy."

Tables 14,15, 16, and 17 give some idea of how uniform certain types of behavior are in a number of street corner groups. These tables report on only four types of street corner activities: "hanging," fighting, stealing,

TABLE 14
FIGHTING

GROUP		SURE TO BE THERE	THEY WOULD DEPEND ON HIM BUT HE MIGHT NOT SHOW	HE MIGHT OR MIGHT NOT; THEY WOULDN'T DEPEND ON HIM	HE'D CUT OUT FOR SURE	NOT ASCERTAINED OR UNKNOWN	TOTALS
Older Mexican Groups							
Erls		23	2	2		2	29
Regents		8	10	6	1		25
Subtotal	N	31	12	8	1	2	54
	%	57	22	14	2	4	100
Younger Mexican Groups							
Junior Erls		7	4			2	13
Stylists		16				2	18
Barracudas		6	9		2		17
Roman Dukes		1	4	11			16
Subtotal	N	30	17	11	2	4	64
	%	47	27	17	3	6	100
Oldest Negro Group							
Magnificent Gallants	N	8	10	6	1	1	26
	%	31	38	23	4	4	100
Younger Negro Groups							
Rapids		4	2	4	1	1	12
Midget Gallants		4	9	2			15
Gutter Guys		6	10	3			19
Subtotal	N	14	21	9	1	1	46
	%	30	46	20	2	2	100
Oldest Italian Group							
Junior Contenders	N	13	11			2	26
	%	50	42			8	100
Youngest Italian Group							
Meteors	N	10	8	2		1	21
	%	48	38	10		4	100
TOTAL	N	106	79	36	5	11	237
	%	45	33	15	2	5	100

TABLE 15

"Hanging"

Group	He's sure to be there if anyone's there	Usually there; they expect him to show	Might or might not be there; they wouldn't depend on him	Would be there only if something special was happening	Rare; they'd never depend on him or wait for him	Almost never there; they'd be surprised to see him show	Never hangs with them	Not ascertained or unknown	Totals
Older Mexican Groups									
Erls	11	8	4	3	1			2	29
Regents	6	9	5	4	1				25
Subtotal N	17	17	9	7	2			2	54
%	31	31	17	13	4			4	100
Younger Mexican Groups									
Junior Erls	4	2	2	2	1		2		13
Stylists	8	7	2				1		18
Barracudas	7	5	2	3					17
Roman Dukes		6	5	5					16
Subtotal N	19	20	11	10	1		3		64
%	30	31	17	16	2		5		100
Oldest Negro Group									
Magnificent Gallants N	3	3	6	9	1	3		1	26
%	12	12	23	35	4	12		4	100
Younger Negro Groups									
Rapids	8	2		2					12
Midget Gallants	8	2	2	3					15
Gutter Guys	7	7	4	1					19
Subtotal N	23	11	6	6					46
%	50	24	13	13					100
Oldest Italian Group									
Junior Contenders N	7	8	8				1	2	26
%	27	31	31				4	7	100
Youngest Italian Group									
Meteors N	9	5	3	1	2			1	21
%	43	24	14	5	10			5	100
Total N	78	64	43	33	6	3	4	6	237
%	33	27	16	14	3	1	2	3	100

and drinking. All of the judgments were made with the help of local adults working with each group as a social worker or sponsor. The final figures in each table were arrived at after three of more interviews. On the first interview, the worker was simply asked to make certain judgments on each boy.

TABLE 16

DRINKING

Group	Sure to be there; they wouldn't believe it if he turned it down	More likely than not; they'd depend on him	Might or might not; they wouldn't depend on him	Doubtful; would be surprised if he showed up	Doesn't drink	Not ascertained or unknown	Totals
Older Mexican Groups							
Erls	9	9	8			3	29
Regents	6	6	6	3	4		25
Subtotal N	15	15	14	3	4	3	54
%	28	28	26	6	7	6	100
Younger Mexican Groups							
Junior Erls	5	2	4			2	13
Stylists	7	4	3	3		1	18
Barracudas	7	5	3	2			17
Roman Dukes	4	3	1	5	3		16
Subtotal N	23	14	11	10	3	3	64
%	36	22	17	16	5	5	100
Oldest Negro Group							
Magnificent Gallants N	5	1	8	3	8	1	26
%	19	4	34	12	34	4	100
Younger Negro Groups							
Rapids	2	1	4	4	1		12
Midget Gallants	7	3	2	1	2		15
Gutter Guys	4	6	7	2			19
Subtotal N	13	10	13	7	3		46
%	28	22	28	15	7		100
Oldest Italian Group							
Junior Contenders N	10	10	3	1		2	26
%	38	38	12	4		8	100
Youngest Italian Group							
Meteors N	3	6	7	4		1	21
%	14	29	33	19		5	100
TOTAL N	69	56	56	28	18	10	237
%	29	24	24	12	7	4	100

The second interview repeated the same request. This time, however, discrepancies between the first and second judgments were discussed with the informant. An agreement was reached to have the group sponsor observe closely those boys on which there were discrepant judgments. Later a third set of judgments was made. If there were no discrepancies between the

TABLE 17
STEALING

GROUP		SURE TO BE IN ON IT; THEY'D WAIT FOR HIM	LIKELY; THEY'D ASK HIM BUT HE MIGHT NO 1-11 GO WITH THEM	MIGHT OR MIGHT NOT; THEY WOULDN'T DEPEND ON HIM	DOUBTFUL; THEY WOULDN'T EXPECT IT OF HIM	ALMOST NEVER; THEY'D BE SURPRISED IF HE DID	NOT ASCERTAINED OR UNKNOWN	TOTALS
Older Mexican Groups								
Erls		5	7	7	7		3	29
Regents		6	6	5	6	1	1	25
Subtotal	N	11	13	12	13	1	4	54
	%	20	24	22	24	1	8	100
Younger Mexican Groups								
Junior Erls		5	2	1	3		2	13
Stylists		3	8	2	3	2		18
Barracudas		6	4	2	2	2	1	17
Roman Dukes		1		4	6	5		16
Subtotal	N	15	14	9	14	9	3	64
	%	23	22	14	22	14	5	100
Oldest Negro Group								
Magnificent Gallants	N	3	5	10	4	2	2	26
	%	12	19	38	15	8	8	100
Younger Negro Groups								
Rapids		4	2	4	1	1		12
Midget Gallants		4	4	6		1		15
Gutter Guys		9	4	4	2			19
Subtotal	N	17	10	14	3	2		46
	%	37	22	30	7	4		100
Oldest Italian Group								
Junior Contenders	N	10	4	8	1	1	2	26
	%	38	15	31	4	4	8	100
Youngest Italian Group								
Meteors	N	3	6	7	1	3	1	21
	%	14	29	33	5	14	5	100
TOTAL	N	59	52	60	36	18	12	237
	%	25	22	25	15	8	5	100

second and third set of judgments, they were accepted as valid. Otherwise, the boys were placed in the "unknown" category.

The figures in these tables do not indicate how frequently the boys actually indulged in these various types of behavior. Instead they measure each boy's behavior according to whether or not the others could depend on him *if* one of the four activities was in progress. Thus, questions and answers were always framed in this way: if the boys are drinking, (1) he's sure to be there; (2) they'd wait for him and expect him to show; (3) he might or might not show but they wouldn't depend on him; (4) he wouldn't show, or they would be surprised if he did; or (5) he doesn't drink.

There are minor variations between ethnic groups, but in all of them fighting is the one activity which most nearly draws the boys together into concerted behavior. About 78% of all group members are either "sure" to be present or considered "dependable." Only about 2% are sure to "cut out" and not fight. In most other activities there is considerable variation ranging from extreme deviance to extreme conformity. Generally, the most "dependable" end of the scale claims the largest single grouping: 33% in the case of "hanging" and 25% in the case of stealing. Only about 2% of the boys never "hang" with the remainder, and only 5% never steal. Still, within these limits, there is great variability. Only 47–60% are "dependable" participants in "hanging," drinking, and stealing. A sizable proportion fall into an intermediate range where their behavior is unsure. For stealing, this reaches 40%; for drinking, it declines to 24%.

Whatever the source of this variation, it is not easily explained on the basis of age or group membership. The younger boys in each ethnic group are not consistently more or less dependable than the older ones. In no group are boys uniformly dependable or undependable in all activities. In the case of "hanging," drinking, and fighting there are some differences between ethnic groups. The Italian boys are somewhat more concentrated in the two "dependable" categories.[4] The Negro boys are the least concentrated in these two categories, while the Mexicans fall between them and the Italians (see table 18). These differences tend to follow other patterns discernible in each ethnic section, the Italians being the most solid territorial unit, while the Negroes are the most transient, anonymous, and

[4] This sort of formalism was most noticeable among the Magnificent Gallants, the only group which possessed a "war counselor." This was also the least uniform group in its behavior. Only between 23 to 69% fall into "dependable" categories. For the same activities, this range is somewhat higher for all groups except for the Roman Dukes.

While on this point, it is worth mentioning that almost any attempt to reduce formal social ruling to the personal dispositions of individuals flies in the face of reason. So long as personal dispositions seem to support existing norms, their formalization seems purely gratuitous. It is only when we doubt the "good intentions" of other people that we erect the strictures of formality. This is the central fault of Homan's and Schneider's attempt to reduce formal social rules to personal inclinations (*Marriage, Authority and Final Causes: A Study of Unilateral Cross-Cousin Marriage* [Glencoe, Ill.: Free Press, 1955]). If personal inclinations tended to coincide with formal rulings, the latter would seem only a redundant "projection."

TABLE 18
PROPORTION OF BOYS WHO ARE CONSIDERED DEPEND-
ABLE PARTICIPANTS IN FOUR SPECIFIC ACTIVITIES
(FIRST TWO CATEGORIES IN TABLES 14–17)

ACTIVITY		NEGRO	MEXICAN	ITALIAN
Fighting	N	70	112	45
	%	74	77	90
"Hanging"	N	71	116	44
	%	40	61	62
Drinking	N	71	112	44
	%	40	57	62
Stealing	N	70	111	44
	%	49	45	49

distrustful. Among the adolescents themselves, the Negro boys were the most likely to resort to an explicit and formal attempt to insure uniform behavior. The Italian and Mexican groups openly resisted attempts to establish formal offices or rules that could compel uniform behavior. Apparently it is those groups whose members can least depend upon one another that resort to the more forceful tactics of formalization.

As a group activity, stealing stands out because of the small number of boys that it seems to draw together. Among all three ethnic groups, just less than half the boys are "dependable" participants. Among the Mexicans and Italians this is the lowest figure for any activity. Among the Negroes it is about the same as for drinking and "hanging," although the proportion involved is about the same as for the other ethnic groups. Thus, in all groups, stealing cannot be carried out under the automatic assumption that all the other members will cooperate, offer support, or "go along" with the activity. It must be especially important, then, that the members in each group "feel out" one another before going headlong into such mercenary ventures. Such a procedure is unlikely to result in much planned theft or heavy group involvement in stealing. Instead, most Addams area groups seem drawn together more by private pleasures ("hanging" and drinking) and conflict than by some instrumental task.

One conclusion from these findings seems almost inescapable: within each group great uniformity of behavior is not expected, nor does it occur. Only the few understandings listed below reach such a level of explicitness that they could be called "rules" or "norms."

1. The group has a "hangout" where one member can expect to find at least some of the others.

2. Some groups are allied with girls' groups or younger boys' groups by shared names.

3. Among the Negro groups there is usually a president and, in one group, a "war counselor." Among the white groups, formal offices are either lacking or acknowledged only during meetings with an adult sponsor.

4. Occasionally, *ad hoc* alliances develop between groups for some specific purpose or for a limited time period.

5. Within each ethnic section, age-grading establishes a stable hierarchy in which older groups are not challenged by younger ones.

With such a meager list it is fairly obvious that the boys rely on something other than explicit rules to establish common procedures and goals. Typically, when some of the boys arrive at their hangout during the afternoon, there is no previous agreement about what they are going to do. Generally, the practice is simply to "come on the scene" and ask "what's happening." From then on, joint activities emerge crescively as situations present themselves. Probably the most frequent activity is gossiping about people in the neighborhood. On a Friday (payday) some of the older boys may "chip in" for some beer or wine. From time to time they may start "rapping" or insulting one another. Sometimes they pitch pennies for an hour or two. During weekends there may be a local dance or social, and some of them may go there. Often someone in the older groups will own a car, and all the guys will "pile in" and go for a ride around the neighborhood, yelling and waving at the girls and other boys they know.[5] Occasionally, all those present will rise and go to the nearby beefstand, the Tastee Freeze, the Good Humor truck, or a hot dog stand. If there is a fight, a fire, or wreck, everybody—adults and adolescents—runs to see it. Sometimes there are games: "babies," "ringoliva," "war," and so on.

During the summer, ball games attract a sizable audience. If a policeman stops someone, everyone around gathers to see what will happen. Three or four boys may wander over to the home of one of their girlfriends and sit with her on the front steps. A few times each week their social worker will drop by and take them for a ride or get them to hold a meeting. Peddlers come by and sell a nickel's worth of peanuts or pistachios. One week each year the Italians' carnival draws many boys to the rides, dart games, and improvised roulette wheel. The Mexicans' fiesta and parade last a day each. In early 1964, glue-sniffing became popular, but by the next summer it was

---

[5] The Italians seem to have greater access to cars than any other group. The Italian girls may have a car, and it is common to see a group of them driving back and forth on Taylor Street. The usual practice is to drive around the neighborhood and, especially, up and down Taylor Street. Some boys spend the entire evening at it.

almost out of fashion. Card playing in doorways, roughhousing, and record playing are more enduring activities.

Accompanying all these little episodes is a continuing line of conversation —bawdy, irreverent, and earthy. Often they talk about each other, and there is a good deal of boasting and insulting anecdotes. Among the Negro and Mexican boys, when such banter becomes highly stylized, it is called "signifying." When other people in the neighborhood come up for discussion, they are treated in much the same disparaging way.

Lacking anything like a daily agenda or a clearly defined set of group values, each group operates largely with a set of amoral assumptions and precedents that help define each situation. These assumptions and precedents, however, are equally well-known by the older residents. There is, for example, the general belief that each named group is up to something, acting tough, or in need of a strong hand. Specific group antagonisms are well-known, and group reputations are widespread. The location, movement, and age of each group can be interpreted by most of the residents. For instance, if a Mexican group is seen around Sheridan Park, people assume they are looking for trouble. When the boys enter a store, the management immediately takes precautions against shoplifting. If a group of boys are seen "hanging" in a dark alley, it "means" they are drinking. If the boys approach a girl, they are "on the make." When they "hang on the corner" they are just "wasting their time."[6]

Expectations of this kind are shared by all the street-corner groups, but neither the boys nor the adults would describe such behavior as desirable or socially acceptable. Instead, they are convinced that such behavior is an unavoidable fact of life, and arguments to the contrary are dismissed as "soft-headed." Since these assumptions are held with such strong convictions and are often couched in a naturalistic vocabulary of motives, they are seldom doubted in the same way that moral rules or formal agreements are challenged. To the residents they are a law of nature rather than laws invented by man. One cannot "break" such "laws" any more than one can violate the laws of physics. Thus, the residents tend to meet each situation with a definiteness that usually excludes any attempt to alter or redefine the situation.

[6] These expectations are shared equally by the police, sociologists, judges, lower class adults, and the boys themselves. Thus, it makes little sense to ask how delinquent "values" originated unless we consider both the street-corner group *and its audiences.* What is at issue is the definition of a set of *signs* associated with a named male, adolescent congregation that has certain distinctive styles of dress, deportment, and language. As to the interpretation of these signs, one could argue that the police, sociologists, and "invaded group" have been more active than the street-corner groups themselves in assigning such a meaning to their appearance.

Personal Identities

Despite the amoral nature of these expectations, they are nonetheless effective in regulating the boys' behavior. From the boys' point of view, the problem they face is whether they will "live up" to these expectations or "back down" from them. To those confronting the boys, the immediate problem is to adopt some sort of defensive maneuver that will "put the boys back in their place." Thus, on either side there is a tendency to resort to coercive methods, since it is assumed that normative solutions have already been cast aside.[7] Denials, disbelief, protestations, appeals to morality, and attempts to be friendly take on the appearance of evasions or cowardice.

These expectations are usually sufficient to define the street-corner group's relations with others in the neighborhood. It is very rare, however, for these widespread beliefs and stereotypes to concern the internal arrangements of each group. A very few boys are widely known for their leadership; in all other cases, however, relative rank, prestige, and leadership have to be settled by the boys themselves. Also, there are such problems as internal disputes, new members to be accommodated, and the simple decision of what to do among themselves. In meeting these exigencies the boys must have some sort of prior understanding of what they can expect from one another. Obviously, these expectations are not grouped together and designated by formal roles or a set of all-embracing rules.

Despite the absence of explicit rules and any impersonal division of labor, the boys seem to possess a vast and detailed set of preconceptions about what each member is apt to do. In the eyes of a boy, however, these are not "role expectations" but a sure knowledge of each other's "true," personal character. In this sense, their expectations are tailored to each individual by the precedents, promises, and commitments laid down in his known history.

This importance attached to "remaining true" to one's established identity is readily apparent in most groups.[8] If a member behaves inconsistently in terms of what is expected of him he is not criticized or disturbed about doing something "wrong," but merely disbelieved or suspected of being "phony" or a "con artist." When street workers attempt to introduce explicit roles, like president or secretary, the boys tend to think them

---

[7] Throughout most of the literature there is a tendency to identify all "expectations" with *socially approved expectations*. However, a vast number of our expectations are completely amoral. Where relationships are defined by such expectations, the problem for either side is purely technical. Within this limited context, both parties have lost any public image of self that could be preserved by moral propriety. In this case, incidentally, it becomes quite inappropriate to characterize each party's role as a set of "rights and duties."

[8] See R. Turner, "Role Taking: Process Versus Conformity," in *Human Behavior and Social Processes*, ed. A. Rose (Boston: Houghton Mifflin., 1962), pp. 20–40.

very funny. Apparently, the incongruity of someone "playing his part" is too much for them and "breaks them up." Thus, when elected to an office, most boys find it almost impossible to keep a "straight face."

Effective authority within the group is almost always exercised as a personal prerogative. Authority is vested in the individual rather than in a formal role and a person's leadership is justified by his force of character instead of by his agreed-upon duties and situational requirements.[9] From the boys' point of view this is entirely reasonable. They have great faith in each other's personal character and in the interests which lead people to "act big," seek their own advantage, or become greedy. Someone who claims to be acting only out of a sense of duty or to serve their common welfare is thoroughly suspect. One who claims to be acting out of altruism is seriously questioned, while an overt "strong man" is considered far more dependable and effective.[10]

By tailoring their expectations to each other's personal character, it should not be assumed that the boys have actually discovered one another's basic personality or "true" self-concept. Here, these terms are used in their colloquial rather than their technical sense.[11] What the boys seem to do is to select out of their common history certain "diagnostic events" which they dramatize into signs that foretell one's "true" self and potential patterns of behavior. Just what these diagnostic events might be and the variety of self-concepts they can yield is still something of a mystery.

In this connection, it is profitable to look back at one of the classical experiments carried out by Lippitt, Polansky, and Rosen.[12] In this study, several lower-class boys who were unknown to each other beforehand were taken to a summer camp. A similar number of middle-class boys were taken to a different camp. In each group, after the boys had a chance to look one another over, they were asked to judge each other's fighting ability. At this time, both groups made choices based primarily on physical size.

---

[9] Robert D. Hess, ("Culture and Cognition," unpublished paper, delivered at the Symposium of The Committee on Human Development, Center for Continuing Education, University of Chicago, June 4, 1965) has shown that demands and disciplinary statements among lower income groups generally take the form of unjustified imperatives rather than requests which are "explained" as situational or collective necessities.

[10] These views lead to what seems a curious complaint about many school teachers. Often the boys will condemn a particular teacher because she can't "make nobody behave." On the other hand, a teacher who is a strict disciplinarian is often respected. Apparently, the boys have little faith in others behaving properly without the presence of a "strong man."

[11] For more extensive discussion of this problem see Hsien Chin Hu, "The Chinese Concepts of Face," *American Anthropologist*, 46 (January–March, 1944): 45–64. The distinction here is between an emic and etic concept of personality.

[12] Ronald Lippitt, Norman Polansky, and Sidney Rosen, "The Dynamics of Power," *Human Relations*, 5 (Winter, 1952): 37–64.

Subsequently, however, a second set of judgments on fighting ability yielded a positive correlation with physical size only among the middle-class subjects. Lippitt and his associates conclude quite reasonably that among the middle-class subjects, "where fighting hardly ever occurs, the perception of fighting is really a perception of potential fighting ability and is based on the most obvious cues of physical size." Among the lower-class subjects, "where a good deal of fighting takes place, the perception is actually based on performance which probably does not correlate very highly with physical size or age in such a relatively homogeneous age population as a cabin group."[13]

In minor form this experiment dramatizes the difference between the situations that confront middle- and lower-class adolescents. Middle-class youths can and do depend upon public signs as a basis for establishing a reliable "pecking order" which they never question afterwards. The lower-class youths, on the other hand, have to test these stereotypes or live with the dangers attached to their apparent poverty, low ethnic status, residential locations, and the like. In a small way the lower-class boys created a piece of what we call a "sub-culture," a set of private understandings about one another's fighting ability, while middle-class boys continued to behave on the basis of public stereotypes. This is the difference between deduction and induction, between idealism and realism, between nominalism and operationalism. It is also the difference between having a "rep" and having a role, between what is and what ought to be, and between a "subculture" and "the culture."

The study of Lippitt and his collaborators suggests that on the second set of judgments the lower-class boys accurately estimated each other's actual fighting ability. In fact, any two boys probably fought only once or twice and many of the boys may have inferred their relative fighting ability by assuming something like a "law of transitivity."[14] From a statistician's viewpoint their sampling may have been miserable and their assumption of transitivity unwarranted. Thus, the "pecking order" established by the lower-class boys was probably as arbitrary as the *a priori* one of the middle-class boys. The fact that their judgments may not be absolutely accurate, however, need not disturb this order so long as everyone accepts it.

Once a group in the Addams area has determined the character of its members, the members can maneuver in a well-known order with some certainty. Some boys are known to be good fighters, others are said to be able to talk to adults, or to "get the guys serious." To the boys, these talents

[13] *Ibid.*, pp. 56–58.
[14] The use of such rules is discussed at length by Roger Brown, *Social Psychology* (Glencoe, Ill.: Free Press, 1965), pp. 21–43.

are personal gifts and cannot be conferred by elections or arbitrary assignments. In actual fact, of course, their discovery of these personal gifts may be based on quite trivial and exceptional observations. To the boys, however, their personal identities provide a real social world; and whether their place in the group tends to be a favorable or unfavorable one, they are not believed if they attempt to escape it. The condemnation for being a phony is far greater than that for being a "nobody." What is important for the group is the preservation of a common order, not one's particular place in it.

Such a personalistic social order has some obvious weaknesses. For one thing, members cannot be shuttled about arbitrarily to fit all those places necessary to the group. Good fighters cannot be made by acclamation. Leaders cannot be elected. The task of moderator cannot simply be assigned. Over time, each of these capacities must be discovered among their membership. When someone leaves, he cannot be replaced until another is discovered. Similarly a new member cannot be placed within the group until he is "really" known. Thus, transiency, attrition, or a flood of new recruits are apt to disrupt the group's pattern of cohesion far more than in a formal organization where people can simply pass through a series of permanent positions.

Pattern of Cohesion

Since Addams area street corner groups lack a well-defined set of roles for establishing mutual obligations, their pattern of cohesion must be worked out in face-to-face relations with one another. The result is a combination of affiliations which overlap one another and extend in somewhat separate directions. Of the twelve groups closely studied over a two-year period, the Erls provide an illustrative case that includes all the complexities observed. In 1963, the Erls included eighteen Mexican boys and one Polish boy (see figure 1). In the view of the other named street corner groups, the Erls were a Mexican group, the oldest and most prominent north of Taylor Street. They were allied with the Junior Erls and Erlettes. The Regents, another Mexican group that "hung" south of Taylor Street, were their competitors but not their enemies.

The Erls had no formal roles until a street worker pressed them to elect officers. At the time, the boys complied by electing K-Man president and Baker vice-president. At their next meeting with the street worker a week later, Baker did not attend, and K-Man at first refused to act as president and later joined the others in tearing up all the furniture in the meeting place. A week later, in the continued absence of Baker, the boys conceded reluctantly to elect a vice-president, but K-Man refused to act as president.

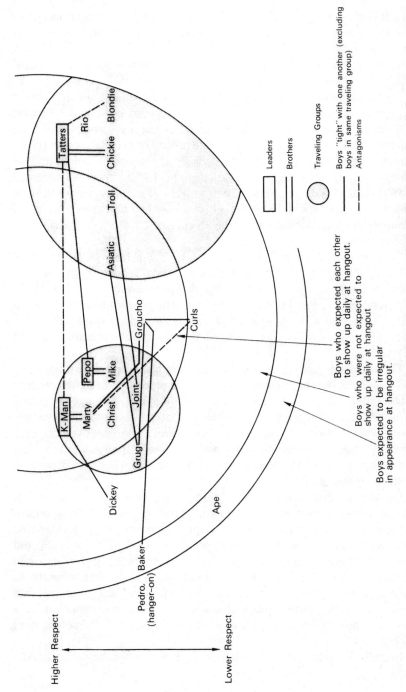

Higher Respect

Lower Respect

Tatters

Rio

Blondie

Chickie

Asiatic

Troll

Groucho

K-Man

Pepo

Marty

Christ

Mike

Joint

Grug

Curls

Dickey

Ape

Pedro.
(hanger-on)

Baker

Leaders

Brothers

Traveling Groups

Boys "tight" with one another (excluding boys in same traveling group)

Antagonisms

Boys who expected each other to show up daily at hangout.

Boys who were not expected to show up daily at hangout

Boys expected to be irregular in appearance at hangout.

FIG. 1. Pattern of Relationships Among the Erls: 1963

At a fourth meeting, all the boys refused to acknowledge these roles, referring to them as a "bunch of bullshit." From then on the status of officers
was forgotten.

Of the nineteen boys in the group, nine were almost always at the Erls'
hangout, and their absence was an occasion for inquiry: "Where's Pepo?"
"Hey man, what were you doing last night?" Seven other boys were almost
as regular in their attendance at the Erls' hangout but could be truant
without arousing comment. Their infrequent absences were accepted for a
variety of individual reasons. Dickey had a brother outside the group with
whom he spent some of his time. Grug worked and was the sole supporter
of his family. Curls had several girlfriends. Rio had a fiancée. Chickie was
a good student and had to study. When absent, Tatters was assumed to be
with his brother Chickie. Blondie, a Polish boy, had no close friend in the
group except for Chickie, and in the absence of Chickie, no one asked his
whereabouts.

Two boys in the group, Baker and Ape, were irregular in their attendance
at the Erls' hangout, and the other members did not plan on their appearance on every occasion. Ape was regarded as generally unreliable; Baker
was very trusted but known to have interests (illegal) elsewhere. Pedro
was a hanger-on with the group and included as a participant only on his
own initiative or when the absence of other members made his help
necessary.

These "hanging groups" were an important basis for anticipating future
activities since they established who would be present. When attempting to
foresee whom they could depend on in case of a fight, a dance, or meeting
with their street worker, the boys would tick off names in a definite order:
those "sure to show," those "usually here," and those "guys you can't tell
about." Since the boys seldom plan activities, these "hanging groups" are
the most stable basis the boys have for deciding whom they can depend on
in the near future.

Usually the Erls moved around the Mexican section as a single group,
but occasionally they split up into two "traveling groups." These groups
revolved around the two most prominent boys in the group, K-Man and
Tatters. Both traveling groups were consistent in their membership but
excluded six boys in the "hanging group." These traveling groups existed
in the sense that most of the boys in each considered themselves to be
"tight," to have a strong mutual trust in one another. These groupings were
also a part of the boys' expectations and were used in explanation for a
boy's absence; for instance, "He must be with K-Man" or "Guess he went
with Tatters."

In each traveling group, K-Man or Tatters was the boy who usually initiated group activities. When all the boys were together, K-Man usually took the initiative, but Tatters could always thwart "K's" efforts. In initiating activities K-man usually mentioned them first to Pepo, whose enthusiasm or ratification became the occasion for other boys to join in. Tatters, on the other hand, served only occasionally to veto moves proposed by K-Man.

The relationship of tightness within each traveling group was supplemented by several kin ties. There were three pairs of brothers in the Erls, and each pair remained in the same traveling group. Joint, a uterine cousin of Pepo and Mike, also belonged to the same traveling group. Boys related by kinship were quick to support each other, although they also felt free to take extreme liberties with one another. Kin relations also provided a bond between this group and others around their hangout. Tatters, Chickie, Grug, Joint, Ape, and Curls had sisters in the Erlettes. Grug and Christ had brothers in the Junior Erls.

The separation of the Erls into different "hanging" and "traveling" groups and the plurality of leaders were potentially divisive forces within the group. Additional relationships among the boys, however, tended to cross-cut these divisions and mollify their consequences. The two traveling groups were joined by three pairs of boys who were tight with one another: Tatters and Pepo; Grug and Asiatic; Joint and Troll. Baker and Curls, boys who belonged to no traveling group, were tight with Groucho who was, in turn, tight with Grug. Dickey did not appear regularly at the Erls' hangout and belonged to neither traveling group. But Dickey was related by marriage to K-Man, one of the leaders of the group. Only Ape and Pedro were not tight with anyone else in the group. Except for these two boys, all the others were "tight" with at least one other boy and all the segments they belonged to were joined by this type of relationship.

There were also strong and divisive antagonisms in the Erls. Each of these antagonisms, however, was muted by a third party loyal to both antagonists. Curls and Marty did not get along, but both were "tight" with Groucho. Tatters and Blondie were competitors, but Tatters' brother Chickie was Blondie's best friend. Also, Tatters and K-Man signified (insulted) with one another in an uneasy and ominous manner, but Pepo was a mutual friend of both boys.

While the boys in the Erls refused to accept a hierarchical set of roles, they varied a great deal in the respect they received from one another. K-Man was almost the smallest boy in the group but was reputed to be an excellent fighter. He was also the oldest boy in the group and had once belonged to the Eminents, a group notorious for a fight with the Taylor Barons (Italian). K-Man frequently gave direction to group activities but had no illusions about his ability to control the Erls. In confidence he said he could only "play it by ear" and propose what "the guys'll go along with."

Joint and Grug were openly insulted and made fun of by the other members. Joint was a skinny, toothless little boy with a notorious appetite for wine. Grug was homely and said to be stupid. Both boys were well liked and devoted to the group. Joint was killed one night when he tried to rob a Chinaman in order to obtain funds needed by the Erls to rent a storefront. All the Erls, Junior Erls, and Erlettes attended his wake and mourned his passing. When Baker was elected as vice-president and failed to come to the meetings, Grug was suggested as a replacement because he was "the only *real* Mexican" in the group.

Ape, Groucho, Curls, Baker, and Pedro were also low status members. Ape was not trusted by any of the boys because he had a reputation for "shooting off his mouth" and being undependable. Groucho was known to be rather cynical and often sneered at the other boys' enthusiasm. Curls was somewhat younger than the remaining members. He was quite handsome and spent a good deal of his time away from the group where he could be admired by the girls. The other boys kidded him about being a "pretty boy." Baker was the only boy in the group that was seriously preoccupied with criminal ventures. The other boys respected Baker's rational approach to these ventures but seemed to assume that Baker's interests withdrew him from the recreational and expressive character of the group. Pedro was only a "hanger-on" who spent most of his evenings at the Erls' hangout.

Mike, Christ, Asiatic, and Troll were highly respected and very active in the group. These boys were the performers in the group and provided much of its entertainment by making exaggerated claims and posturing for the benefit of the other boys. Frequently these boys were the butt of their own jokes and the first to laugh.

Pepo was especially respected because he was so generous and quick to be friendly with any boy in the group. Dickey and Marty were not nearly so well liked. Both, however, were related to K-Man and seemed to be protected somewhat by this relationship.

Rio looked older than most of the members and was respected for his maturity. He was quiet, dressed meticulously, had a girl picked for his wife, and was saving money for his marriage. Rio's opinions were respected, and his manner with the other members was friendly and paternalistic.

Chickie was a quiet boy who made very good grades in school. Like Pedro, he took a rational approach to life, and after graduation from high school he began to earn more tnan three dollars an hour. Chickie was liked by the other members, but he was remote and less effusive than they. His kinship to Tatters seemed to enhance his status.

Blondie was Polish and the only non-Mexican in the group. He was also the largest boy in the group. Tatters was the next largest boy in the group and was celebrated for his strength. Tatters and Blondie traveled together, and each was very quick to respond to what the other said or did. Their relationship, however, was strained by frequent speculations on their strength and fighting ability. The discomfort of this relationship was one reason Blondie decided to leave the group. When he announced his decision, however, it became the occasion for a serious fight between Blondie and Tatters. The fight ended in a draw after the intervention of a local street worker. Blondie then left the group, and except for Tatters' brother Chickie, none of the other boys would speak to him.

The major structural features of the Erls are present in most of the twelve Addams area groups that were known in some detail. In two very small groups, the Patricians (eight members) and Junior Meteors (ten members), there were no separate traveling groups. Among the Negro boys, traveling groups were sometimes explicitly acknowledged by the terms "running partners," but this was used to indicate dyads and triads as well as the larger unit of which they were a part. Among the white boys, traveling groups were evident only in the members' tacit expectations about who would be with whom.

In all groups, members were differentiated according to the extent they could be depended upon "to show" at the group's hangout. In a few rare instances a boy was not expected to "hang" with his group at all; he was expected to show only if there was "something going on": trouble, a dance, payday, or a ballgame. Hangers-on occurred in most groups, but not all.

Kinship occurred in all groups, and it tended to draw boys into the same "hanging" and traveling groups. An exception was the Meteors, all of whom thought they were related, although they could not always trace their kin lines. The boys' parents denied many of these relations but were pleased to know that the boys thought themselves akin.

Two or more boys able to exercise leadership or to veto the other's efforts were present in all twelve groups. Among the Negro groups, leadership was formally acknowledged by the offices of president and vice-president. These offices, however, were mentioned only to outsiders and were never used as forms of address within the group. Indeed, in all groups, terms of address indicating kinship, respect, or office were ignored in favor of first names. In all groups nicknames had replaced about a half to a third of the boys' given names. The general tendency, then, is away from society-wide categories and toward a more personal or local designation.

In all groups the cleavages due to separate "hanging" and traveling sections were counterbalanced by strong dyadic loyalties. From 1963 to 1965 there was no instance of segmentation based on these two cleavages. Two groups (Junior Contenders and Cardinals) in the Addams area, however, included a minority of boys from another ethnic group, and despite strong dyadic loyalties between boys of different ethnicity, the minority members left as a unit. Where a Mexican or Italian group included only one or two minority members, they were not a divisive force within the group.

Personal antagonisms that were not counterbalanced by a common friendship were very rare and quickly led to one boy leaving his group. What remained then was a stable, intransitive network of relations in which antagonisms and cleavages could not be expressed without endangering someone's loyalties and friendships as well. Indeed it is possible that the stable membership of these named groups in the Addams area was the remainder of a much larger network of social relations in which cleavages and antagonisms were not all counterbalanced by tertiary relations.

Such an intransitive network of relationships tends to subdue conflict and forestall segmentation. For the same reason, however, this structure impedes the open exercise of authority, the demands of rank, and an explicit decision-making process. In the Erls, as in other groups in the area, members were arrayed in a hierarchy according to the respect shown them. Yet this structure did not wholly coincide with the one produced by "hanging groups," traveling groups, kinship, and "tight" dyads. As a result, leaders had to temporize lest resistance from one boy reverberate throughout the group and force a choice between respect, friendship, or association. Leaders were also hamstrung by equalitarian relations that reached down from themselves to others less respected. Even such a simple rule as a "majority vote" was impracticable because it would force at least some boys to "choose sides" when their loyalties and antagonisms extended to both parties.

The consequence in these groups was an avoidance of explicit decision-making and a good deal of by-play to achieve consensus or a common direction. Banter, joking, and uproarious fantasy introduced possible choices as a way of seeking agreement. Boys would privately "feel one another out" before "showing their hand"; and sometimes, when they were all together, each member seemed to be waiting for the other "to make a move."[15] A rumored fight or street argument might weld them all together and produce immediate consensus. Otherwise each group could spend days simply "hanging," joking, gossiping, and waiting for something to happen.

---

[15] The boys sometimes speak of this as "sounding," and while the term is not used frequently, it is widely understood by the boys in the area.

11

The Boys' World
and the Wider Society

Alongside the standing arrangements that help define relations within and between street corner groups, there are a number of broader social processes that include both the groups and the wider community. On the one hand, there is the constant circulation of rumors which often upset the existing relationship of groups and their members. Since these rumors usually disrupt the balance between different groups, they often draw in a number of "peacemakers" from the wider community and the local neighborhood.

The wider community also intrudes directly upon the local street corner groups through police activity. While the boys do not openly disavow legal rulings, they take into account many additional "facts" of local social structure and history. This again produces a pattern of arrests that reflects the area's provincialism and its points of tangency to the wider community.

Rumors and Rumbles: Tragetore

Literally, the term "*tragetore*" means the "author of the tragedy." The local Italians, however, use it to indicate anyone who starts a rumor to which others react with tragic consequences. Whether the rumor is true or false is not too important. To tolerate such rumor-mongers is a sign of one's incapacity to halt their efforts. Traditional notions of honor call for the death of such rumor-mongers. In the Addams area, however, residents seldom resort to such drastic measures.

Usually, *tragetori* in the Addams area started rumors that fall into one of three types. First, there were those which simply impugned the character of single individuals; suspected abortions, illegitimacies, family troubles, involvement in illegal activities, etc. Such doubtful items of information are initially exchanged as a "secret," even when practically everyone eventually hears of them. So long as they are exchanged as "private information" and not told openly to the person involved they have little consequences except to expose morality as the exception rather than the rule. For example, a girl who is said to have recently lost her virginity will be treated much as she always was. Indeed, almost everyone goes into a sort of collusion to

195

maintain her public honor while talking behind her back. Where this kind of "secrecy" is maintained, she remains marriageable and appearances are well observed.[1] However, once she is brazenly confronted with such a rumor in front of others, she is ruined—unmarriageable and subject to advances by any male. There are no more than a dozen such girls in the Addams area. If one believes the rumors that circulate among the street corner groups, all the girls in the area should be in the same position. Yet, the boys go on to marry these girls and to treat them with local respect. Thus, it is not a girl's physical condition or a mere rumor which divests her of her virtue.

A second type of rumor was far more extensive in circulation and concerned the relationship of the Addams area and the wider community. Below are a few examples of these rumors:

1. The urban renewal program was a way of keeping the First Ward and the Loop out of the Negroes' hands.
2. The university location was undertaken because nobody had any faith in the Italians' ability to renovate the area from its status as a slum.
3. Negro families are being transferred arbitrarily from the projects to make the neighborhood safe for the university students.
4. The urban renewal plan's building codes will be altered to suit the private plans of the realtors and politicians.
5. The older people who move away from the neighborhood are dying from grief and the loss of their old friends.
6. They're going to rename Taylor Street "University Avenue." They don't want it associated with all the hoods that used to live here.
7. The plots of land available in the area are intentionally sold in such large units that it excludes any local residents from buying them.

There were many other such rumors, some of them more, some of them less plausible than these. To the residents they were simply rumors; items of information which were credible but never certain. Perhaps this is the most striking feature in the relationship between the inner city and the

---

[1] Malinowski (*Crime and Custom in Savage Society* [New York: Harcourt, Brace, 1932]), records a similar observation on incest among the Trobrianders. So long as the illicit sexual relation was kept a shared "secret," neither the deviants nor the community took action. However, once exposed in public, it became necessary for both to take action. The male party to the incest committed suicide, while the community denounced his partner.

In the Addams area a girl is sometimes her own worst enemy, especially when she confronts her accusers and demands they acknowledge her purity. Most often, however, she is the most eager of those who maintain secrecy.

wider community. The quality of available information about the actions of the wider community never seems to go beyond that of a vague rumor. The uncertainty of this information is itself enough to cripple most attempts at civic action. Thus, it becomes far more foolish to respond to such rumors than to do nothing at all.[2]

The third type of rumor is also rather extensive but involves only local people. Since the assumed protagonists are included within the local neighborhood, residents are more likely to feel they can "do something about it." Rumors of this type tend to follow a fairly standard course. First, they arise from some sort of objective circumstance or occasion which is taken as evidence. The reliability of this evidence may or may not be very great. Every spring for example, there were several rumors which preceded the closing of school: for instance, the Negroes are going to cause a riot in the Italian section, or vice versa; two gangs are going to have it out; the students from Crane High School are going to march on the neighborhood. These rumors do not seem to be simple inductions from past occurrences. If you ask people why the suspected event should occur, they do not cite past events of a similar nature. Instead, they dwell on the assumed designs, intentions, and grievances of the parties that have been implicated by the rumor. Also, while the rumors tend to be recurrent, the events they presage often fail to mature.

Second, these rumors seem uniformly to arise from traffic patterns, institutional schedules, and social congregations that do not follow the local order of segmentation. These "precipitating events" are due largely to institutional practices that lie outside local control: the closing of a school, the placement of movie theaters and beaches, open dances held by street workers, and so on. These traffic patterns and events produce gatherings that Addams area residents would not convene or condone. They can do little about them, however, because of the institutional incompleteness of their ethnic sections and the power of the wider community to establish contravening patterns.

Third, once under way, these rumors always implicate groups and persons whose antagonisms are already known to exist. Thus, while these rumors grow out of social patterns dictated by the wider community, their transmission and consequences follow a course determined by structural arrangements within the neighborhood.

Fourth, the mere inception of a rumor seldom progresses exactly as a

---

[2] This may help explain the apathy of lower income people towards explicit and formal attempts to alter political decisions, while they eagerly seize upon every avenue of informal political influence. Certainly, the information they have available does not warrant an explicit public confrontation but only a cautious inquiry in a "smoke-filled room."

"self-fulfilling prophecy."[3] Once such a rumor has started, it is neither believed nor disbelieved in a strict sense. Instead, it is taken as "likely," and people begin to prepare "just in case." When people begin to alter their own behavior to suit the rumor, however, it gains credence and moves on toward being a "certainty." The steps involved here are often quite intricate and involved. Sometimes there is police activity which testifies to the seriousness of the situation. This may be accompanied by the gathering of onlookers trying to find out where the "action" is. Others may draw away, hoping to "stay out of it." In the meantime, each party to the potential confrontation is faced with the problem of denying or corroborating the rumor. Often they attempt to control the situation by appealing for help, taking defensive maneuvers, and creating an impression that they are more than capable of meeting the occasion. This may produce additional rumors which incite further maneuvers that implicate new people. In general the pattern is one in which (1) more and more people are involved in the anticipated conflict and (2) agents of social control, such as the local street workers or policemen, are drawn in to negotiate or forestall serious conflict. The following cases from my notebook describe some of the better documented versions of this progression.

(1) G and his girlfriend (Mexican) were returning from a movie when they encountered some of the Red Ambers (Negro) on the south side of Roosevelt Road. G, a member of the Regents, was wearing his club sweater, and some of the Red Ambers said something derogatory about the Regents. Without contesting the issue, G and his girlfriend ran across the street into the Addams area. Once they were inside the Addams area, the other Mexican kids asked why they were running. They explained that the Red Ambers had tried to stop them because G was a Regent.

Within the same evening a rumor developed that (1) the Red Ambers "had it in" for the Regents, (2) the Red Ambers had tried to "jump" G and his girlfriend, and (3) the Regents were likely to retaliate against the Red Ambers. The rest of the Regents gathered around G, and there was the ominous feeling that "something had to be done."

Fearful that something would happen, and still indignant, G went to E, a Negro street worker who knew both the Regents and Red Ambers. E went to see the Red Ambers. From the beginning he knew that the Red Ambers were no longer a group and had broken up almost a year beforehand. After inquiring, E found out that those who had insulted G included two ex-members of the Red Ambers and some other boys who happened to be with them at the time. According to these boys, they had nothing in particular against the Regents and only intended to frighten G who was outside his own neighborhood. In fact, they hardly knew of the Regents and had no plans regarding them. E assured them that he could talk to the Regents and that they need take no precautions.

[3] Robert K. Merton, "The Self-Fulfilling Prophecy" in *Social Theory and Social Structure* (Glencoe, Ill.: Free Press, 1957), pp. 421–36.

Returning to the Regents, E explained the situation and spread the counter-rumor that the Red Ambers were not involved and that nothing was going to happen. G continued to be outraged but eventually the issue failed to attract the attention of others.

(2) In the late spring of 1962 there developed the rumor that the Negro students from Crane High School were going to march on the Addams area. The closing of Crane High School is always accompanied by some rumor that develops around the credible antagonism between whites and the more than 5000 Negro students who go to Crane. This year, the rumor was that they would march.

Before school let out, students at Crane were feeling each other out about what they were going to do. "Are you going to march?" "I don't know. I guess so if everybody else does."

On the eventful day when school let out, thousands of students milled about outside the school. Eventually, such a large crowd assembled that the streets were full. Traffic stopped. After a while they faced towards the Addams area. Someone started to walk. The others followed. Their trek was guided and charted by a course well-laid out by police cars and barricades. If there were leaders they were unnoticeable in the straggling crowd. Along the way the whites sat on their stoops and eyed them, waiting for something to "break out." Policemen were everywhere, stopping traffic and guiding the marchers to the Village where most of them lived. Once there the Crane marchers disappeared mysteriously into their homes. Next year the same rumor occurred, but students were released at several different times throughout the last day of school. There were no further marches after this.

(3) A social worker procured tickets to a rock-and-roll concert at McCormick Place. Some he distributed among the Barracudas, and the remainder among the Stylists. Later he transported both to McCormick Place and left them there. During the concert, which both groups enjoyed, there was no problem. Later, however, as they waited for a bus home, words were exchanged between members of the two groups. A fight broke out and the two groups fell upon one another. The police arrived, but all the Stylists escaped. Some of the Barracudas were arrested.

Next Monday morning many Addams area youngsters had heard of the fight and freely speculated on what the Barracudas would do to "get back" at the Stylists. Both groups were mindful of the delicacy of their position. About three days later some of the Stylists were walking down Harrison Street when they came upon some of the Barracudas at the latter's hangout. The Barracudas, thinking they were being attacked, started throwing bricks. The Stylists returned their bricks, and a short artillery battle resulted until the local adults and police broke it up. No one was hurt except one boy who was bruised by falling off a roof while trying to heave a brick.

Later, the boys held a number of conferences presided over by local street workers. Eventually there was a settlement, and the rumors died down—at least until another confrontation occurred.

(4) Over the weekend some of the Barracudas went to the Eleventh Street beach where they met some of the Roughshods from Eighteenth Street. A few pointed

remarks were exchanged. Later, when the Barracudas got back home, they related the occurrence to others in the area. Word spread that the Roughshods might "do something" to get back at the Barracudas. There was a good deal of talk, and the Barracudas were "touchy."

Later Monday night a car came careening down Harrison Street just past the Barracudas' hangout and stopped just beyond them where a group of Mexican girls were "hanging." The Barracudas "cut out" and went to where they had their "artillery" cached away on the other side of Harrison Street.[1]

When the Barracudas came back, the car sped off. Immediately some of the Barracudas went over to "Greek Town" to see the Potentates (Mexican), hoping that they might help them. Some of the Potentates agreed and came over toward the Barracudas' hangout.

In the meantime, someone had consulted with the Mexican girls to see who was in the car. As it turned out they were not from the Roughshods but were some friends of these girls and were trying to impress them. In the meantime, however, some adults had seen the congregating teenagers and called the police. Just after the Potentates left, the police arrived. A good many of the Barracudas were arrested for carrying weapons, for curfew violation, and for being disorderly.

Quite possibly the Roughshods spent an uneasy night on Eighteenth Street waiting for the Barracudas to show.

(5) In the winter of 1964 a Mexican from Eighteenth Street was badly hurt by someone who tied him to a telephone pole and ran a car into him. Three Italians were arrested as drivers of the car but later released. Among the Mexicans on Eighteenth Street, the rumor was that the "Outfit" had "got off" the three Italians. To this was added the general view that "someone from around here's gonna get one of those Dagos." Implicitly this meant any "Dago" in the Addams area. Being Italian and living in the Addams area is equivalent to belonging to the "Outfit" so far as those from Eighteenth Street are concerned.

This rumor circulated on Eighteenth Street until late spring when an open dance was held in the Addams area. A large number of boys from Eighteenth Street attended. Outside the dance, boys congregated and eyed one another. A group of Mexican boys congregated at one location only a few yards from several Italian boys. A shot rang out and Snout, an Italian boy, fell wounded. A policeman no more than a few yards away gave chase and wounded one of the assailants. The rest got away.

Immediately, there was a gathering among the Italian boys in the Addams area, and the question of "what will be done about those Spics on Eighteenth Street" arose. On this occasion, however, they waited for a report on Snout's condition. No one was badly hurt. Later another rumor developed among the Italians: "Our (Italian) policemen are going to take care of it." From that point on, no one felt any need to retaliate against Eighteenth Street. The fact that there was no subsequent evidence that the Italian policemen had done anything did not lessen their faith in the outcome.

[1] This account is not a reconstruction. I happened to be with the Barracudas throughout most of the evening. All the other accounts are partial reconstructions, although I viewed portions of each.

(6) One late afternoon, about dark, someone reported seeing an older Negro boy point a pistol at a six-year-old Italian boy. Once word of this reached a local Italian group, they set out looking for the Negro boy. None of them had seen the event, but they had been supplied with descriptions and suspects. Eventually, someone "fingered" A, a Negro boy from outside the Addams area and a member of the Village Deacons. He was located while standing with some of the Magnificent Gallants near the projects. One of the Italian boys pulled a gun on him and made him get to his knees. While A pleaded, the Italian boy snapped the gun twice at A's head. The Gallants looked on without helping or protesting. They wanted A in the area no more than did the Italian boys.[5] Indeed, there was some suspicion that the Gallants helped finger A. Certainly they condoned the Italian boy's behavior.

Next day rumors about a potential conflict between the Village Deacons and the Italians grew apace. Both street workers and police located the protagonists and tried to talk them out of it. A and the Italians both agreed to these counsels, but their commitments were not passed on to other people. Rumors continued to spring up from time to time.

Sometime later Batman from the Satan's Deacons[6] told R that they were going to have to do something about the Italians in the Addams area. R, being from the Addams area, discouraged him. "Look, if you start something up there, they're not going to know you from us. And who's gonna take the rap? Us. If we wanna start something with them we'll start it." Batman and R fell into an argument over this and while in anger Batman shot R. R was not much hurt, but his condition added fuel to existing rumors.

Later this same rumor had several other episodes. For all I know, they are still going on. When I left the neighborhood, the general view was that both the Village and Satan's Deacons were plotting against the Italians.

At some point rumors like the above usually implicate one or more named street corner groups. Frequently this takes the form of a predicted "gang fight." The prediction, however, seldom matures to an actual confrontation. Between 1962 and 1965 there were only two fights that might be called gang fights. More commonly the boys descend to a type of guerrilla warfare in which groups withdraw into their own territory and "jump" anyone they think is a member of the opposing street corner group. The boys make no pretense that these measures are fair and explain them as an attempt to "warn" the other group. Sometimes these attacks are a mistake and draw in another street corner group or the victims' friends.

In any case there is a tendency for such rumors to spread widely and to implicate additional people. The spread of a rumor and its variants, however, follows a very selective path. The ordered segmentation that exists

---

[5] The choice of A was hardly a random selection. He belonged to a group from below Roosevelt Road, but frequently came into the Addams area. It is doubtful that the Italians would have suspected a Negro from the immediate neighborhood.

[6] A group from the area to the west of the Village. The Village Deacons borrowed their name from this group, and there was a vague feeling of kinship between them.

within the neighborhood places several strictures on communication, and rumors that start among the young males in two ethnic sections are a long time in reaching other people. After a rumor has spread among the younger males, it tends to cross ethnic and sex boundaries at the same age level. Although the rumor may then spread downward among the young children, it seldom reaches upwards to their parents before a number of street workers and policemen have heard some version of the rumor. The street workers place themselves in the confidence of local teenagers. In turn, they are able to call in the police where their own efforts falter.

By contrast, local parents, adults, and priests are among the last to learn of impending fights among the youngsters. This does not imply that the adults are lax and indifferent about the behavior of teenagers. Often, it is just the opposite; the adults set such a high level of morality for adolescents that the latter can never tell them what is "really happening." Thus, the adults are usually excluded from any active role in adolescent affairs that reach beyond the immediate household.

In their onset, circulation, and conclusion, these rumors show again the internal segmentation of the Addams area while also demonstrating those points of tangency it shares with the wider community. The precipitating events that give rise to these rumors are, as has been said, often determined by external arrangements: teenage dances held by a local social agency, the closing of a school, and traffic patterns dictated by wider economic considerations. Once under way, these rumors seem to invariably implicate groupings that are already acknowledged in the area. Moreover, the time at which groups learn of these rumors also follows the local order of segmentation. The residents have no standing mechanism for handling these disruptions, but a number of local street workers and policemen can generally intervene to forestall serious conflict.

Encounters with the Police

Between July, 1963, and June, 1965, 390 Addams area boys below the age of seventeen were arrested. Thirty-three of these arrests were for running away from home, a family quarrel, or being ungovernable. These are generally offenses that arise out of domestic problems, and they are not considered here.

Ethnicity of Offenders

Table 19 gives a breakdown of all offenses according to the ethnicity of each offender. The figures must be regarded with caution. The Negro boys account for a little over a third (36%) of these offenses. In 1960 the Negroes made up about 14% of the population. By 1965, however, they probably

TABLE 19

PROPORTIONAL DISTRIBUTION OF ARRESTS ACCORDING TO ETHNIC GROUP
MEMBERSHIP OF THE OFFENDERS AND TYPE OF OFFENSE: JULY 1963 TO JUNE 1965

TYPE OF OFFENSE	NUMBER OF ARRESTS	NUMBER OF OFFENSES	ETHNICITY OF OFFENDERS				
			MEXICAN	ITALIAN	NEGRO	PUERTO RICAN	OTHER*
Drinking Disorderly Glue-Sniffing Disturbance	7% (24)	7% (13)	54% (13)	4% (1)	25% (6)	17% (4)	... ...
Malicious Mischief Property Damage	9% (31)	9% (17)	42% (13)	29% (9)	10% (3)	3% (1)	16% (5)
Subtotals	16% (55)	16% (30)	22% (26)	27% (10)	7% (9)	15% (5)	15% (5)
Carrying Weapons	4% (14)	4% (7)	21% (3)	7% (1)	64% (9)	... ...	7% (1)
Fighting Assault Affray	11% (36)	14% (26)	22% (8)	11% (4)	39% (14)	6% (2)	22% (8)
Subtotals	15% (50)	17% (33)	9% (11)	14% (5)	19% (23)	6% (2)	26% (9)
Theft Burglary Purse-Snatching Strong Arming	54% (184)	48% (92)	33% (60)	7% (12)	43% (80)	12% (22)	5% (10)
Subtotals	...	...	52%	32%	65%	65%	29%
Trespassing	2% (6)	3% (5)	33% (2)	17% (1)	17% (1)	... ...	33% (2)
Lewd Fondling Attempted Rape Intercourse	2% (8)	3% (6)	13% (1)	25% (2)	25% (2)	13% (1)	25% (2)
Curfew	7% (24)	8% (16)	46% (11)	17% (4)	8% (2)	8% (2)	21% (5)
Fire Crackers Turning on Fire Hydrant False Fire Alarm	5% (16)	5% (10)	31% (5)	19% (3)	31% (5)	13% (2)	6% (1)
Unclassified	14		Records lost, unavailable or incomplete				
Runaway Incorrigible Ungovernable	33	33	33% (11)	24% (8)	36% (12)	3% (1)	3% (1)
TOTALS	390		127	45	134	35	35

* Twenty-four of these arrests were among Southern Whites, two were Rumanian Gypsies, one was a Pole, and the remainder are unknown.

constituted around 21% of the population because the destruction in the area had removed many private dwellings which had housed white residents.[7] In either case their arrest rate is comparatively high.

For the other ethnic groups it is far more hazardous to make any suggestion about the relative rate of arrests. In 1960 the Puerto Ricans made up about 8% of the population.[8] By 1965 they had probably declined to about 5% of the population. Their arrest rate is probably somewhat higher than the average.

Estimating the arrest rate of the Italians and Mexicans presents an even more difficult problem because many of their parents were born in this country and the 1960 census figures do not include them as a separate group.[9] However, taking these figures into account and judging from the number of homes destroyed, the arrest rate among the Mexicans is probably somewhat above their share, while the Italians undoubtedly have a rather low arrest rate.

Only the obvious difference between the Negro and Italian boys stands out. In the Addams area, however, this is fairly easy to understand: both were being handled by policemen and youth officers who were predominantly Italian. Certainly this does not mean that the Italian policemen were corrupt. In approaching an Italian boy they often knew both him and his parents. A Negro boy was a stranger and his parents unlikely to accede to the justice of a "sidewalk trial."[10]

In the 1960 census only 60% of the local population is classified in one of the four dominant ethnic groups. According to table 18, however, 90% of all arrests included boys who were labelled as Negro, Italian, Mexican, or

[7] This estimate is made on the basis of the number of homes destroyed in the Addams area. It assumes that the number of white boys below seventeen years of age is proportional to the number of buildings left standing.

[8] Assuming there are no third or fourth generation Puerto Ricans in the area.

[9] The 1960 census figures for the Addams area giving the following numbers:

Total Population	..	20,524	100%	United Kingdom,			
White		16,982	83%	Ireland, Norway,			
Negro		2,968	14%	Sweden, Germany	..	208	1%
Other		28	0.1%	Czechoslovakia,			
Born in Puerto Rico	..	1,057	5%	Austria, USSR ..	..	271	1%
P.R. Parentage ..	..	705	3%	Canada	..	53	0.2%
Total Foreign Stock	..	8,977	44%	Italy..	..	4,519	22%
Native, Foreign or				Mexico	..	3,352	16%
Mixed Parentage	..	5,485	26%	All other and Not			
				Reported	..	574	3%

[10] Often a policeman simply gives a boy "hell" or "takes him in the alley." When carried out by a member of one's own ethnic group, this may be accepted practice. Otherwise it becomes a cause for great concern and many recriminations. The Italian policemen in the Addams area were very cautious about handling Negro boys in such an informal way. It was much easier and safer just to arrest them.

Puerto Rican. This disparity is probably due to the police records including ethnicity despite generational depth. The same practice is followed by the local residents, and the 90% figure gives a good idea of how thoroughly these four ethnic groups dominate the area.

Most of the boys responsible for the remaining offenses were incongruous in the Addams area. Twenty-four of these offenses were committed by Southern whites. There are very few Southern whites in the area, and all of these offenses were committed by boys from just six families. Two Gypsy boys from the only Gypsy family in the area account for two more offenses. The one American Indian family known to be in the area had a son who produced two known offenses. It is possible that the marginal ethnic status of these boys placed them in conflict with others in the neighborhood. However, I knew almost all the Southern white boys, and they seemed well accepted by the Mexicans, among whom they spent most of their time. One Southern white boy gave me quite a different explanation for the number of times he had been arrested: "Look, everytime somebody with blond hair does something in this neighborhood, they come and bust me."

Types of Offenses

While differences between the arrest rate in each ethnic group are relatively small, there are some distinct differences in the types of offenses each commits.

Drinking, disorderly, glue sniffing, disturbance, curfew, malicious mischief, and property damage. Arrests for these offenses make up a relatively high proportion (24%) of the total among the Mexican and Italian boys. By contrast, arrests for these types of misbehavior are relatively low (7% of all arrests) among the Negro boys. In part, this may reflect the extent of Mexican and Italian street life. The relatively low proportion of such arrests among the Negro boys, however, may be due to their location in public housing. The Jane Addams Projects form many sheltered courts and small yards that cannot be seen from the streets. Policemen seldom enter these areas, which form something like sanctuaries for Negro boys who are drinking, keeping late hours, or marking up a wall.

Carrying weapons, assault, affray, and fighting. Arrests for these offenses are relatively high among Negroes (19% of all arrests) compared with whites (12% of all arrests). Both of these findings follow national trends, which show a high rate of weapon-carrying and assault among Negroes.[11] In the

---

[11] Harry E. Barnes and Nagley K. Teeters, *New Horizons in Criminology* (Englewood Cliffs, N.J.: Prentice Hall, 1959), p. 173.

Addams area this seemed to grow out of the mutual fear and distrust common among the Negroes.

Theft, burglary, purse-snatching, and strong-arming. Arrests for these offenses make up about half (54%) of the total. This does not mean that the boys in the Addams area specialized in the more utilitarian forms of deviance. Offenses of this sort are most likely to arouse the victim and subsequent police activity. In the Addams area, 85% of the victims to these offenses made a complaint to the police. Only about 47% of the arrests for other offenses were made upon the insistence of a complainant other than the police themselves.

According to table 19, arrests of this type make up a relatively high proportion (65%) of all Negro offenses. On the other hand, such arrests are relatively scarce (32% of all arrests) among the Italian boys. These figures differ sharply from the local assumption that the Italian boys are heavily involved in the more mercenary forms of delinquency. In part, this is probably due to the favored position of the Italians relative to police enforcement. In addition, however, the Italians may be constrained by their own dominance in the area. Within the neighborhood, and especially their own section around the park, most of the local businesses are owned or operated by Italians. These may be fair game to the Negro, Mexican, and Puerto Rican boys, but to the Italians they are "off limits."

Arrests of Females

Addams area girls under the age of eighteen were arrested sixty-eight times between July, 1963, and June, 1965 (table 20). The most outstanding observation was the large proportion of arrests of Negro girls. The ratio of female to male arrests among the Negroes was about 1 : 3.2. Among the Mexicans it was much lower (1 : 7.5), and among all whites it was still lower

TABLE 20
ARRESTS FOR PERIOD JULY 1963 TO JUNE 1965: FEMALES UNDER 18 ONLY

	ETHNIC GROUP MEMBERSHIP OF OFFENDER					
	NEGRO	MEXICAN	ITALIAN	PUERTO RICAN	OTHER	TOTAL
Number of Arrests	41	17	1		9	68
Ratio of Female to Male Arrests	1:3.2	1:7.5	1:45		1:3.9	
		All Whites Combined 1:9				

NOTE: All ratios are computed by including runaways among male offenses. Thus, male offenses total 376.

(1 : 9). Except for the Puerto Rican girls, these ratios tend to follow the pattern of cross-sex relations in the Addams area. The Negro girls and boys are the most equalitarian and unconstrained in their relationship. The Italian girls tend to view the boys as an intractable danger and avoid any unprotected contact with them. The Mexican boys and girls are, again, a people in the middle.

These cross-sex relations are probably best expressed by the relationship among the named groups in the Addams area. Among the Negroes, the girls possess their own groups unaffiliated with those of the boys. The Mexican girls have groups of their own, but they are always affiliated with a male "protector" group. The Italian and Puerto Rican girls have no groups of their own. Thus, in the Addams area the proportion of female offenses tends to increase as girls are progressively emancipated and sex role differentiation declines.[12]

Location of Offense

Table 21 gives the location of 192 offenses for which 343 boys were arrested. When there are two or more offenders, the location of each offense is determined by the distance from the place of the offense from the nearest residence of the offenders. The residence of the nearest offender was selected because it was thought that in the case of some offenses the boys would be more hesitant to victimize someone who lived close to any one of them. As will be pointed out later, this assumption seems to have some validity, particularly in the case of property offenses.

As can be seen in table 21, almost two-thirds (65%) of all offenses were committed within the Addams area. Nearly one-half of these (31%) were committed less than a block from the home of the nearest offender. Generally, this merely reflects the localism and provincialism that pervades the entire area. Usually the boys do not stray far from their homes, and most of their grievances and activities are contained within the neighbor-Some offenses, however, are more likely than others to be committed within the local neighborhood.

Trespassing, carrying weapons, curfew, and loitering. Compared with arrests for other offenses, arrests for these offenses are the ones which are most likely to occur outside the local neighborhood. Altogether, 54% of them occurred outside the Addams area. In the case of curfew, trespassing, and loitering, this may be mostly a function of police handling. So long as a boy is only a few blocks from home, the police are likely only to warn him

---

[12] Edwin H. Sutherland and Donald R. Cressy, *Principles of Criminology* (New York: J. B. Lippencott, 1955), pp. 111–14.

TABLE 21

DISTANCE BETWEEN PLACE OF OFFENCE AND RESIDENCE OF NEAREST OFFENDER

TYPE OF OFFENSE	NUMBER OF OFFENDERS	NUMBER OF SEPARATE OFFENCES	DISTANCE							
			LESS THAN 1 BLOCK	1.1–2 BLOCKS	2.1–3 BLOCKS	3.1–4 BLOCKS	4.1–5 BLOCKS	6 OR MORE BLOCKS	OFFENSE COMMITTED OUTSIDE ADDAMS AREA	UNKNOWN
Trespassing	2% (6)	3% (5)		40% (2)	20% (1)				40% (2)	
Carrying Weapons	4% (14)	4% (7)	29% (2)			14% (1)			57% (4)	
Drinking Disorderly Glue-Sniffing Disturbance	7% (24)	7% (13)	23% (3)	8% (1)	16% (2)			46% (6)		8% (1)
Lewd Fondling Attempted Rape Intercourse	2% (8)	3% (6)	50% (3)		17% (1)				17% (1)	17% (1)
Curfew Loitering	7% (24)	8% (16)	19% (3)	13% (2)	7% (1)				56% (9)	7% (1)
Fire Crackers Fire Hydrant Fire Alarm	5% (16)	5% (10)	40% (4)	60% (6)						
Malicious Mischief Property Damage	9% (31)	9% (17)	41% (7)	23% (4)	6% (1)	6% (1)	12% (2)	6% (1)	6% (1)	
Fighting Assault Affray	11% (36)	14% (26)	39% (10)	23% (6)	12% (3)		4% (1)		15% (4)	8% (2)
Theft Burglary Purse-Snatching Strong-Arming	54% (184)	48% (92)	29% (27)	13% (12)	5% (5)	7% (6)		1% (1)	37% (34)	8% (7)
TOTALS	343	192	31% (59)	17% (33)	7% (14)	4% (8)	2% (3)	4% (8)	29% (55)	6% (12)
			65% (125)						29% (55)	6% (12)

and see to it that he goes home. Certainly, on any warm night the police could pick up innumerable boys who are lounging in front of their homes after curfew. Generally, they do not; and, in fact, the curfew law seems intended to keep boys near their homes rather than in it.

Although the number of separate arrests for carrying weapons is very low (seven cases), the tendency for this offense to occur outside the area probably reflects the boys' view that it is prudent to carry a weapon once outside one's home territory.[13]

Theft, burglary, purse-snatching, and strong-arming. These are the offenses next most likely (37%) to be committed outside the area. All of them are impersonal forms of exploitation with some possibility of gain. Given their fears, distrust, and amoral view of outsiders, the boys have few reservations about exploiting persons or businesses outside their neighborhood. As will be made apparent later on, it is less likely for a boy to take such an amoral view of someone who lives close by.

Drinking, disorderly, glue-sniffing, disturbance, shooting fire crackers, turning on fire hydrants, and false fire alarms. All arrests for these offenses occurred within the Addams area. From the boys' point of view, they are local forms of entertainment and an integral part of street life. Drinking, glue-sniffing, and making noise are usually group activities carried out at their local hangout. False fire alarms bring a little excitement when a young group is having a dull afternoon. Shooting fire crackers and turning on fire hydrants are extremely common activities and often encouraged by the adults. Sometimes an adult will give a young boy a wrench and tell him to turn on a fire hydrant, explaining, "If the police catch you, they won't do anything. You're just a kid." Then the adults use the water to wash their cars. On hot summer days practically all the fire hydrants in the area are turned on. The boys put an old tire around the hydrant and lodge a plank between the tire and the outlet. This creates a tremendous fountain that arches across the street, and the young children all go bathing. In the evening the water department comes around and turns the water off. Rarely do they bother to remove the tire.

Similarly, fire crackers are sold to the boys by local adults who do a lively business for about a month preceding the Fourth of July. The boys shoot off the fire crackers around their house and hangout for their own amusement.

Fighting, assault, affray, lewd fondling, attempted rape, intercourse, malicious mischief, and property damage. The vast majority (82%) of these offenses

---

[13] Going to school within the area is also considered dangerous in some cases because a few of the schools draw boys from several neighborhoods.

occurred within the Addams area. Most are offenses which presuppose some prior acquaintance and sufficient intimacy for persons to acquire grievances or attractions. As a rule, the boys in the Addams area do not go about wantonly destroying property, making sexual overtures to unknown girls, or beating up strangers. Instead, they usually do so only after a certain measure of intimacy has been established. By and large, the attainment of this level of intimacy is most likely with people who either enter the neighborhood regularly or live there.

Victims and Complainants

While the boys commit most of their offenses within the neighborhood, their victims and complainants are more likely to come from somewhere else. As table 22 indicates, curfew violations, loitering, shooting fire crackers, turning on fire hydrants, and making false fire alarms seldom arouse a local complainant. Ninety-two per cent of the time the complainant is simply the policeman who apprehends a boy while he is committing the offense.

Theft, burglary, purse-snatching, and strong-arming are offenses that the boys are more likely to commit outside the area and that very seldom (8% of the time) victimize a local resident of common ethnicity. While the residents complain of these offenses, most of the victims (61% of all cases) are either persons who live outside the area or large business firms, schools, and public facilities.

As pointed out above, certain offenses seem to presume a prior level of intimacy and occur largely within the Addams area. Malicious mischief, property damage, fighting, assault, affray, and sex offenses most often (74% of the time) victimize a local resident, a high proportion (33%) being people from the same ethnic section and same ethnicity as the offenders.

In general the following pattern emerges: (1) instances of interpersonal conflict are concentrated within the area, (2) offenses for gain victimize outsiders, and (3) the remaining offenses do not arouse local complaints.

Changes Through Time

As can be seen from figure 2 the number of offenses between July, 1963, and June, 1965, shows no decline despite the continuing efforts of local youth workers and a gradual decrease in the total population due to urban renewal and the clearance for the University of Illinois. In fact, the arrest rate seems to be increasing: the first twelve months produced only 159 arrests (41% of the total), while in the second twelve-month period, there were 231 arrests (59% of the total).

The most prominent pattern is one attributed to seasonal variations. During the summer vacation (July through August), the average number of arrests per month is 20, or about twice as high as in the dead of winter, (December through February), when the average number of arrests per month is 9.2.

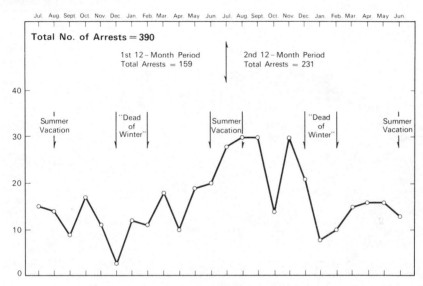

FIG. 2.
Number of Arrests for Period of July 1963 to June 1965:
Males under 17 Years of Age

The rise in the number of arrests is rather surprising because the population probably declined by about 20% during this period. Thus, the increase in the arrest rate is greater than might be inferred from figure 2 alone. Calculations based on the amount of destruction in the area produce the approximate arrest rates given in table 23.[14] These figures do not change

[14] These estimates were made by assuming that the population decline was directly proportional to the number of cleared lots in each separate block, that is,

$$\sum \frac{\% \text{ of occupied lots, February 1963}}{\% \text{ of occupied lots, 1960}} \cdot \begin{array}{l} \text{No. of males sixteen years of age} \\ \text{and below, 1960} \end{array}$$

for all city blocks in the Addams area.

For 1960, the number of occupied lots was determined from material provided by the local office of urban renewal. Two other counts were established by the author, one in February, 1963, and another in August, 1965. The figures given in table 23 are very rough and assume (1) the number of males sixteen and under are evenly distributed in each city block, (2) the age structure did not change during this period (1960–65), and (3) the destruction of homes proceeded at a regular pace throughout the same period. All of these assumptions are doubtful, but provide the only available basis for judging the arrest rate.

TABLE 22

SELECTED CHARACTERISTICS OF OFFENDERS, VICTIMS, AND COMPLAINANTS

| TYPE OF OFFENSE | NUMBER AND PERCENTAGE OF OFFENDERS | NUMBER AND PERCENTAGE OF OFFENSES | DISSIMILARITIES BETWEEN OFFENDERS | | | | | POLICE, CORPORATE PERSONALITY OR NO VICTIM |
			1 DIFFERENCE OF ETHNICITY ONLY	2 NONRESIDENT IN OFFENDER'S SECTION OF ADDAMS AREA	3 NONRESIDENT IN ADDAMS AREA	1,2	1,3	
Curfew Loitering	7% (24)	8% (16)						100% (16)
Fire Crackers Fire Hydrant Fire Alarm	5% (16)	5% (10)						100% (10)
Subtotals	(40)	(26)						100% (26)
Malicious Mischief Property Damage	9% (31)	9% (17)	18% (3)	12% (2)		12% (2)		29% (5)
Fighting Assault Affray	11% (36)	14% (26)	8% (2)		8% (2)	8% (2)	27% (7)	4% (1)
Lewd Fondling Attempted Rape Intercourse	2% (8)	3% (6)			17% (1)		34% (2)	
Subtotals	(75)	(49)	10% (5)	4% (2)	6% (3)	8% (4)	18% (9)	12% (6)
Trespassing	2% (6)	3% (5)					40% (2)	60% (3)
Carrying Weapons	4% (14)	4% (7)						100% (7)
Drinking Disorderly Glue-Sniffing Disturbance	7% (24)	7% (13)			8% (1)		16% (2)	69% (9)
Theft Burglary Purse-Snatching Strong-Arming	54% (184)	48% (92)	9% (8)	3% (3)	12% (11)	16% (15)	33% (30)	16% (15)
TOTALS	343	192	7% (13)	3% (5)	8% (15)	10% (19)	22% (43)	34% (66)
					49% (95)			34% (66)

TABLE 22—*Continued*

| AND VICTIMS | | DISSIMILARITIES BETWEEN OFFENDERS AND COMPLAINANTS | | | | | | | |
| | | 1 | 2 | 3 | 1,2 | 1,3 | | | |
NO DIFFERENCES BETWEEN OFFENDER AND VICTIM	UNKNOWN	DIFFERENCE OF ETHNICITY ONLY	NONRESIDENT IN OFFENDER'S SECTION OF ADDAMS AREA	NONRESIDENT IN ADDAMS AREA			POLICE, CORPORATE PERSONALITY	NO DIFFERENCE BETWEEN OFFENDERS AND COMPLAINANT	UNKNOWN
		7% (1)					93% (15)		
							90% (9)	10% (1)	
		4% (1)					92% (24)	4% (1)	
18% (3)	12% (2)	18% (3)	12% (2)		6% (1)		35% (6)	18% (3)	12% (2)
38% (10)	8% (2)	12% (3)		8% (2)	8% (2)	23% (6)	15% (4)	35% (9)	
50% (3)				17% (1)		34% (2)		50% (3)	
33% (16)	8% (4)	12% (6)	4% (2)	6% (3)	6% (3)	16% (8)	20% (10)	31% (15)	4% (2)
						40% (2)	60% (3)		
							100% (7)		
8% (1)				17% (1)		34% (2)		50% (3)	
8% (7)	3% (3)	11% (10)	3% (3)	12% (11)	15% (14)	34% (31)	15% (14)	5% (5)	4% (4)
12% (24)	4% (7)	9% (17)	3% (5)	8% (15)	9% (17)	22% (43)	35% (67)	11% (22)	3% (6)
12% (24)				51% (97)			35% (67)	11% (22)	3% (6)

TABLE 23

ESTIMATED ARREST RATES FOR NEGRO AND WHITE BOYS
FOR TWO TWELVE-MONTH PERIODS

	July 1963– June 1964	July 1964– June 1965
Estimated number of Negro boys 16 and under	576	561
Number of arrests among Negro boys 16 and under	45	96
Estimated arrest rate among Negro boys 16 and under	.078	.171
Estimated number of white boys 16 and under	2584	2262
Number of arrests among white boys 16 and under	115	131
Estimated arrest rate among white boys 16 and under	.045	.058
Estimated arrest rate among all boys 16 and under	.051	.080

what is already apparent: the number of arrests increased, especially among the Negro boys.

The first explanation that could be offered is that the destruction occurring in the neighborhood disrupted its internal organization and social controls. However, the urban renewal and clearance programs occurred almost wholly among the white residents in the area. Yet table 23 and figure 3 show an increasing arrest rate among both white and Negro boys. Among the whites, the number of arrests was about the same for both twelve-month periods despite a decline in population; among the Negroes, the number of arrests doubled, while the population remained about the same.[15]

The increase in arrests during the second twelve-month period is not evenly distributed across all twelve months but is concentrated in the months July to December, 1964. Otherwise there is little in the way of a systematic discrepancy between the two twelve-month periods (see table 24). Thus, whatever the reason for this rise in the offense rate, it seems to have occurred during the last half of 1964.

One common reason for a sharp change in arrest rates is an increase in police activity. The Addams area is a part of the Chicago Fourth Police

[15] These tables include runaways, but they do not affect the general trends. Eighteen occur in the first twelve-month period and fifteen in the second.

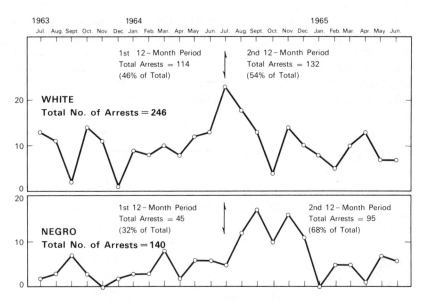

FIG. 3.
Number of Arrests per Month for Negro and White Boys

TABLE 24
MONTHLY DIFFERENCES BETWEEN NUMBER OF ARRESTS FOR
TWO TWELVE-MONTH PERIODS

	NEGRO BOYS			WHITE BOYS			DIFFERENCE BETWEEN 1ST & 2ND PERIOD FOR NEGRO AND WHITE BOYS
MONTH	1ST 12-MONTH PERIOD JULY 1963– JUNE 1964	2ND 12-MONTH PERIOD JULY 1964– JUNE 1965	DIFFERENCE BETWEEN 1ST AND 2ND PERIOD	1ST 12-MONTH PERIOD JULY 1963– JUNE 1964	2ND 12-MONTH PERIOD JULY 1964– JUNE 1965	DIFFERENCE BETWEEN 1ST AND 2ND PERIOD	
July[a]	2	5	+3	13	23	+10	+13
August[a]	3	12	+9	11	18	+7	+16
Sept.[a]	7	17	+10	2	12	+10	+20
Oct.[a]	3	10	+7	14	4	−10	−3
Nov.[a]	0	16	+16	11	14	+3	+19
Dec.[a]	2	11	+9	2	10	+8	+17
Jan.[b]	3	0	−3	9	8	−1	−4
Feb.[b]	3	5	+2	8	5	−3	−1
Mar.[b]	8	5	−3	10	10	0	−3
Apr.[b]	2	1	−1	8	13	+5	+4
May[b]	6	7	+1	13	7	−6	−5
June[b]	6	6	0	14	7	−7	−7

[a] Sequence of month during which number of arrests tended to be higher in 2nd period than in 1st period.
[b] Months during which number of arrests show little or no systematic difference between two periods.

Area, and all of its youth officers are administered through this area.[16] If the offense rates of the Addams area are a function of police activity, then they ought to fluctuate with the other arrests throughout the area. A comparison of figures 2 and 4, however, show that except for seasonal variations, there is no systematic correspondence between the number of arrests in the Addams area and in the Fourth Police Area.

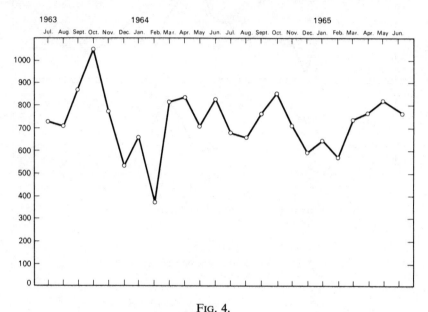

FIG. 4.

Number of Arrests in Fourth Area from July 1963 to June 1965:
Males and Females Excluding those Arrests Occurring
in the Addams Area

Another explanation of this increase in the number of arrests is of a more historical and local nature. About the middle of the spring of 1964, the four oldest Negro groups[17] became seriously involved in the civil rights movement and were drawn into formal groupings. At the same time these older street corner groups declined until they were almost nonexistent. However, while the older boys were occupied with civil rights, certain other changes

---

[16] The Addams area is also located in a smaller unit called the Twelfth Police District. Police officers are attached to the district headquarters, but youth officers are attached to area headquarters. Since the youth officers make most juvenile arrests, the Fourth Area was chosen for comparison.

[17] Magnificent Gallants, Patricians, Rapids, and Midget Gallants. In addition, the Bon Ton Fillettes took a leading role in this movement.

began to occur. First, the boys from the Village began to enter the Jane Addams Projects and created a number of incidents. In addition, they also felt obliged to contest with the Italians around Sheridan Park.

Second, the disappearance of the older Negro groups thrust the Gutter Guys and Etruscans into the position of being the oldest Negro groups in the Addams area. Both of them were much younger than the boys from the Village and were unable to fend them off. At the same time, however, they became extremely active and took a leading role in the street life around the projects. In due course they became involved in a number of fights, several minor thefts, and quite a bit of mischief. Some of the offenses were clearly an attempt to keep the Village Boys out of their territory. Other offenses, however, developed into a form of collective behavior: the boasts and defiant manner of the Gutter Guys drew other youngsters into the same misbehavior. For the most part, these were other Negro boys who lived in the same area. To some extent, however, white boys were also affected, either as antagonists, victims, or observers.

Table 25 gives the number of arrests occurring in each six-month period among the Gutter Guys and Etruscans as well as all other boys affiliated with a named street corner group. As can be seen, the number of arrests in these two street corner groups climbs sharply in early 1964 and reaches a peak in the last half of that year. Negro boys who were unaffiliated with a named street corner group follow a similar course for the last half of 1964. Although the increase in arrests is somewhat delayed and less severe among the white boys, there are similar trends, with arrests reaching their highest point in the last half of 1964.

One unexpected finding on table 25 is that it is only among the Negro and white boys unaffiliated with a named street corner group that the number of arrests follow the same pattern as among the Etruscans and Gutter Guys. Among the other Negro groups and among all Mexican and Italian groups the number of arrests remains fairly stable over the entire two-year period. Although unexpected, these results may fit a well-known pattern. Assuming that the territorial defense by the Gutter Guys and Etruscans approximated a form of collective behavior, such behavior would, for the most part, draw in boys who had no firm commitments elsewhere and who were free to play the adventurer without jeopardizing the fortunes of others. A boy who is a member of a named street corner group cannot act as a completely free agent but must consider his role as a group representative.[18] Thus, he is unlikely to be captured so easily by his own personal indignation or by a bit of temporary opportunism. In fact neither the Gutter Guys,

[18] L. M. Killian, "The Significance of Multiple Group Membership in Disaster," *The American Journal of Sociology*, 57 (January, 1952): 309–13.

TABLE 25

NUMBER OF ARRESTS OCCURRING AMONG AFFILIATED AND UNAFFILIATED BOYS WITHIN
EACH ETHNIC GROUP (FOR ALL BOYS ON WHICH THERE IS COMPLETE INFORMATION)

	PERIOD				
ETHNIC GROUP	JULY–DEC. 1963	JAN.–JUNE 1964	JULY–DEC. 1964	JAN.–JUNE 1965	TOTAL
Gutter Guys & Etruscans (Negro)	0% (0)	26% (17)	59% (39)	15% (10)	66
Unaffiliated Negro Boys	22% (13)	7% (4)	52% (30)	19% (11)	58
Subtotal	10% (13)	17% (21)	56% (69)	17% (21)	124
Unaffiliated Italian Boys	26% (8)	23% (7)	35% (11)	16% (5)	31
Unaffiliated Mexican Boys	25% (13)	19% (10)	31% (16)	25% (13)	52
Unaffiliated Puerto Rican Boys	14% (4)	24% (7)	48% (14)	14% (4)	29
Unaffiliated "Other"	9% (1)	27% (3)	55% (6)	9% (1)	11
Subtotal	21% (26)	22% (27)	38% (47)	19% (23)	123
Members of Italian Groups	22% (4)	28% (5)	33% (6)	17% (3)	18
Members of Mexican Groups	21% (22)	29% (30)	28% (29)	23% (24)	105
Members of Negro Groups Other than Gutter Guys & Etruscans	25% (4)	44% (7)	13% (2)	19% (3)	16
Subtotal	22% (30)	31% (42)	24% (33)	23% (31)	136
TOTAL	69	90	149	75	383

the Etruscans, nor the Village Boys were apt to offend openly, cajole, or
exploit someone who was known to be a well-established member in another
local group. With an older group, this could be dangerous. In any case,
however, it was probably regarded as futile.

By December, 1964, all the groups had drawn back as street life lapsed
for the winter. The Gutter Guys were somewhat wiser for the experience

because they tried to change their name "after what happened last summer." Their reputation, however, was established, and no name change took place. Next spring they were at least somewhat older and better able to defend the Jane Addams Projects.

In their defense of their local ethnic section, the Gutter Guys were tailoring their behavior to the maintenance of the ordered segmentation that characterizes the Near West Side. The police were an intrusion, but a necessary one because the age of the Gutter Guys left them incapable of protecting the area. A prior intrusion by civil rights workers had truncated the orderly succession between age grades.

The police and these civil rights workers represent one of the most direct ways in which the provincialism of the Addams area is punctured by the actions of the wider community. Once under way, however, the consequences follow a course that is constricted by local structural arrangements. Most of the rumors that get started in the Addams area are incited by recreational events, institutional schedules, and traffic patterns which are determined by the wider community. After their inception, however, these rumors travel in a circuit that is confined by age, sex, territorial, and ethnic groupings. As a result, the local neighborhood cannot react as a unit, and visiting street workers seem necessary to keep the peace.

The police intrude most directly when they arrest boys for a few minor offenses that are rather well accepted in the area: staying up late at night, shooting fire crackers, turning on fire hydrants, and making false fire alarms. The police also intervene between the local residents and those people or organizations which Addams area residents regard as "fair game." Inter-ethnic conflicts within the area and relations with outsiders are often predatory, and only the police seem able to dispose of them.

Within the Addams area, relations among the young people are often very intimate and lead to many private disputes. Older Addams area residents have no way of understanding or dealing with these private quarrels, and the intervention of the police may be necessary to help forestall the youngsters' attempts to take the law in their own hands.

Thus, at the inception and at the conclusion of local conflicts, the wider community plays a prominent role. While the conflict is in progress, the ordered segmentation of the neighborhood seems to channel the course of rumor and conflict. The boys attack intimates and exploit outsiders. The girls hang back and avoid conflict except in the case of the Negro girls whose status most nearly approaches that of the boys. Territorial groupings assume the truth of spurious rumors, and ethnic differences add fuel to their circulation. The local adults are unable to intercede because they have no first hand acquaintance with the boys' world. Thus, in various ways, age, sex, residence, and ethnicity continually reappear to define participant and onlooker, victim and victimizer, the ignorant and the wise, and the trouble-maker and the peacemaker.

As the wider community intervenes to prevent serious consequences of local conflict, the street corner group is often selected as the most likely convert or culprit. Street workers seek out its members and try to wean them away from their past alliances. The police single them out as trouble makers and argue that their removal would save the Addams area from its continual troubles.

Neither conversion nor removal of the named street corner group seems a likely solution to the conflicts that go on within the Addams area. In the area, a high proportion (47%) of arrests involved boys who did not belong to a named street corner group. Judging from the population figures, this is only slightly below what might be expected on the basis of their numbers. While granting the inexactitude of these figures, the proportion of arrests among boys who are not members of named street corner groups remains rather large.

In any case it is doubtful that the conflicts within the Addams area will abate simply because a few members of its street corner groups are conver-ted to conventional purposes while others are thrown into jail. The street corner group provides a way of ordering people into a manageably small number of social aggregates. If its members are removed, then others will have to take their place until anonymity and uncertainty is again erased. The function of the named street corner group is rudimentary and primi-tive: it defines groups of people so that they can be seen as representatives rather than individuals.

Part 5

The Meaning of Morality

12

Practicality and Morality

The Addams area is less than one-half square mile in size and contains fewer than 20,000 residents. It is probably a more orderly slum than many others and departs sharply from the common image of an atomized and unruly urban rabble. For all its historical uniqueness, the neighborhood does establish the possibility of a moral order within its population. The reoccurrence of the circumstances that led to its organization is as uncertain as the future of the Addams area itself. In spite of all these uncertainties, the Addams area shows that slum residents are intent upon finding a moral order and are sometimes successful in doing so.

Provincialism

The most general characteristic of the Addams area is its provincialism. This provincialism, however, is not total, nor does it constitute an unqualified rejection of societal values and norms. A belief in the stereotypes held by the wider society is what arouses so much mutual distrust among the residents and drives them to find another basis for a moral order. Even so, the residents organize themselves on the basis of distinctions that are widely made in American society: age, sex, ethnicity, territoriality, and personal reputation. In the Addams area these distinctions are emphasized to the exclusion of occupational, educational, and other attainments that are more appreciated in the wider society. The process, however, is more nearly one of reversion than inversion or outright rejection.

In the Addams area there are also numerous dependencies and attachments to the wider community. The resident policemen have a strong interest in maintaining stable relations both with the other residents and with their department. The local store owners and managers want the streets safe for their suppliers and customers. The area's politicians take a protective attitude toward the neighborhood and are active in acquiring patronage. Some of the churches are part of a nationwide structure, and street workers have been accepted into the neighborhood since the early days of the Chicago Area Project.[1] Adult crime tends to be organized within an "Outfit" which extends into many portions of the city.

In fact, these structural links between the Addams area and the wider community are essential to its provincialism. Until 1960, the Italians were partially able to fend off the destruction of dwellings preliminary to the development of industry and urban renewal. The control the Italians exercised through the wider community allowed them to become the most provincial ethnic group in the Addams area. The Negroes possess far less control over their ethnic section and are much less provincial than the Italians.

An essential condition to the provincialism of the Addams area is some control over land usage and population movements. This control, however, need not extend over vast areas because of the segmental structure of the neighborhood. The Addams area consists of four ethnic sections in which the residents are dependent primarily upon persons in the same section. Changes in land usage and population shifts, then, tend to disrupt only one section at a time.

The Addams area has been subject to continuous inroads as the Medical Center, the University of Illinois, industry, and the Chicago Housing Authority have occupied contiguous pieces of land at its boundaries. The extent to which this has limited or disrupted the internal organization of each ethnic section has varied a great deal. The location of the Negroes in public housing has made it impossible for them to develop a complement of ethnic institutions; and they remain heavily dependent upon the nearby shopping area, religious establishments, and educational facilities. Public housing is probably the most serious impediment to the developing provincialism in the Addams area. The same effect, however, may be present in other neighborhoods where "absentee" control of land usage makes it impossible for a local group to lay claim to a full complement of the establishments necessary to its day-to-day life.

The Italians in the Addams area have lost several portions of the neighborhood to other ethnic groups and to nonresidential usage. Because they are in private housing, can obtain control over relatively small building spaces, and are not too constrained by zoning laws, the Italians continue to preserve a range of local facilities adequate for daily life. Despite their loss of previous sections of the neighborhood, they are more able than any local ethnic group to restrict their relations to one another.

The Mexicans and Puerto Ricans in the Addams area are also situated

[1] Solomon Kobrin, "The Chicago Area Project—A Twenty-five-Year Assessment," *Annals of the American Academy of Political and Social Science*, 322 (March, 1959): 20–29.

in private housing and, like the Italians, they have been able to acquire at least a portion of the facilities to serve their everyday requirements. The success of their efforts is incomplete primarily because of the time it takes Addams area residents to readjust facilities to their own demands and to assimilate themselves to one another. Each ethnic section in the Addams area is able to incorporate a limited number of newcomers in a brief time. The new Puerto Rican and Mexican establishments are only gradually building up a clientele through the credit, informality, and license they permit their patrons. The street groups, named gangs, establishment groups, families, and SAC's are equally slow at accepting a new resident until his personal identity is known. The Mexican and Puerto Rican sections of the Addams area have neither fully developed those groupings which can function to incorporate newcomers nor have they had time to satisfy their doubts about the trustworthiness of many new arrivals.

These variations in the provincialism of each ethnic section reflect gradations in the balance between involvement in the wider community and continued participation in the local neighborhood. Until the beginning of this study, the Italians had maintained enough power in the wider community to protect their ethnic establishments, but they were not so involved with "outsiders" as to detract from their relations with their fellow residents. The Negroes in the housing projects have little voice in the wider community and less to say about how their local facilities are managed. The provincialism of the Addams area qualifies but does not exclude many relations with the wider community. Up to a point, then, an exchange with the wider community is complementary to the provincialism of the Addams area. Moreover, an absence or decline of provincialism in each ethnic section does not mean an increasing compliance with the mores of the wider community. In the Addams area the alternative to provincialism is a pervasive anonymity, distrust, and isolation.

Ordered Segmentation

Each ethnic section of the Addams area differs from the others in the extent to which it possesses a standardized routine for managing safe social relations. There is, however, a general agreement upon the social categories beyond which associations are not pursued. The boundaries of the neighborhood itself form the outermost perimeter for restricting social relations. Almost all the residents caution their wives, daughters, children, and siblings against crossing Roosevelt, Halsted, Congress, and Ashland. Within each neighborhood, each ethnic section is an additional boundary which sharply restricts movement. Adults cross ethnic boundaries to shop or go to work, while children do so in running errands or attending school.

Free time and recreation, however, should be spent within one's own ethnic section.

Further territorial partitions are present in each ethnic section and maintain a degree of segregation between age, sex, and residential groupings. The general pattern is one that fans out from the household and is partitioned according to the age and sex of the residents. Females and children are in closest proximity to the household. Males move progressively beyond this perimeter depending on their age.

These territorial allotments produce only social aggregates which are defined by their spatial proximity. They afford an opportunity for interaction, but each ethnic section differs in how far these face-to-face relations have become a routine basis for association. In all ethnic sections the youngsters form regular play groups, and except for the Puerto Ricans, there are named gangs among the adolescent males. Only among the Italians, however, has this spatial ordering of age and sex aggregates been thoroughly embraced as the basis of group life. The Italian named street corner groups continue into adulthood as a SAC. All of the Italian boys' groups preface their name with either the term "Taylor" or the name of some other street in the area. Italian girls, on the other hand, are kept so close to home that they aggregate in only small unnamed groups. In the evening the Italian adults regularly reassemble at their favorite tavern, doorway, or stoop.

Among the Negroes, the spatial ordering of sex and age groups is not nearly so distinct, and social aggregates are not closely identified with the areas they occupy. Adolescent Negro girls range almost as far from their households as do the boys. The Negro girls also have named street corner groups like those of the boys. Street groupings among the adult Negroes shift a great deal in their membership, and in general, social relations are more transient than elsewhere in the area. The projects themselves seem simply to lack establishments and locations that can be clearly assigned to each age, sex, and residential grouping.

In the Puerto Rican and Mexican sections, spatial aggregation has produced many separate age and sex groups that regularly assemble. The Puerto Rican section is so small that these groups are still known by their membership rather than by some shared title. In the more populous Mexican section both the girls and boys have named groups, but the girls always retreat within the area occupied by an allied boys' group. The adult males and females in both the Puerto Rican and Mexican sections have their regular stoops, taverns, and other places where they expect to congregate in their leisure hours.

Unlike the Italians, the Puerto Ricans and Mexicans have not yet developed any adult SAC's. As they reached adulthood in 1965 both the Erls and the Regents made faltering attempts in this direction but failed when their members were unable to contribute equally to a storefront. The failure of the Mexicans and the Puerto Ricans to follow fully the pattern laid out by the Italians results from some of the same conditions that impede group formation among the Negroes. The Italians are able to command the facilities of their ethnic section; and territorial aggregations repeatedly face one another in the same grocery store, tavern, recreational establishment, and church. The Puerto Ricans and Mexicans cannot always afford a local storefront, and many of their transactions take them outside the local neighborhood. Face-to-face relations among the Negroes are confined largely to the streets; and commercial, religious, and recreational requirements often scatter them beyond their local ethnic section.

Conflict and Order

The social order produced in the Addams area is always partial, and there are many occasions for conflict between ethnic sections. When there is trouble with an adjacent neighborhood, all four ethnic groups show their greatest unity. At other times their cohesion is expressed in such limited forms as a common voting pattern, a respect for territorial arrangements, and joint resistance to the clearance for the University of Illinois.

The residential segregation of ethnic groups is compounded by incomplete communication and a number of cultural differences. The older Italians, Mexicans, and Puerto Ricans find their English an embarrassing and inadequate means of handling inter-ethnic relations. Real and inferred differences in dialect, gestures, posture, and eye movements are a continual source of friction and uneasiness. It is doubtful if these communication differences reflect much variation in basic cultural values, and the residents themselves are only perplexed. As one Negro girl put it, "Maybe they [Italian women] don't mean anything by staring at you, but how can you tell?"

These cultural differences are only partially due to separate historical traditions. The provincialism of the Italians creates an expressive order in which they express their solidarity by disregarding the clothing fads, novel language, and new dances of the wider society. The Negroes are very quick to pick up new dances, dress styles, and the novelties of youthful slang. The result is two expressive orders that make it difficult for either ethnic group to accommodate itself to the other. The Puerto Ricans and Mexicans have an especially difficult time since they are neither so "hip" as the Negroes nor so "square" as the Italians.

While these cultural differences are real enough, the major distinctions between these ethnic groups arise from social conditions within the

neighborhood itself. The expressive order of the Italians fits into their provincialism, while the Negroes find the recent fads, dances, and linguistic
novelties useful in more anonymous circumstances. The variation among
ethnic groups is increased by their cultural differences, but it rests
essentially on the same conditions that produce varying levels of provincialism within each ethnic section.

The divisions between age, sex, and territorial groups are another source
of conflict between and within ethnic sections. Trouble between ethnic sections often starts when peer groups of the same sex confront one another
and gradually draw in other age and sex groupings. Within each ethnic section, named groups of about the same age are frequently at odds and occasionally threaten combat. If a girl goes very far out of her territorial
confines, she invites the attention of predatory males. The strictness of age
ranking in each ethnic section allows the older boys to "push around" the
younger ones if they become obstreperous.

All of these instances of conflict, however, are an inevitable and necessary
accompaniment to the area's segmental order. Individuals in the Addams
area achieve a positive association with coresidents of the same age, sex,
and ethnicity primarily because conflict with other persons forces them together into small face-to-face groupings. Otherwise, people might remain
almost wholly isolated, associate indiscriminately, or be dependent on such
dyadic relations as they could form.

So positive a role for conflict cannot be appreciated unless it is placed in
a developmental sequence. At the outset, parents, and children in the
Addams area do not prescribe a definite set of persons with whom the
family are to associate. Instead, they voice a variety of proscriptions:
"Don't go out of the neighborhood"; "I thought I told you to stay off
Taylor Street"; "Don't you get off the block"; "Stay by the house, like I
told you." Injunctions of this sort do not initially produce positive associations but only territorial aggregates confined together in an enduring relationship because of the restrictions on other associations.

The result is a pattern of movement that brings together coresidents of
the same age and sex. These small and continuous face-to-face aggregations
furnish the occasion for people to get acquainted and to inquire into each
other's personal history. In this context they can provide the assurances
that relieve their apprehensions. Without some principal of selection, however, the residents could wander from one person to another while failing to
establish a firm relation with anyone. Conflict between age, sex, and territorial groups, however, forces the residents to throw their lot in with a
definite group of people.

The social order that emerges in these small congregations does not consist of a series of highly standardized role capacities. Addams area residents relate to one another primarily by a personalistic morality in which individual precedent is the major standard for evaluation. The most incongruous of people become associated and continue to remain safe companions. Judgments of worth and social sanctions are individuated and tailored to past commitments. Normative rulings, then, do not apply to a fixed role apart from the incumbent; they can be developed only as individuals have the time and occasion to become familiar with each others' past history and future intentions.

Such a personalistic morality is obviously limited in the number of people it can include because of the time and effort it takes to become so intimately acquainted. Once under way, however, these discrete groupings can be complemented by a growing maze of intergroup relations. The conflict between age, sex, and territorial groups, then, sets the stage so that dyads can relate entire groups of people.

The Extension of Face-to-Face Relations

While face-to-face relations and a personalistic morality are the main forms for association, they are extended by a number of other devices. Kinship functions to create an extensive web of connections between informal groups. Children who become closely acquainted seem tacitly to assume some trust and respect for each others' parents. Having a brother, a cousin, or parent in another group is perhaps the most frequent reason given when a resident says, "It's OK, they won't bother me."

Similar intergroup relations are established where different kinds of territorial groups overlap but do not coincide in their membership. This type of connection is most evident among the Italian adults where street groups and establishment groups only partially coincide in the people they include. Since the Negroes have extremely few establishment groups, this type of structural bridge between groups is rare.

There are, however, a variety of ways in which affiliations spread beyond each local group of peers. When people change residences within the neighborhood, they usually become associated with a new street group without, however, losing contact with prior friends. In the Italian section a single church draws people from practically every social grouping and allows for some measure of acquaintance. The local parochial schools serve much the same function among the Italian youngsters. Residents in the other three ethnic sections are more fragmented by the churches and schools they attend; still, these institutions afford some opportunity for association among different street groupings.

The most stable form of intergroup relations occur among the named street corner groups and adult SAC's. Within each ethnic section of the Addams area, the named street corner groups form an age-graded hierarchy with clear dominance relations. The younger groups do not challenge the dominance of their seniors, and the older groups are patronizing toward the younger ones. Shared names and debette groups extend these affiliations and clarify them to other groups. Potential conflict, then, is restricted to groups which are at about the same age level. Even among these groups, however, there are mechanisms that forestall full-scale fights. Among the Italians, the adult SAC's are powerful groups and do not hesitate to quell the youngsters when they get too rowdy or threaten to draw the police into the area. A half dozen or so resident Italian policemen take an equally active role in supressing disturbances among the youngsters. Local members of the "Outfit" are especially heavy-handed when they think the youngsters will "bring heat on the neighborhood."

The other three ethnic groups in the area do not have these means of dealing with conflict among the youngsters. In part, the area's street workers are able to fill the same role. As among the Italians, however, the pattern of group affiliations is such that most instances of conflict are truncated short of a "gang fight." As grievances and questions of dominance between groups accumulate, other people are notified by a series of rumors. Sometimes this will result in other groups taking sides. Often this process of accretion will progress until the dominant group in the ethnic section becomes implicated. In the Addams area, the Erls, Regents, and Magnificent Gallants were clearly dominant and able to intimidate antagonists within their own ethnic section. If they allied themselves with a particular faction, opponents within their own ethnic section grumbled but gave in.

A far more common pattern was one in which rumors anticipated gang fights and thus became the occasion for intervention from a number of sources. Once alerted by these rumors, street workers, the police, parents, shop owners, and priests took a hand in separating the antagonists. As a result, actual conflict was usually restricted to one of two circumstances. First, a few boys might "jump" a member of another group, following rumors of a "gang fight." Second, segments of two groups might unwittingly run into one another and start a row. Full-scale "gang fights" seem very rare, and only two were known to occur in the three years between 1962 and 1965. Both were very brief encounters and left no one seriously injured. In each case two groups had independently strayed out of their local territory and accidentally met.

The discrete groupings and intergroup affiliations that occur in the Addams area produce an ordered segmentation in two senses. First, ethnic, age, sex, and territorial groupings establish an order within which people can be related directly or indirectly to the entire neighborhood. Second, there is a sequential order in which these groupings can be combined through a process of accretion when there is a threat of trouble. Neither of these structural arrangements are fully able to stave off all instances of violence and conflict. The result in the Addams area, however, is a far cry from an atomistic situation in which every person must work out his associations one at a time.

An integral part of the neighborhood's ordered segmentation is its named adolescent street corner groups. Despite widespread apprehension about adolescent gangs, those in the Addams area have gone far toward creating an order which includes a large number of people. Within each ethnic section, age-grading, a dominant group, and explicit alliances establish stable relations between several hundred youngsters, some of whom scarcely know one another. Where kinship and friendship might otherwise establish safe relations among those immediately concerned, the street corner group turns these affiliations into a guarantee of safety between entire groups of boys. The adolescent gang, then, may be less an anarchistic rebellion than the first step toward a social solution to individual relations.

Reality and Morality

The understandings, myths, rumors, gossip, prejudices, and social divisions shared by Addams area residents make up a highly localized subculture. Its content, however, is not easy to characterize with the general concepts of "role," "value," and "norm." The residents themselves tend to describe their relationships in highly personal terms, starting with a series of facts they regard as valid, and then proceeding to detail their behavior as a necessary consequence. Occasionally, reference is made to what people should be like, but a far more common concern is the actual character of people and one's own affiliation with them. There is, then, an explicit recognition of the ideal status of public morality and its undependability when applied to "real people."

The "real people" that Addams area residents are most concerned about are their neighbors. What they know from general sources, however, only furthers their view that public standards of morality are not a safe guideline for conduct. According to general stereotypes and public channels of communication, their neighbors are an urban rabble prone to riot, pillage, disorder, and crime. The residents know such behavior to be the exception rather than the rule. But it is only by going beyond the stereotypes, evaluations, and norms of public conduct that the residents can determine who is the exception and who fits the rule. Thus, cognitive rather than moral considerations dominate the residents' interests.

The resulting subculture consists of a wide range of personal information, shared understandings, ethnic customs, and mutual disclosures. The young boys, the old ladies, men, and adolescent girls all become intimately involved with one another to the point that their omissions and shortcomings are shared and act as pledges to further securities. Ethnic origins are appealed to and kinship is emphasized in the absence of other assurances of affiliation and safety. Gossip, slander, and innuendo are closely attended and serve as a common basis for determining someone else's social character.

Since Addams area residents share many suspicions and common failings, the content of their subculture is limited in the direction it takes. First, there is a great deal of concern about illegal activities, the "Outfit," and criminals. Those involved in these activities are small in number, but the residents are anxious to make peace with them or, if possible, to avoid them. Because they inquire so thoroughly into this issue, the residents are uncommonly aware of each other's illegal activities. The result is a sort of social compact in which respectable residents and those not so respectable are both tolerant and protective of one another.

A second focus of interest is in each other's trustworthiness, sincerity, or loyalty. Addams area residents are very interested in gaining rapport with one another; but they hesitate to reveal too much about themselves, lest they become vulnerable. Thus, "finks," "con-artists," "phonies," and "jitter bugs" are stronger terms of condemnation than "unemployed," "poor" or "felon." By taking each other into their confidence, the residents risk a great deal. Trustworthiness, then, is valued far more than some formal appellation that connotes high morals and good character.

Third, the residents share a number of apprehensions over the exercise of brute force and the physical attributes assumed to divide the weak from the strong. Physical size, age, sex, and numbers enter fully into the residents' calculations and are a strong consideration for assigning superordinate or subordinate statuses. Generally these signs of physical prowess are accepted out of hand or settled after a single demonstration. Leadership, social rank, and associations, however, are partially based on shows of strength which, in turn, lead to some measure of violence and force.

The subcultural commonalities of the Addams area consist primarily of a selective search for private information rather than the invention of normative ideals. The residents express admiration for unrelenting respectability, complete frankness, and a general restraint from force. In the real world they live in, however, the residents are willing to settle for a friend of doubtful repute, guarded personal disclosures, and the threat of force to meet force.

The subculture of the Addams area is more nearly a means of gradually discovering a moral order than a set of rules which one mechanically obeys. As the residents fan out from their households, they are very cautious, arranging their social relations to minimize the assumed dangers. The outcome is an ordered segmentation of age, sex, ethnic, and territorial groupings bound together by common disclosures and personal loyalties. Even this order takes time to construct and can be upset by circumstances that continually recur in slum neighborhoods.

Sources of Instability and Change

Under very idealized circumstances, it is possible to imagine a social order in the Addams area which is far more inclusive and determinate. Given sufficient control over the facilities in the area, stable boundaries for each ethnic section, and a slow rate of population change, the residents might create a very provincial but also a very orderly neighborhood. So far only the Italians have been able to realize so complete a social order. Looking to the future, it is tempting to predict a convergence between the Italian section and the other three ethnic sections. Such a speculation would be hazardous for a number of reasons.

First, the future of the Addams area itself is uncertain, since urban renewal and institutional building plans threaten to disband its population. Once they are scattered, the residents will have to start anew rather than simply advance from where they stand.

Second, as new economic and political policies gain ground, the entire complex of inner-city life may change its character. Except for the projects, the land and buildings of the Addams area are broken into many small and independent units which allow for the interlarding of religious, commercial, recreational, and domestic life. The growth of public housing and the sale of large blocks of land for special usages is likely to separate these functions. The construction of huge housing developments, uniform in style, size of dwelling unit, and rental costs, may produce a series of residential compounds appropriate to only a period of the family life cycle. If these policies are implemented on a large scale, the centrifugal forces may be so great that slum residents can no longer maintain the integrity of their territorial groups and provincial way of life.

Added uncertainties accumulate as we consider possible changes in the occupational structure and a variety of programs aimed at reacculturation. In the particulars of its ordered segmentation, then, the Addams area may be less a model of the future than a reflection of the past. In a broader sense, however, the Addams area is an example that has direct relevance to the future of all slum neighborhoods. Addams area residents are not engaged in an attempt to create an illusory world that merely denies the one which the wider community has established. The residents are impelled by a far more basic task of finding an order within which they can secure themselves against common apprehensions. So basic is this burden that few slum residents can ignore it or retreat fully into sheer fantasy, opportunism, or defeatism.

The moral order created by Addams area residents does not meet either their own ideals or those of the wider society. The local people recognize as much and view their way of life as a practical exigency. For all its shortcomings, however, the moral order they have developed includes most, if not all, of their neighbors. Within limits, the residents possess a way of gaining associates, avoiding enemies, and establishing each others' intentions. In view of the difficulties encountered, the provincialism of the Addams area has provided a decent world within which people can live.

Bibliography

Addams, Jane. *Twenty Years at Hull House*. New York: New American Library, 1961.

Anderson, Nels. *The Hobo*. Chicago: University of Chicago Press, 1923, Phoenix edition, 1961.

Banfield, Edward C. *The Moral Basis of a Backward Society*. Glencoe, Ill.: Free Press, 1958.

Barnes, Harry E., and Teeters, Nagley K. *New Horizons in Criminology*. Englewood Cliffs, N. J.: Prentice-Hall, 1959.

Bell, Daniel. *The End of Ideology*. New York: Collier Books, 1961. See especially pp. 39-45, 127-50.

Berger, Bennett M. *Working Class Suburb*. Berkeley: University of California Press, 1960.

Brown, Roger. *Social Psychology*. New York: Free Press, 1965.

Burgess, E. W. *Urban Areas of Chicago: An Experiment in Social Science Research*. Edited by T. Smith and J. White. Chicago: University of Chicago Press, 1929.

Carney, Frank J. "Experimental Area III-X (Addams)." Unpublished report. Chicago Youth Development Project, 1961.

Cartwright, Dorwin, and Zander, Alvin, eds. *Group Dynamics*. White Plains, N.Y.: Row, Peterson, 1953.

Chicago Board of Education. "Montifiori Special School Report." Unpublished report. Chicago, 1942.

Cloward, Richard A., and Ohlin, Lloyd E. *Delinquency and Opportunity: A Theory of Delinquent Gangs*. Glencoe, Ill.: Free Press, 1960.

Cohen, Albert K. *Delinquent Boys: The Culture of the Gang*. Glencoe, Ill.: Free Press, 1955.

Croce, Benedetto. *Politics and Morals*. New York: Philosophical Library, 1945.

Duncan, Otis Dudley. "A Critical Evaluation of Work in Community Stratification." *American Sociological Review* 15 (1950): 205-15.

Evans-Pritchard, E. E. *The Nuer*. Oxford: Clarendon Press, 1940.

Fortes, Meyer, and Evans-Pritchard, E. E. *African Political Systems*. London: Oxford University Press, 1940.

Frazier, E. Franklin. *Black Bourgeoisie*. New York: Collier Books, 1962.

Goffman, Erving. *The Presentation of Self in Everyday Life*. Garden City, N. Y.: Doubleday, 1959.

Gold, Martin. *Status Forces in Delinquent Boys*. Ann Arbor: University of Michigan Press, 1963

Gouldner, Alvin W. "Reciprocity and Autonomy in Functional Theory." In *Symposium on Sociological Theory*, edited by L. Gross. White Plains, N. Y.: Row, Peterson, 1959.

Grimshaw, Allen D. "Urban Racial Violence in the United States: Changing Ecological Considerations." *American Journal of Sociology* 66 (1960): 109–19.

Gross, Llewellyn, ed. *Symposium on Sociological Theory*. White Plains, N. Y.: Row, Peterson, 1959.

Hess, Robert D. "Culture and Cognition." Unpublished paper delivered at the symposium of the Committee on Human Development, Center for Continuing Education, June 4, 1965. Chicago: University of Chicago.

Homans, George. *The Human Group*. New York: Harcourt, Brace, 1950.

Homans, George, and Schneider, David. *Marriage, Authority and Final Causes: A Study of Unilateral Cross-Cousin Marriage*. Glencoe, Ill.: Free Press, 1955.

Hsien, Chin Hu. "The Chinese Concepts of Face." *American Anthropologist* 46 (1944): 45–64.

Hymes, D. H. "Lexicostatistics So Far." *Current Anthropology* 1 (1960): 3–44.

Killian, Leslie M. "The Significance of Multiple Group Membership in Disaster." *The American Journal of Sociology* 57 (1952): 309–13.

Kinsey, Alfred, *et al. Sexual Behavior in the Human Male*. Philadelphia: W. B. Saunders, 1948.

Klein, Malcolm W., and Myerhoff, Barbara G., eds. *Juvenile Gangs in Context*. Los Angeles: University of Southern California Press, 1964.

Kobrin, Solomon. "The Chicago Area Project—A Twenty-five Year Assessment." *Annals of the American Academy of Political and Social Science* 322 (1959): 20–29.

Kobrin, Solomon. "The Conflict of Values in Delinquency Areas." *American Sociological Review* 16 (1951): 653–61.

Komarovsky, Mirra, "The Voluntary Associations of Urban Dwellers." *American Sociological Review* 11 (1946): 686–98.

Kvaraceus, William, and Miller, Walter. *Delinquent Behavior: Culture and the Individual*. Washington, D.C.: National Education Association, 1959.

Landesco, John. *Organized Crime in Chicago*. Chicago: Illinois Association for Criminal Justice, 1929.

Levy, Marion J. *The Structure of Society*. Princeton, N. J.: Princeton University Press, 1952.

Lewis, Hylan. *Blackways of Kent*. New Haven, Conn.: College and University Press, 1964.

Lippitt, Ronald, *et al.* "The Dynamics of Power." *Human Relations* 5 (1952): 37–64.

Litwak, Eugene. "Occupational Mobility and Extended Family Cohesion." *American Sociological Review* 25 (1960): 9–21.

McDavid, Raven, and McDavid, Virginia. "The Relationship of the Speech of American Negroes to the Speech of Whites." *American Speech* 26 (1951). 3–17.

Machiavelli, Niccolo. *The Prince and the Discourses*. New York: Modern Library, 1940.

Malinowski, Bronislaw. *Crime and Custom in Savage Society*. New York: Harcourt, Brace, 1932.

Mattick, Hans, and Caplan, Nathan. *The Chicago Youth Development Project*. Ann Arbor: University of Michigan Press, 1964.

Merton, Robert K. *Social Theory and Social Structure*. Rev. ed. Glencoe, Ill.: Free Press, 1950. See especially pp. 161–94, 421–36.

Merton, Robert K., and Lazarsfeld, Paul F., eds. *Continuities in Social Research: Studies in the Scope and Method of "The American Soldier."* Glencoe, Ill.: Free Press, 1950.

Morland, John Kenneth. *Millways of Kent*. New Haven, Conn.: College and University Press, 1965.

Orphan, Constantine D. "Good Bye Greek Town," *Inland, The Magazine of the Midwest* Chicago, (Spring, 1963): 24ff.

Orwell, George. *The Road to Wigan Pier*. New York: Harcourt, Brace, 1963.

Pareto, Vilfredo. *The Mind of Society*. New York: Harcourt, Brace, 1942.

Park, Robert E., Burgess, Ernest, and McKenzie, Roderick D. *The City*. Chicago: University of Chicago Press, 1967.

Parsons, Talcott. "Age and Sex in the Social Structure of the United States." In *Essays in Sociological Theory*. Glencoe, Ill.: Free Press, 1954.

Plant, James. *Personality and the Cultural Pattern*. New York: The Commonwealth Fund, 1937.

Powdermaker, Hortense. *Hollywood, the Dream Factory*. Boston: Little, Brown, 1950.

Radcliff-Brown, A. R., and Forde, Daryll, eds. *African Systems of Kinship and Marriage*. London: Oxford University Press, 1950.

Reiss, Albert J., Jr. "Rural, Urban and Status Differences in Interpersonal Contacts." *American Journal of Sociology* 65 (1959): 182–95.

Rose, Arnold, ed. *Human Behavior and Social Processes*. Boston: Houghton Mifflin, 1962.

Roy, Donald. "Banana Time: Job Satisfaction and Informal Interaction." *Human Organization* 18 (1959–60): 158–60.

Schumpeter, Joseph A. *History of Economic Analysis*. New York: Oxford University Press, 1954.

Shaw, Clifford R., and McKay, Henry D. *Juvenile Delinquency and Urban Areas*. Chicago: University of Chicago Press, 1942.

Shils, E. A. "Primary Groups in the American Army." In *Continuities in Social Research: Studies in the Scope and Method of "The American Soldier,"* edited by R. Merton and P. Lazarsfeld. Glencoe, Ill.: Free Press, 1950.

Short, James F., Jr., *et al.* "Perceived Opportunities, Gang Membership and Delinquency." *American Sociological Review* 30 (1965): 56–67.

Steward, Julian H. *Theory of Culture Change*. Urbana, Ill.: University of Illinois Press, 1955.

Sutherland, Edwin, and Cressey, Donald. *Principles of Criminology*. New York: J. B. Lippincott, 1955.

Suttles, Gerald. "Public Housing and the Problem of Family Impression Management." Unpublished paper, delivered to Illinois Academy of Criminology, December, 1964.

Thrasher, Frederick. *The Gang*. Chicago: University of Chicago Press, 1926, rev. ed., 1963.

Turner, Ralph H. "Role-Taking: Process Versus Conformity." In *Human Behavior and Social Processes*, edited by A. Rose. Boston: Houghton Mifflin, 1962.

Warringer, Charles K. "The Nature and Functions of Official Morality." *American Journal of Sociology* 64 (1958): 165–68.

Welfare Council of Metropolitan Chicago. *Community Area 28—The Near West Side*. Chicago, 1953.

Whyte, William Foote. *Street Corner Society*. Chicago: University of Chicago Press, 1961.

Wirth, Louis. *The Ghetto*. Chicago: University of Chicago Press, 1956.

Wolfgang, Marvin. "Victim-Precipitated Criminal Homicide." *Journal of Criminal Law, Criminology, and Police Science* 48 (1957): 1–11.

Wolfgang, Marvin, Savitz, Leonard, and Johnson, Norman, eds. *The Sociology of Crime and Delinquency*. New York: John Wiley, 1962.

Young, Michael, and Willmott, Peter. *Family and Kinship in East London*. New York: Pelican Books, 1962.

Zorbaugh, Harvey. *The Gold Coast and the Slum*. Chicago: University of Chicago Press, 1929.

Index

Addams, Jane, 18
Addams area
—selected as target area by CYDP, 18
—rate of delinquency in, 18, 18*n*
—ethnic division of, 9, 22
—possible future of, 100, 233–34
—geography of: boundaries, 13; ethnic
    neighborhoods surrounding, 27; im-
    personal domains in, 36–37; no-man's
    lands in, 36; portion controlled by
    Italians, 99
—history of, 15–20, 102; and business
    establishments, 84–85; Italians' poli-
    tical control, 119–20
—provincialism of, 223–25
—unique characteristics of, 223
—and wider community: opposition to,
    22, 31; relations with, 223–24; re-
    putation among, 24–25; as deviant
    from, 3
Age grading, 162–63; and personal identi-
    ties, 83; deviations from modal age in
    street groups, 163; encouraged by
    parents, 163; in Negro street groups,
    132–33; in Italian named groups,
    107–12
Age groups
—segregation of, 74–75, 88–90
—in Italian named groups, 107–12;
    supremacy of adults among, 117–
    18
Arrest rate: annual increase of, 211, 214;
    of ethnic groups, 202–5; of females,
    206–7; and police activity, 214–15;
    and location of offense, 207–10; and
    residence of victim, 210; seasonal
    variations of, 210–11; and types of
    offenses, 205–6
Athenians (Mexican group from Eigh-
    teenth Street), 31

Barracudas (Mexican street group): con-
    flicts with Italians, 113–16; ethnic
    composition of, 164–65; fight with
    Stylists, 199; residence in Italian sec-
    tion, 166–67, 167*n*; rumored fight
    with Roughshods, 199–200
Bryan school, and dispute between Ne-
    groes and Italians, 58
Business establishments: criteria for ethnic
    classification of, 46–47; groups of in
    relation to street groups, 88; Negroes'
    lack of control of, 88; social relations
    in, 23–34, 83–88. *See also* Commer-
    cial exchanges

Catholics: Italians as, 42; Mexicans as,
    42; Negroes as, 43; parochial schools
    of, 56–58; Puerto Ricans as, 42
Catholic churches. *See* Our Lady of Pro-
    vins; Our Lady of Vesuvio; Sacred
    Domesticus; St. Assisi
Capone, Alfonse, 13, 18
Chicago Youth Development Project
    (CYDP): and decline in Negro gang
    membership, 132–33; purpose of in
    Addams area, 11; target area, 18
Church of the Valley (Puerto Rican
    storefront), 44
Civil rights movement: effect of on age
    grading, 219; relation to arrest rate
    of Negroes, 216–17; draws Negro
    boys from street group membership,
    133–34; Italians' resentment of, 102–
    3; swim-in at Sheridan Park, 144;
    and West Side Christian Mission, 43–
    44
Commercial exchanges: "guests-and-
    hosts" relation, 49–51; "mutual ex-
    ploitation" relation, 52–54; "mutual

239